THE BUSINESS
OF
MAY NEXT

JAMES MADISON
and the Founding

THE BUSINESS
OF
MAY NEXT

JAMES MADISON
and the Founding

W<small>ILLIAM</small> L<small>EE</small> M<small>ILLER</small>

University Press of Virginia
Charlottesville and London

THE UNIVERSITY PRESS OF VIRGINIA
Copyright © 1992 by the Rector and Visitors
of the University of Virginia
First published 1992

Library of Congress Cataloging-in-Publication Data

Miller, William Lee.
    The business of May next : James Madison and the founding /
William Lee Miller.
        p.   cm.
    Includes bibliographical references (p.   ) and index.
    ISBN 0-8139-1368-3 (cloth)
        1. Madison, James, 1751–1836—Political and social views.
2. United States—Consitutional history. 3. Political science—
United States—History—18th century.   I. Title.
E342.M55   1992
973.5'1—dc20   91-32785
                                                              CIP

Printed in the United States of America

for
ANDREW HORTON MILLER
not as father to son
but as one writer-scholar to another
with gratitude, admiration, and love

Contents

THE BUSINESS OF MAY NEXT

JAMES MADISON
and the Founding

A Word to the Reader

THIS BOOK GREW OUT OF A LARGER PROJECT that had as its subject, and working subtitle, "the moral foundations of the American Republic." The working main title was the phrase from Lincoln's First Inaugural, "The Better Angels of Our Nature." As that project developed it came to include historical narrative, and it expanded to have four parts, of which this book is one. As Herman Melville—or the narrator of *Moby-Dick*—exclaimed, "This book is but a draught! Nay, but a draught of a draught! Oh, Time, Strength, Cash, and Patience!"

These pages tell the story of some important years in the work of an important American founder, not for their historical and biographical interest only but also to convey something of that larger theme: the moral and intellectual underpinnings of the American nation.

Among the meanings concentrated in those years and in that founder are these: that good fortune offered this nation an unusual chance at ideal nation-forming and that some honorable leaders seized that chance; that this nation was founded not only, as all nations, on the triumphs and heroes of the battlefield and the palace and the podium but also on the quiet work of thinking and reading; that this reading and thinking did not start from the ground but built upon centuries of Western history; that the version of Western history that it particularly drew upon had a shape and featured a distinctive strand, the best short name for which is *republicanism;* that the Americans did not so much invent the received republican ideals as give them new and lasting institutional expression; that this republican institution-making was not the work solely of scholars in their studies but also of men with experience in the institutions they were thinking and writing about; that this thoughtful republican institution-making was not the work of one man only, a single great lawgiver, but was a collaboration; that the institutions thus designed were not complete but contained within themselves provision for their own continuing alteration; that the revisions made possible by these changeable institutions included the overcoming of great evils the founders themselves only partly—but partly—recognized; that a primary insight underlying this collaborative thought-and-experience-based republican institution-making was a sober wisdom, which is not the same as cynicism or pessimism, about the conduct of human beings in the large and across time in the great matters of collective life.

James Madison's research project was neither one of those great events in the world of affairs, like a victory on the field of battle, on the outcome of which the fortune of nations turn, nor one of those tremendous solo accomplishments of thought or art, by which a single mind leaves behind a book or a poem or a play or a treatise that will benefit readers forever—it was not even a work of original political philosophy—but it was an accomplishment of a mixed and different kind, as worthy in its way as these others may be, and a story that Americans ought to keep telling themselves as long as the nation it helped to form may last.

Introduction
Big House in Orange County

IF WHEN TRAVELING SOUTH from the nation's capital you leave the interstate at Fredricksburg and go west on Route 3, turn south through the
Battle of the Wilderness, turn right at the Big T Burger Tastee Freeze near
Orange, and proceed into the town of Orange itself, and then turn left
(south) again, you will come after four miles to a railroad station named
Montpelier. And if you park and pay and take the shuttle bus you will be
taken to the estate that was the home, all his life, of the fourth president
of the United States, James Madison.

Madison, like all the other great founders, ended his life in financial
difficulties; his house, like the houses of the other great Virginia founders—Monticello and Mount Vernon—had to be sold out of the family,
and eventually rescued from neglect by public-spirited citizens. (The
Adamses, up in Quincy, did hold on to the old house, but it was not easy.)
Dolley Madison, like Mozart's widow selling off pieces of music by the
note, or like Mary Todd Lincoln auctioning her clothes and begging Congress, had to sell off Montpelier—first, this piece of land, and then that
piece of land (the estate now has 2,780 acres), and finally the house itself.
Montpelier changed hands six times after Dolley Madison sold it in
1844, before it was acquired by William duPont in 1901.

Although the house is not distinguished, the site and the grounds are
beautiful. If you come there on the right day and look from the porch out
across the rolling green expanse to the west you will learn how the Blue
Ridge Mountains got their name.

Montpelier is tied not only to what is worthy in Madison's generally very worthy life but also to its limitation and tragic shading. Montpelier was a Virginia tobacco plantation operated by 100 slaves. Madison, as the heir, would be a slaveowner on a large scale. In his youth, imbued with the ideals of the Revolution and the Enlightenment, he would endeavor to free himself from the institution which all his life he condemned—notably at the Constitutional Convention, in which he was a leader in insisting that "property in men" not be explicitly acknowledged. But he never did free himself, from slavery or from this house, and in his old age his ideas as they touched slavery and regional conflict would shift subtly as he settled for being a Virginia planter.

He came back to the house intermittently, and returned permanently after retiring from the presidency, and died at Montpelier. Additions to the home were made in his lifetime, but when the duPonts acquired the place at the start of the twentieth century their alterations dwarfed what the Madisons had done. They put another story on top of the wings, added large new sections, took out walls and made new rooms, switched entrances and windows, brought Wedgwood from England to make a fireplace, and got Corning glass for a fireplace in what now became Marion duPont's horse-and-jockey room, put in large new bathrooms, brought the kitchen in from an outer building. They made a new house out of Montpelier, something approaching a mansion, a much different place.

William duPont, the purchaser of the property in 1901, had two children, a boy, William, Jr., and a girl, Marion. Marion duPont spent essentially all her life at Montpelier; she kept the place, almost until the bicentennial of the United States Constitution, as "one of the last great sporting stables." When in the days before it was open to the public you were taken through the empty rooms of the old house, there came a moment when there was a pause, and a warning: a surprise was coming. The opening of a door then suddenly revealed a room quite unlike anything else in the house: 1930s art deco, filled with pictures of twentieth-century racehorses and jockeys. In place of a chandelier there was a device to show the direction of the wind, for the purpose of pointing the hounds' noses for fox hunts.

There on the wall of the house in which James Madison's Memorial and Remonstrance was written is a whole panel of pictures devoted to Battleship, the first American horse to win the English steeplechase. The graves closest to Montpelier turn out to be not those of James and Dolly Madison, or other Madisons, but of Battleship and two other horses. A huge picture book called *Montpelier,* published by Scribners, has not only an author (Marion duPont Scott) but also, with their names in large letters on a page in the front, a designer, an editor, and—quite unusual for books—a producer. The jacket of this book tells us that "Montpelier is, obviously, a very special place for horses and for horse people."

It is a very special place for constitutions, and constitution people, too, but that is harder to make visual and dramatic—harder to put into a big picture book with a photographer and a producer.

Once Montpelier was open to the public, the bus tour up to the house would indicate the duPont additions. The steeple chase. The race track (Montpelier Hunt Races are still held on the first Saturday in November). The many barns and buildings of a horse farm: the stud barn (very important), the blacksmith shop, the dog kennels. The greenhouses. The sawmill. The bowling alley. The two and one-half acre formal garden. The dairy and the train station. Many of the barns, one is told, were purchased by Mrs. Scott from the Sears, Roebuck catalogue. There is a cockpit, a sort of a miniature coliseum—not open to the public—in which the duPonts and their guests would watch cockfights.

What James Madison did, partly in that house, and always with a connection to that house, is worthier and more lasting than what others did, but it is less susceptible to dramatization and to quick comprehension, or even to proper attention and respect.

Marion duPont's married name was Scott; the horsewoman of forty years was Marion duPont *Scott*. The Scott who had been her husband, very briefly in 1936–39, was none other than the Randolph Scott of the movies—the cowboy actor. The actor—the star—you used to watch, up there on the silver screen, if you are old enough, in some Rialto or Roxy or Loew's cinema palace, riding horses and engaging in gunplay with cattle rustlers, in Westerns like *When the Daltons Rode, Thunder over the Plains, Western Union, Hangman's Knot, The Man behind the Gun, Comanche Station,* and *Ride the High Country*—*that* Randolph Scott. It turns out that he was a Virginian, born in fact in Orange, and a genuine horseman.

On moving to Charlottesville and reading about Montpelier, thirty miles away in Orange County, and about Mrs. Randolph Scott, a duPont heiress, who now owned Madison's house, one would say: Can these things be? Can they be juxtaposed? Randolph Scott with his six-shooter on the screen, the duPonts with the monstrous wealth from chemicals, and—James Madison? Yes, they can be, and are, here in America, and in Orange County. That is, Orange County, *Virginia*—not to be confused with other Orange counties. This Orange County, which goes back before the Revolution, was named for the house of Orange, William of Orange, the William of William and Mary, the sovereign brought to the English throne after the Glorious Revolution. It is not named for *oranges*.

Thomas Jefferson's house, Monticello, in Albemarle County, also in the Piedmont, and now in the days of the motorcar not far from Montpelier—thirty miles—is justly a great tourist attraction, as troops of Americans and others made their way through the house, and grounds, of the drafter of the Declaration of Independence. Monticello is revealing of Jefferson and intensely interesting: he was the *architect*, after all, and the planner of all the exhibits and gadgets: the pen machine with which he could sign multiple letters, the pulley arrangement to tell not only the time but the day of the week (on which he made a mistake so that Saturday is relegated to the basement), the busts of Alexander Hamilton and himself facing each other through the ages.The distant kitchen, and the distant quarters for slaves: it is a house of a slaveowner who did not have to worry about how close the kitchen was to the dining room. The graceful grounds and graceful pillared Palladian front. The dome. Another lovely view, from a higher elevation than Montpelier's, although not as direct a view of the Blue Ridge. It is all Jefferson, the many-sided drafter of the Declaration of Independence, author of the Virginia Statute for Religious Freedom, and founder of the University of Virginia. But Montpelier? Madison? He founded no university, although he was the first rector of the one Jefferson founded. He wrote no statute for religious freedom, although he wrote (anonymously) the Memorial and Remonstrance that furnished the arguments for the one Jefferson wrote, and was the legislative leader who got Jefferson's bill through the General Assembly while Jefferson was in Paris. He drafted no Declaration of Independence, nor any particularly memorable ringing phrases, although he followed the work of the first round of founders with some careful thinking, and persistent politicking, to build a lasting government on the foundations they had laid. How does one dramatize that?

After Mrs. Scott bequeathed Montpelier to the National Trust, a member of the committee on what to do with it mused that perhaps in order to attract any tourists it would be necessary to advertise the place as *Dolley* Madison's house. Millions of Americans have in their minds, in any picture of "the Madisons" at all, a picture of Dolley at a party in the White House.

Dolley, with her vivacity as a hostess; duPont with his multimillions, his cockpit, his Wedgwood fireplace, and his grand house; Thomas Jefferson with his felicitous and well-known phrases, his architecture, his many-sidedness, and his intriguing gadgets; Battleship, with his wall of trophies, his ancestry and progeny and string of victories; Marion duPont Scott, with her hunt race, her stud barn, and her jockeys and trainers; Randolph Scott with his six-shooter on the silver screen; Sears, Roebuck with its fascinating catalogue filled with everything from barns to rubber boots—will all, in their widely various concrete and external and easily accessible ways, be a good deal more enticing to the republic that James Madison helped to construct than will Madison himself. Montpelier was not a house he designed; in any case it has no great distinction, and was upstaged by additions made by richer people. He devised no gadgets. He left no collection of great art. In which room did he write the Memorial and Remonstrance against Religious Assessments? The room does not exist any more; maybe along about in here.

After Montpelier was opened to the public one could tour it in a lonely splendor that was not possible at Monticello. At Monticello, even when the schools are in session, and on a cold day in winter, there are troops of people of all kinds, of all ages, from all over the world, packing the shuttle buses, waiting in line outside the entrance to the house, filing through the house in tour-group bunches, twenty minutes through the downstairs, starting in the hall in front of the clock, through the library, past the bed (seems short, they always say), around the chair where Jefferson read while waiting for the others to come to dinner, past the pictures of Locke and Newton, in front of the busts, through the underground passage by which the slave brought the food all the way from the kitchen (will the tour guide say "slaves" this time, or "servants"?). Lots of people crowding through. At Montpelier, by contrast, thirty miles away, even on a lovely day, it is not at all difficult to have a ride in the shuttle bus all by oneself, and to get a personal tour, by default, taking one's own pace, seeing all that one wants to see, with the volunteer tour guide all to oneself, to answer every question, and the shuttle bus at one's call to take one back in royal solitary comfort.

James Madison was called a "scholar," either in praise or in derision, all his life, and in the planning stage some said that the best use of Montpelier would be as a center for scholarly undertakings. Scholars and educators will understand his significance and his intangible presence.

But will the great public ever come to Montpelier? Some families come. In the summer. They do all the presidents' houses: Monticello, Ashlawn (a nearby home of James Monroe), Montpelier. Some families systematically do the American League ballparks, some do presidents' houses. But James Madison was not so great a president; what he did that was most important came long before he was president or secretary of state—indeed, before those offices, which he helped to create, existed. Also long before he met Dolley, whom he married in 1794, when he was forty-three.

Tell me, mummy, why are we looking at all these empty rooms in this boring house? Well, son, once there lived in this house a Virginia family, rather ordinary except that the oldest child was a very bright boy. That boy sat in his room, wherever here exactly it was, somewhere over by that staircase, and he read and thought hard and made notes for himself. One summer—1785—he wrote the best defense of religious liberty his country would ever see. The following spring, 1786, probably in that same space, surrounded by books his friend Jefferson had shipped to him from Paris, he started—as has been said—the most fruitful research project any American has ever undertaken. He studied what was wrong with republics, old ones and new ones, including the newly independent American state governments—how they had failed and were failing. He studied what was wrong, and why republics failed, so that he could build a republic that would *last,* and he pretty much did. The books he read and the notes he made and the thinking he did shaped James Madison's own ideas, which ideas shaped the so-called Virginia Plan, which plan shaped the United States Constitution, which Constitution shaped the new nation's institutions, which institutions affect all these people (and perhaps all these horses) here at Montpelier, whether they know it or not, and also elsewhere in Virginia, and also elsewhere in the new republic, and also even, indirectly, around the world. He started thinking here with his books, but he continued thinking in argument with others in conventions and legislatures, changing and adapting to their ideas; before his collaborative "new modeling" of this government was completed, in 1791, he had changed his mind about a written federal bill of rights, and had become its most important sponsor. So when James Madison, Jr., began his research project here in Orange County, Virginia, he was embarking on no small endeavor.

The poet Thomas Traherne, a metaphysical poet, as English departments call them, of the early seventeenth century, wrote that "he who thinks well serves God in His inmost court." That is not the way the unpoetic Madison, who in his adult life avoided nonobligatory references to God, would have put it, and not what the modest Madison would have claimed about himself. But he did think well, and silver screens, hunt races, chemical fortunes, great sporting stables, inventive statesmen, sawmills and bowling alleys, big picture books put out by producers, 1930s art deco, universities of Virginia, mail order catalogues, Orange counties named for oranges, religious freedom, cinema palaces, National Trusts, parties with vivacious hostesses, the ending of slavery and the ending of cockfights, and family tours of famous houses, have all grown in the fertile soil of the lasting institutions of liberty.

I

A Child of the Revolution
Reads Some Books

❧

One

IN THE SPRING AND EARLY SUMMER of 1786, James Madison, Jr., was at home in Montpelier for an extended period as he had not been for many years, and as he would not be for a long time again. He already knew he would be a Virginia delegate to the convention of the states that had been called for Annapolis in the fall of 1786. He proposed such a convention in the Virginia General Assembly, of which he was a member and, as often happens in these cases, the Assembly said, all right, you attend it. He did not know exactly what that Annapolis convention would lead to; its stated purpose was a modest consideration of commercial conflicts. But radical revisions in the relationships among the states were being talked about, by, among others, Madison himself. Some rough beast was slouching toward Philadelphia to be born.

And so, in preparation for the Annapolis convention and what might follow, surrounded by his books, Madison undertook his study of the constitutions of ancient and modern republics.

Madison was the intelligent son of a tobacco planter in the Virginia Piedmont who, although he rode some horses and shot some guns, liked books and study all his life. He was fortunate in the tutors who gave him his early education. Madison in later life is reported to have said of one of these tutors, a Scotsman and an Anglican clergyman named Donald Robertson, "All that I have been in life I owe largely to that man."

Madison seems to have been one of those persons for whom college was the right place. Apparently he liked hearing lectures, taking notes, and reading books. No doubt he was one of those who some in a later generation would call a "grind," but often such appellations tell more about the caller than about the callee. The president of the College of New Jersey, the Reverend Dr. John Witherspoon, added to the problems not so much of Madison as of Madison's biographers by making a remark, apparently in Jefferson's hearing, intended, to be sure, as praise, that "during the whole time" Madison was in his (Witherspoon's) "tuition," he never knew Madison "to do, or to say, an improper thing." This of course has put modern biographers, historians, and researchers busily to work trying to find improper things that Madison did, or said, particularly during his stay at Princeton. They have had moderate success, if you define "improper" as it might have been by Dr. Witherspoon: some bawdy verses and horseplay. But perhaps the point about this sonorous remark of Witherspoon's is that Jefferson kept repeating it, as a way of ribbing his friend Madison. Seen in that light it speaks well for both of them—for Jefferson, who generally did not have much of a sense of humor, but in this case seems to have shown that he could engage in some gentle joshing; and for Madison, who is shown being able to take it. If Madison had really been as stuffy as the quotation implies, then the atmosphere would not have been such as to allow his good friend to rib him about it.

Madison "tested out," as they say now, of his freshman year, started college as a sophomore, completed the three remaining years in two, and when he was graduated in September 1771, asked his father to allow him to stay on until the following spring as what we would call today a graduate student, continuing to study a variety of subjects, including Hebrew, with Dr. Witherspoon. He clearly was intellectually excited by the place—by what he was reading, by his professors, by his fellow students, by ideas. He did not get much sleep, but perhaps for reasons somewhat different from those of some other students, then and later. This was one of several times in his life when he felt he endangered his health by overworking. When he finally did come back home from college to Montpelier in Orange County, Virginia, in April of 1772, he felt let down. He felt sick and thought he might die young. He rattled around the house, taught literature to his younger siblings, and wondered which vocation to follow. He mused on the subject in letters to his friend Billey Bradford in Philadelphia and to other Princeton friends.

But the years were 1774, 1775, 1776, and the gathering storm of great political events was to answer that question for him. He was indeed to be, in Edmund Randolph's phrase, a "child of the revolution."

Although he was by temperament, by superior abilities, and by education rather a pure example of the intellectual worker, the tides of history, and Madison's own effort of will, made him over into a practical politician, in one of the most practical of political settings, the legislative body. He became committed to politics and never looked back, for a sixty-year career. One of Madison's biographers remarks that although Madison's friend Thomas Jefferson repeatedly said he wanted to leave public life and retire to the joys of private life in Monticello, with his books, his friends, his violin, his experiments, and his azaleas, no such remark was ever heard from James Madison. He chose public life and stuck to it.

But that does not mean he left his intellectual life behind; he took it with him. The time and place of his life meant that while active in politics he could be thinking through the fundamental principles of government. The opportunity to do that was in the air, in these colonies considering their rights, considering independence, considering self-government, and James Madison took the opportunity to the full.

In 1774, when he was twenty-three, he had been chosen, because he was a son of the local squire, to the local organ of the patriot resistance, the Orange County committee on Public Safety. When he was twenty-five, in the tremendous year of 1776, probably still through family connections, he went as delegate to the convention over in Williamsburg that declared Virginia's independence and constructed its new independent government. He went on to serve once in the General Assembly. When he lost that seat at the next election (the only time he ever did—by reports, because he declined to supply the free liquor the electorate expected), he was appointed to the council that advised the governor, in which role he met his lifelong friend and collaborator Thomas Jefferson. Then—most significant—he was appointed by the Assembly to be a Virginia delegate to the Continental Congress that met up in Philadelphia mostly. Madison undertook this last role in 1780 and served for four years as—typically—the most conscientious member.

This Congress was the successor to the momentous First Continental Congress that had assembled in September 1774, at which Massachusetts had met Virginia and had started the ball of independence rolling. It was the successor also to the Second Continental Congress, which assembled in the following year, at which John Adams got Col. George Washington of Virginia appointed commander of the American forces, and at which in the year after that John Adams would propose that the states form new governments and would in his turn meet Thomas Jefferson. Adams had then in that Congress proposed that his new young Virginia friend draft the language in which the new nation would set forth reasons for dissolving the bands that had bound them to the mother country.

But by the time James Madison arrived on the congressional scene in 1780, these moments of high drama were passed. Fairly early in his tenure, in 1781, the last state ratified the Articles of Confederation, and Congress became the uninspired creature of that uninspired instrument. Madison had become a legislative leader and dealt with the continental politics of the years of Revolution—surely a considerable political education. He and his congressional colleagues dealt with appointing generals and drawing boundaries and managing public funds—such as there were—and settling accounts and negotiations with foreign powers and restoring public credit and drawing up commercial treaties and—very often—with the big question of the western lands. They dealt with these matters in a time of war in a purported legislative body composed of representatives of the thirteen newly independent states, jealous of each other, touchy about their sovereignties, stingy about money, which legislative body in fact had no power over these sovereign entities.

When his term as delegate to Congress expired, Madison had returned to Virginia, in the spring of 1784, and had soon been given another assignment in a legislative body, once again as a delegate from Orange County to the Virginia General Assembly. Here, too, he quickly became a legislative leader; among his other services he steered through the Assembly as much as could be of the thorough revision of the Virginia law code, the "Revisal," that Thomas Jefferson had proposed and then, with a committee, written into a long set of new bills. Only a part of this new code could be enacted against conservative resistance, but Madison did manage to shepherd through the Assembly Jefferson's bill establishing religious freedom. (Jefferson himself by that time was in Paris.)

At another time one would not expect a man like Madison to be a political success. He was shy, short—most of his great Virginia compatriots were unusually tall for the time—and he was either sickly or hypochondriacal. He did not have a loud voice; people a few rows away had a hard time hearing him, so he was certainly no match in oratorical skill with his sometime opponent Patrick Henry or with Richard Henry Lee or many others. But Madison—as contemporary testimony reiterates—was regularly the best prepared and the most well read of the participants in the many political events through which he lived for half a century. He persuaded others by having the facts and ideas, the knowledge and the thought, already worked out more deeply and thoroughly than any one else present.

A legislative body can be an instructive political environment, and that particularly toothless and afflicted legislative body, the Continental Congress, trying to run a war and settle a peace with nothing to run it or settle it with, must have been instructive to a high degree. One can learn something political from executive and command positions (among other things, that obedience to commands on the part of actual human beings is far from automatic. Think of the wise old General Kutuzov in *War and Peace*, quite aware that the war would take its course outside the reach of anything he could do. Think of President John F. Kennedy, in that putative center of immense world power, the celebrated oval office, saying to some earnest petitioner: "*I* agree with you. But will the United States government agree with you?"). One can learn something political from the insides of that great application of "rationality" to human organization, the bureaucracy (one learns among other things, perhaps without knowing the sociologist's terms for it, that the informal organization is vastly different from the formal one on the chart). One can learn a great deal from courts and the legal system, where general principles of social ordering intersect individual and concrete cases; it is no accident that the courtroom has been the most appealing arena of government for the drama and novel. But perhaps one can learn most about the ground and nature of politics in general, about the human being as a political animal, and also about politics in a republic, by participation in a legislature. A legislator going the rounds of bills and disputes and committees and second readings in a legislative body does not have command or superior authority, or a defined office with its piece of a putatively rational division of labor, or the explicit guidance of the law. In a "republican" legislature equal representatives of equal peoples must deal with each other as (more or less) equals, to persuade and deal and compromise and cast votes, and to mingle facts and values, interests and social goods in whatever proportions, and finally to decide collectively on the policy for a people.

When one reads about the leaders of the French Revolution, one is struck particularly by the stark contrast on this point: their total lack of practical political experience in general and of this kind of republican political experience in particular. One scholar of the French Revolution wrote of the most striking group of its leaders, the twelve of the Terror of 1793, none of whom had been formed by the give and take of a parliament: "Their ideal statesman was no tactician, no compromiser, no skillful organizer who could keep various factions and pressure groups together. He was a man of elevated character, who knew himself to be in the right, a towering monument in a world of calumny and misunderstanding, a man who would have no dealing with the partisans of error, and who, like Brutus, would sacrifice his own children that a principle might prevail." Madison and the Adamses and Thomas Jefferson, and James Otis and Peyton Randolph and John Dickinson and Roger Sherman, and virtually all of the American framers and most of the American founders had a shaping experience in legislative bodies, and would not be described by that paragraph. This includes founders whom one might not identify with the practical politics of legislative bodies—Benjamin Franklin, Alexander Hamilton, and George Washington. Although sufficiently supplied with the "right" and with "principle," the Americans also affirmed the tactician, the compromiser, the "skillful organizer who could keep various factions and pressure groups together."

The Robespierres of this world do not realize that in the politics of an actual republican state being right is only half the battle—maybe much less than half. In the work of complex social ordering—politics—there are always considerations beyond the pure "right"—of a sort that escape the moralists' eyes but have some "moral" weight—some value—nonetheless. Order is value, a deep need of human beings in society, even though a value dangerous to liberty and other values; tradition and custom and social habit are values, although dangerous to social ideals. Dealing humanely with those human beings who hold something other than the "right" views is a very important value. One learns in the legislature of a genuine republic exactly to have many and continuous "dealings with the partisans of error." For the Americans—and for the English who were their primary teachers—these tolerations and collaborations and acknowledgings of multiple values were not violations of republican ideals but part of the essence of those ideals. And one of the places that republican ethos would be built into one's spiritual formation was the legislature.

Two

Madison had also had his political education advanced, we may presume to say, by his participation in the climactic episodes of the long struggle of 1776–86 over the religious arrangements in Virginia, which ended in the passage of Jefferson's Statute for Religious Freedom in January 1786. That enormous and consequential struggle entailed a politics not simply of a legislative body but of a whole state. Madison's strategy as the leader of the victorious forces involved a kind of politicking among the denominations, and a recognition of the value in having multiple groups to politic among, that we may infer would leave a lasting mark on his understanding. The Baptists and Presbyterians each had an essential role over against the Anglicans. The Methodists played an important role, too, by pulling away from the Anglicans at a crucial moment. The presence in the state of Quakers, Lutherans, and Moravians presumably helped, too, from Madison's point of view. He had already believed that uniting religious and political power tended to produce oppression, and that each human being has a natural right to conscientious belief; that was his earliest clear-cut political conviction, derived in part from his education among the New Side Presbyterians in Princeton. Now he came to believe, in addition, that the actual existence of a multitude of "sects," with some division and opposition among them, was the realistic way to protect against religio-political tyranny and to secure religious rights. In the midst of the fray in 1784 Madison wrote to Jefferson: "The mutual hatred of these sects has been much inflamed by the late Act incorporating [the Episcopalians]. I am far from being sorry for it, as a coalition between them could alone endanger our religious rights, and a tendency to such an event has been suspected." As the battle reached its climax in 1785 Madison wrote Jefferson: "The Presbyterian clergy have at length espoused the side of the opposition, being moved either by fear of their laity or a jealousy of the Episcopalians." The protection of religious liberty, he would now say, was to be found not only in declarations of rights, in principles and convictions, or even in laws; it was to be found also in a power situation—a division and balance—in which the numbers of, and conflict among, religious groups made overbearing combinations unlikely. Both Madison and Jefferson would say that in a situation of multiple "sects," each would serve as a *censor morum* of the others. Madison's conscientious sobriety of tone had nothing of the acid humor of Voltaire, but Madison nevertheless picked up and like to quote Voltaire's aphorism: "In one religion only were allowed in England, the Government would possibly become arbitrary; if there were two, they would be at each other's throats; but as there are such a multitude, they all live happy and in peace."

At important moments thereafter he would make use of the plurality of religious groups as an analogue for his larger theory. In February of 1788, in New York, working rapidly on his share of *The Federalist*, he made this analogy in a well-known and often quoted passage in *Federalist* 51: "In a free government, the security for civil rights must be the same as that for religious rights. It consists in the one case in the multiplicity of interests, and in the other, in the multiplicity of sects. The degree of security in both cases will depend on the number of interests and sects."

At the Virginia convention considering the ratification of the Federal Constitution, then, in June of 1788, he said, in the new nation the states happily "enjoy the utmost freedom of religion. This freedom arises from the multiplicity of sects, which pervades America, and which is the best and only security for religious liberty in any society. For where there is such variety of sects, there cannot be a majority of any one sect to oppress and persecute the rest."

In other words the analogue or example of religious pluralism ran through his subsequent thinking. The timing was close. The climax of the ten-year fight over religious policy in Virginia came, as noted above, in January 1786, in which month also he was chosen to be a Virginia delegate to the conference on interstate trade squabbles that was to be held in Annapolis the following fall. That Annapolis gathering was the beginning of the sequence of events that would lead to the Federal Constitution.

Three

When Madison began his studies in 1786 his adult life had had just two layers: Princeton and politics. Though still young by our standards today—thirty-five in 1786—he had become by then an experienced politician. At the same time he was still in his heart a scholar, an intellectual. And so in the spring of 1786, at home in Montpelier as he had not often been since his youth, he undertook systematic reading and note-taking and thinking about the kinds of governments the Americans were forming—republican governments—and about the foundations of politics itself.

Those are subjects best studied perhaps after some years and some experience. They have neither the exactitude nor the pure passion that is available and most appealing to the young; politics is neither mathematics nor lyric poetry nor pure moral philosophy. The inherent inexactitude of the subject was memorably noted not only by Aristotle but by Madison himself in *Federalist* 37. Politics as an intellectual subject is unavoidably tied to the humanities as we today divide the subject matter of the intellect; it cannot be an exact science with exact meanings and ironclad proof. The words that it uses are not denotative, utterly precise, the same across the centuries and the cultures, absolutely convincing to those who understand the terms, as in mathematics and those studies that properly rest upon mathematics. No such perfection attends our reflections on politics.

By the time he came to undertake his studies James Madison had spent ten years, virtually all of his adult life since college, in the most difficult and exacting kind of politics, in a most exhilarating and auspicious moment of political history. Such an experience makes one think.

So Madison did think. He was at home in Montpelier in Virginia for an extended stretch as he had not been since he went to Philadelphia in 1780 as a delegate from Virginia—he was a bachelor still—and although he became now a delegate to—a leader in—the Virginia Assembly there was more time, and more time at home with his books, than before.

He set about obtaining every treatise he could find on "confederacies"—on governments that bore some resemblance to the one in which he had been participating, with all its painful difficulties. When his friend

Thomas Jefferson went to Paris in July of 1784 he and Madison came to an understanding about services they could render to each other while Jefferson was abroad. Madison would look after the education of Jefferson's nephews, while Jefferson would make certain purchases for Madison. These included, as it turned out, various gadgets and devices that reflected the inventive spirit of the times, but most importantly—books. Madison asked Jefferson to obtain books on several subjects,and first on the list were books about ancient and modern republics, ancient and modern confederacies. Adrienne Koch, who included in her book on "the great collaboration between Jefferson and Madison" a chapter on this Jeffersonian supply of books to Madison, wrote that "Madison specifically requested Jefferson to purchase for him 'Treatises on the ancient and modern Federal Republics, on the law of Nations, and the History, natural and political, of the new World,' adding to these subjects 'such of the Greek and Roman authors, where they will be got very cheap, as are worth having, and are not on the common list of school classics."

There followed a remarkable exchange between the two young Virginia intellectuals. To quote Professor Koch again: "Jefferson's thoughtful provision of books for Madison, including some thirty-seven volumes of the coveted *Encyclopédie methodique,* which Madison called 'a complete scientific library,' treatises on morality, and histories of European countries, surely made Madison the most cosmopolitan statesman never to have quit American shores. Indeed, it was often remarked a few years later that Madison was probably the best-read and best-informed member of the Constitutional Convention." By January of 1786 James Madison, in Montpelier in Orange County, Virginia, had received two trunks of books bought in Paris by Thomas Jefferson.

Working in Montpelier with his books, Madison made his study of the history of confederacies. He specifically referred, according to the editors of his Papers, to twenty-one works, some of them multivolume collections. The notes that he left from this venture resemble the work of many a bright bookish list-making young person, with sharpened pencils copying onto fresh pieces of paper the populations of the major cities or the top ten songs on the hit parade or the batting averages of the Detroit Tigers. But Madison, although only in his thirties, and certainly bookish and studious, was no innocent secluded youngster—not any longer. These lists of ancient "confederacies," culled from books and lined up on the page—the Amphictyonic and the Achean confederacy of ancient Greece; the Helvitic confederacy of fourteenth- to fifteenth-century Switzerland; the Belgic confederacy after 1679; the Germanic confederacy—somewhat irrelevant as they may seem to us today—were an important part of his thinking through his problem. In each case he made a list of the identifying features, often with numbered sequences; and an analysis of the "federal" authority. Always the last section is a listing of the "vices" of the system. (for example, "1. disparity in size of cantons. 2. different principles of Government. in difft. cantons. 3. intolerance in religion. 4. weakness of the Union"). The overriding "vices" of all of these past confederacies were the jealousies and "sovereign" defiance of the component parts and the weakness of the central authorities, too weak to control these parts.

It is to be noted that young Madison, the child of this first successful modern revolution, concentrated his studies upon the vices—the faults and defects and dangerous tendencies—of the kind of government he was supporting. And on the past. That is not usual with revolutionaries; ordinarily they concentrate only on the present and the future, and on the vices exclusively of the regimes they oppose. The regime they propose often is all roses and moonlight, slogans, ideals and dreams. It has, by implication, no past. If these modern revolutionaries look back at the experience of humankind before they arrived on the scene, they do so only to invoke some largely imaginary golden age, to which they propose by their revolutionary upheaval to return: this past is but the deposit of their utopianism. They are not analytical about it. They do not characteristically examine it critically, to instruct themselves about the pitfalls they too must face, or the defects they themselves might represent.

The world has had a plentiful supply of revolutions and revolutionaries since Madison's day. The modern revolutionary, with his clenched fist and his barricades, his marching songs and his banners, has characteristically attributed the perennial problems of politics to the corrupt old order that he clenches his fist against; once that is overthrown, he implies, then humankind will awake in a springtime of the human spirit, when the problems of power, conflict, and interest have evaporated. Once the colonial oppressor is cast into the sea, once the royal tyrants are overthrown, once the dispossessors have themselves been dispossessed, once the working men of the world have united and thrown off their chains, once the white man with his racism has been replaced, once the arrogant males with their violence have been tamed by the soft sound of another voice, once the last king has been hanged in the entrails of the last priest, *then* the problems of power, the problems of self-interest, perhaps even the fact of social *evil* itself will be gone. It will depart with the departing oppressors and their evil system.

If you look at the world in that excessively revolutionary way, then you do not much examine the perennial and ubiquitous sources of the political problem. You do not see them as they appear even in your own revolutionary movement—even in yourself. But you should look around you. Notice those factions and conflicts, egotisms and power plays, present there in your own revolutionary movement. Will they disappear, "come the revolution?" On the contrary: they will grow. If you attribute the entire stock of the world's social evil to the particular order you seek to overthrow, then you and your movement are by implication altogether exculpated. You don't need to look to history; you do not identify with precursors, except as you may make them heroes and heroines in your revolutionary myth. You do not analyze the *vices* of regimes, like your own, that have preceded you. But young Madison *did* look at the vices of his own movement.

He did so not as an opponent, but as a supporter. He did believe deeply in "republicanism"—would devote his whole life to it. Two enormously consequential years after his studies in the spring to 1786—on June 14, 1788, to be exact, at the Virginia convention considering the ratification of the Constitution, he would made a personal testimony to that devotion, in a way that was unusual for him, and with quiet eloquence rare in him, that it may be useful to jump ahead and to quote here: "I profess myself," he said then, "to have had a uniform zeal for republican government. If the honorable member, or any other person, conceives that my attachment to this system arises from a different source, he is greatly mistaken. From the first moment that my mind was capable of contemplating political subjects, I never, till this moment, ceased wishing success to well regulated republican government. The establishment of such in America was my most ardent desire." The popular impression of his countrymen in later times may not suspect James Madison of "ardent desire" and "uniform zeal" for republican government—ardor and zeal not being part of the superficial stereotype of this American founder— and yet those who have examined James Madison's life, early and late, have regularly confirmed that he did indeed have such a zeal, such ardor, and not for the moment only but throughout a long life.

He was therefore, and moreover, a partisan of a progressive movement—a supporter not of the established order but of a change to improve it. However conservative James Madison may look to the eyes of the late twentieth century, he was a progressive in his own setting. On the world scene he was a young supporter of the world's first successful colonial revolt and of a worldwide antimonarchical, antihierarchical, and anti-imperial movement of republicanism spawned by the Enlightenment and Dissenting Protestantism. In his own land he was a supporter of the patriots against the Loyalists when that very weighty choice was made, and in later years when the new nation was established and under way he would be not only a supporter but a founder, along with Thomas Jefferson, of the more progressive of the two parties that contested for power in the new nation. But as a progressive or revolutionary he nevertheless consulted books about the past, and as a republican he nevertheless asked questions about the vices of republican governments.

Examining the past and examining the vices were part of an effort to look beyond the moment of revolutionary ardor to the long future, and to find the forms and principles that would make the results of the Revolution continue through time.

Most revolutionaries of course expect that the new order they hope to establish will last—but few take thought about how that lastingness might be achieved. James Madison *did* think about that: how the American republics, and the American union, might be made to be more stable and lasting than he been those republics and confederacies of past times. He thought about that—and the new American republic has indeed lasted, at least for two hundred plus years.

Four

Madison certainly would make use of those notes on the ancient and modern confederacies. They would appear in his important speech on June 6 in the Federal Convention in Philadelphia, in the summer of 1787, and, rather suddenly, in the following October, in his letter to Thomas Jefferson in Paris giving his summary of the convention, and finally in the following winter in three numbers Madison wrote in the *Federalist* papers.

James Wilson of Pennsylvania, who is often said to have been second in importance to Madison at the Constitutional Convention in Philadelphia, though a collaborator in thought and action with Madison in most of the big points at the convention, apparently did not share his belief that much could be learned from those antique confederacies. Wilson said in his speech about the Constitution in the Pennsylvania convention, a couple of months after the signing, that we know too little about these ancient republics and confederacies, and from what we do know they are so different from the United States as to "have supplied but a very small fund of applicable remark." Perhaps one can picture Wilson rolling his eyes to the ceiling of the Pennsylvania State House when Madison would start in again about the Achean League and the Helvitic Confederacy.

For James Madison, though, they did supply a certain fund of "applicable remark," because when you went through all these repeated experiences of human beings you established a trend. That trend at least illustrated and perhaps strengthened Madison's conviction that in the new republican government in the American colonies there had to be, as in these confederations of other times and places there had not been, strength at the center.

In Madison's important letter to Jefferson of October 24, 1787, which included a fair amount of arguing along with its factual report on the Constitutional Convention, there did appear again, sure enough, suddenly popping into the argument, the Achaean League and the Helvitic system and the German Empire and the Lycian Confederacy.

And then in *Federalist* 18, 19, and 20—not the numbers one rushes out to read perhaps—Madison would once more take up these old notes of his, two years after he had made them, and spill them out into complete sentences. In that setting, in the *Federalist* papers, Madison pointed all his examples from his memo toward his argument in behalf of the Constitution. And that meant his argument against the Articles of Confederation. The defects of those ancient and modern confederations were the defects of the Articles of Confederation, which the Constitution would correct. He said the faulty ancient Greek confederation, for example, "bore a very instructive analogy to the present Confederation of the American states." The fault in both was to be found in the absence of a central controlling authority—like that now provided in the new Federal Constitution. When he had marched through the details of the Greek, German, Dutch, and Belgian confederacies in those three *Federalist* papers he concluded: "I make no apology for having dwelt so long on the contemplation of these federal precedents." Then came a sentence that the scholars would surely tell us is the quintessence of the Enlightenment's belief on these matters: "Experience is the oracle of truth; and where its responses are unequivocal, they ought to be conclusive and sacred." The experience Madison is referring to is not what we might mean today—the necessarily small number of doings and encounters of one lifetime, set over against book learning—but rather almost the opposite: the experience of the *race,* of all the peoples one could learn about, as he did, exactly from consulting books.

And what was the conclusive truth that this kind of experience, "the oracle of truth," had taught? "The important truth, which it unequivocally pronounces in the present case, is, that a sovereignty over sovereigns, a government over governments, a legislation for communities, as contradistinguished from individuals; as it is a solecism in theory, so in practice, it is subversive of the order and ends of civil polity, by substituting *violence* in place of *law,* or the destructive *coertion* of the *sword,* in place of the mild and salutary *coertion* of the *magistracy.*"

In other words, repeated historical experience, the "oracle of truth," had taught that confederation in which the subunits are the sovereign entities, and the central government lacks the power to act directly on individuals, is repeatedly a failure. It does not work. All history shows that it does not work. The solution is implicit in the analysis: the central government must have the power to act, with the "gentle coertion of the magistracy," directly on individuals. Because we are now familiar with it, we Americans do not realize how unusual that idea was in its time—the idea that although Virginia and Pennsylvania would pass laws that a citizen of these states would have to obey, at the same time the United States of America would *also* pass laws that those same Virginians and Pennsylvanians would also have to obey—two governments (Virginia and the United States of America) simultaneously acting upon the same individual. There were those who said that could not be done—that it would not work. But Madison and others said it *would* work—and, moreover, that that power of the central government over individuals was *necessary* in order for a federation of republics to work. Otherwise this American one, like the Achean and Helvitic and Belgic and Germanic and the other fragile confederacies in Madison's memo, would fall into jealous and contending parts, and fail. But the Constitution of 1787 that Madison as Publius was recommending would overcome this fault and provide a new arrangement in which the stronger federal center may exercise its own authority over individuals, and survive.

Five

In the fall of 1786 after he made these first notes, Madison left Montpelier to travel to the Annapolis convention, and there joined with Alexander Hamilton in a story much told in American history books—turning the rather scrawny gathering, which did not even have its quota of states, into a call for a convention of all the states to revise the Articles of Confederation. That call—bold is the word for it—led on then to the convention in Philadelphia, and bold is the word for it, too. That convention in its turn snatched the opportunity and instead of simply revising the Articles pitched them out the window and replaced them with our two-centuries-old Federal Constitution. Madison played a formidable practical role in these events, the two successive bold strokes by which the independent colonies, on their second try, got themselves a workable common government. Madison also played an important role in the events leading up to the convention, for example in persuading the indispensable George Washington to attend.

After the Annapolis convention Madison, the traveling legislator and political scientist, went to a number of other places—to Philadelphia, to Mount Vernon to confer with Washington, to Richmond for the Virginia Assembly, home to Montpelier, to Mount Vernon again, to Philadelphia again—and then finally, in February 1787, to New York, where the old Continental Congress, in its desultory ineffectual way, on its very last legs, was meeting. Madison was to serve once more as a Virginia delegate.

This duty, however, was not arduous, and he continued his studies. He now knew that there would be a convention of all the states in Philadelphia in May and that he would be a Virginia delegate. In preparation, sitting there in New York, he thought some more, and composed another memorandum to himself.

2

"The People"
Can Act Unjustly

One

MADISON CALLED THIS SECOND MEMORANDUM "Vices of the Political
system of the U. States," and he worked on it, off and on, in the late
winter and early spring of 1787 while he was serving in the Continental
Congress of those U. States and observing those vices at first hand. Once
again he focused not on the ideal but rather on what had actually happened in the political life of real republics—this time of Virginia and R.
Island and Massts and the others that had come into being with independence, and on the feeble confederacy through which they were supposed
to collaborate.

The Constitution under which we now live, more than two hundred
years later, was the founders' second try at forming an overarching government, not the first. The Articles of Confederation, agreed to by the last
state—Maryland—so that they could go into effect in 1781, was the first
try, and Madison in particular learned from its defects. Alexander Hamilton and James Wilson, members of the state delegations of New York
and Pennsylvania, respectively, also learned from this participation in
that Congress in the early 1780s. These members of the younger generation in that Congress, dismayed by its defects, talked to each other about
a more effective instrument of republican government for the union, and
before the decade was over they would join together, on the second try,
to build one.

Or one can say that the Confederation under the Articles still was not the Americans' first try at new republican government: the forming of the *state* governments was the first. Back in the tremendous excitements of 1776, on May 10, before the July 4 declaration, Congress, on John Adams's motion, recommended that each of the British colonies in America set up its own new independent and republican government. Exactly in the great year of Independence they began to do that. Virginia had already done so in May of 1776, at a convention in Williamsburg that young James Madison attended, in his first participation in great public events. The Virginia convention both declared the colony (now state) independent of Great Britain and adopted a new state constitution; other states had adopted new constitutions in rapid order through that year and the following year.

Now ten years later, after experience with the state governments, Madison's memo did not celebrate how wonderful these first republics were—how glorious a realization of the great ideals of the late Revolution—but rather itemized what was wrong with them, and with the confederacy that brought them together.

Although Madison accentuated the vices he did not do so destructively or automatically, or out of some personal pique, as one sometimes suspects some radical critics of doing—taking out their own resentments in indiscriminate and sweeping assaults upon "the system." Madison was discriminate, specific, and analytical, as revolutionaries often are not.

By this time he knew that there would be a gathering of all the states in Philadelphia in the summer, and he knew that he would be a delegate. This memorandum was part of his preparation for what he would call in a letter to Randolph "the Business of May next."

The chief vices he found in the confederacy were exactly those that one would expect form his first memo: no strength at the center. The states fail to comply with the Confederation's "requisitions": when states have more power than the union they send troops or money to any common cause when, and only when, they feel like it. This condition "results so naturally from the number and independent authority of the States and has been so uniformly exemplified in every similar Confederacy" that it must be considered inherent. The states encroach on federal authority, violate treaties, trespass on the rights of each other, fail to join in projects of common interest. Such projects "may at present be defeated by the perverseness of particular States whose concurrence is necessary." One state could have a veto. We could not build the canals we needed because the states would not do their part. Even in wartime, as we learned to our sorrow during the "late Revolution," the states would not do their part.

Moreover, they take actions that harm each other: "See the law of Virginia restricting foreign vessels to certain ports—of Maryland in favor of vessels belonging to her own citizens—of N. York in favor of the same."

The states set up their own barriers and patterns of trade, in their own perceived state interest not in the interest of the union. They restrict "the commercial intercourse with other States," and put "their productions and manufactures on the same footing with those of foreign nations"; that "tends to beget retaliating regulations." One gets the picture of a trade war among the states, and also, from other comments, of contending currencies, court practices, treatments of debt, dealings with powers abroad, policies with respect to naturalization and "literary property."

Madison wove into his itemizing of the vices of the confederacy remarks on the foundation of government: "A sanction is essential to the idea of law, as coercion is to that of Government" (this time spelling "coercion" as we do). The government under the Articles is "destitute of both" and therefore doesn't work; it lacks the vital principle. "It is in fact nothing more than a treaty of amity of commerce and of alliance, between so many independent and Sovereign States."

How could such a fatal error have been made? Misplaced confidence in everybody's good faith. Inexperience. But now we know better. "It is no longer doubted that a unanimous and punctual obedience of 13 independent bodies, to the acts of the federal Government, ought not be calculated on. Even during the war, when external danger supplied in some degree the defect of legal & coercive sanctions, how imperfectly did the States fulfil their obligations to the Union?"

Those thirteen clocks would not ever again strike at the same time, if they ever did.

And, Madison asked himself (presumably he was writing this memo mostly for himself), "How indeed could it be otherwise?" He gave a succinct three-point summary of the limitations of "voluntary" coordination in important matters. "In the first place, Every general act of the Union must necessarily bear unequally hard on some particular member or members of it."

So the unequally treated ones scream and probably defy the act. And they estimate the inequalities from their own distorted perspective: "Secondly the partiality of the members to their own interests and rights, a partiality which will be fostered by the Courtiers of popularity, will naturally exaggerate the inequality where it exists, and even suspect it where it has no existence."

And then there will be the acid of suspicion: "Thirdly a distrust of the voluntary compliance of each other may prevent the compliance of any, although it should be the latent disposition of all."

That last is an important political insight: we all have "a latent disposition" to collaborate as well as a resistance to "coercion"; the accomplishment of a successful polity is to bring the latent disposition to the fore, so that it reinforces the obedience to law.

Madison made this analysis stronger by an analogy: Suppose the laws of the states "were merely recommendatory"? How many people would pay their income taxes (these now are my examples) or even drive on the right-hand side of the road, let alone drive under fifty-five miles an hour, if these were just recommendations? Or suppose each county rejudged the state laws?

One can see Madison getting ready to support a constitution for the union that would be "the Supreme Law of the land."

Two

Madison discovered vices not only in the confederacy but in those first republics, the state governments, themselves. These vices included something more disturbing than the "luxuriancy" of the laws they passed ("what a luxuriancy of legislation do they present. The short period of independency has filled as many pages as the century which preceded it") or their "mutability" (the states kept *changing* these laws so fast that the "remoter regions" didn't have time to learn what the new law is before it is changed). Madison as the dutiful, intelligent, and experienced—one might say professional—lawmaker, might be expected to make criticisms of that sort; but other vices he discovered in these new republican states went much deeper—to the core of republican government itself.

One of these deeper issues had to do with "internal violence" within the states, and that matter, in turn, raised the issue of the composition of the electorate—who are excluded and who therefore are inclined to resort to violence. In the winter before these reflections Shays's Rebellion in Massachusetts had startled sober opinion both with the frustration of the excluded and with the possibility of revolt even in a republic. Madison, reflecting in his notebook on these matters, noted that republican theory holds that the majority should rule, but that in certain circumstances a one-third minority in a state—if, say, it has military skill and "pecuniary" resources—may be an "overmatch" for a two-thirds majority. In that case the weak union under the Articles could do nothing about it. A coup or a riot or a minority takeover could lead to an unrepublican government, a tyranny, an oligarchy, a dictatorship as we would later say, in one of the states, and the union would be stuck with that, and all its consequences. (The Virginia Plan presented to the Philadelphia convention a month or two after this memorandum, and the work of Madison as much as any individual, proposed that the union guarantee—with decisively stronger federal power—that every state have a republican form of government. That proposal survives as a provision of the United States Constitution today.)

But providing recourse of the union against unrepublican governments in states does not answer some other troubling questions. His picture of a one-third "minority" overthrowing a two-thirds "majority" went like this (the reader will discern why it is appropriate to use quotation marks): "One third of those who participate in the choice of the rulers, may be rendered a majority by the accession of those whose poverty excludes them from a right of suffrage, and who for obvious reasons will be more likely to join the standard of sedition than that of the established Government."

In other words, the excluded poor, who do not vote and are therefore not counted as part of the legal "majority" of voting citizens, may join a legal "minority," to make an extralegal government: the majority of actual human beings would overmatch the "majority" of property-holding voters. As W. C. Fields was later to exclaim in consternation that "somebody put *pineapple juice* in my pineapple juice," so James Madison in effect remarks that a *majority* might overturn the "majority."

The eighteenth-century majority, even without quotation marks, would be still, as we would be quick to point out in the twentieth century, the larger number only among free white males. Madison did not raise the question of the still larger majority that could outnumber the "majority" if women were included. That question had been raised by Abigail Adams in her famous letters to her husband back in the excitement about "new modeling" government in the spring of 1776. Her husband had responded with lofty and dismissive male amusement, but in letters to others—to male colleagues in the new modelings—John Adams himself then raised the question about why women were excluded in a way that suggested that Mrs. Adams had drawn a little intellectual blood after all. But not much. To raise the question of women's exclusion from the "majority" was too far out of the common thinking in the late eighteenth century for it to be even a speculative possibility. And James Madison had no Abigail writing him probing letters.

Another exclusion, however, was present to Madison's mind. In this memo he made only one very brief and perhaps cryptic reference to slavery, but he did show that he was not unaware of the further contradiction offered to the then current idea of the majority by the presence of large numbers of uncounted black slaves. He wrote: "Where slavery exists the republican Theory becomes still more fallacious."

That is all he said in this memo of 1787. In later notes for himself there was more. Some jottings he was to make in the winter of 1791–92, after the new government was launched, for essays he would write in the *National Gazette,* have been printed in volume 14 of the Madison *Papers* and called to attention by Drew McCoy in *The Last of the Fathers.* In those later notes of 1791 Madison would indicate what presumably he meant in 1787 by republican theory becoming "fallacious" where slavery exists. He would candidly spell out (to himself) the contradiction between slavery and republicanism. He would write that "in proportion as slavery prevails in a state" the government must be aristocratic, even though labeled "democratic." He applied that perception not only to "all ancient governments" but to the current states of the American South— to Virginia itself! In fact he expanded the indictment also to the exclusion of propertyless whites: "The rule of suffrage which, requiring a freehold in land excludes nearly half of the free population." Madison put these points together—excluded slaves and excluded propertyless whites—to say in his notes, in obvious disapproval by an implicit republican standard of majority rule: "At present the slaves and non-freeholders amount to nearly 3/4 of the State. The power is therefore in about 1/4." If it had been present to this consciousness to ask about the exclusion of women, he could have made the fraction that held power even smaller. As an experienced politician, he knew, moreover, that a shift in the base of power shifts outcomes: "Were slaves freed and the right of suffrage extended to all," he would write, in his 1791 jottings, "the operation of government might be very different."

Madison's faulting of governments—specifically that of Virginia— that claim to be republican when they grant power only to one-fourth of the population was confined to his private misgivings, and not made public.

Three

Madison in his memo in 1787 noted a still deeper problem about republicanism. The "majority," however composed, however inclusive—may do great wrong. The "people" may enact unjust laws. How does that square with republican theory?

The fundamental principle of republican government, wrote Madison, was that the *majority* will be "the safest Guardians" of *both* public good and private rights. And yet Madison looked at the new American republics and saw unjust laws passed by majorities. If majorities in these new independent American *republics*—Maryland and Pennsylvania and Virginia and the wild people in Rhode Island and the rest—pass *"unjust"* laws, what is one to say?

Madison expanded and expanded this item in his memo until it was not just a short point any more but a little essay. And it contained the nugget of important ideas that he would take with him in May to Philadelphia and that would then be incorporated in the underpinnings of the United States Constitution.

What causes the evil of unjust laws, enacted by republican states? "These causes lie: 1. In the Representative bodies. 2. In the People themselves."

The first of these, typically, produces another numbered list. Men seek appointment as representatives "from 3 motives: 1. ambition 2. personal interest 3. public good." Now the realist's comment: "Unhappily the two first are proved by experience to be most prevalent." (These notes were not for publication; they would not be read by Madison's colleagues in the representative bodies in which he served.) Self-interested representatives often join "in a perfidious sacrifice" of their constituents' interest to their own. And a succeeding election does not "repair the mischief."

> How easily are base and selfish measures, masked by pretexts of public good and apparent expediency? How frequently will a repetition of the same arts and industry which succeeded in the first instance, again prevail on the unwary to misplace their confidence?
>
> How frequently too will the honest but unenligh[t]ened representative be the dupe of a favorite leader, veiling his selfish views under the professions of public good, and varnishing his sophistical arguments with the glowing colours of popular eloquence?

As in another item Madison implied disapproval of "Courtiers of popularity," so here he indicates that he did not much like "the glowing colours of popular eloquence."

But Madison did not blame unjust laws, as a later American public would have the habit of doing, solely on the "politicians." The most important cause of unjust laws was to be found not in ambitious and perfidious representatives but in the people themselves. To explain that fact Madison looked carefully at that foundation of republican government, "the people." On examination the people proved to be not a simple single unitary body with a common will but a shifting combination of many subgroups. He launched a discussion of the inevitable differences among the human beings that compose any people—an analysis that he would continue to repeat and develop through the decisive years just ahead of him: "All civilized societies are divided into different interests and factions, as they happen to be creditors or debtors—Rich or poor—husbandmen, merchants or manufacturers—members of different religious sects—followers of different political leaders—inhabitants of different districts—owners of different kinds of property &c &c."

So in any "people" there will be divergent interests—"factions," as he would later write.

But when it comes time to compose the public will upon which republican government rests, won't members of these potentially clashing interest restrain themselves, for the larger good? Not necessarily. You cannot depend on it. A devoted republican, Madison nevertheless did not romanticize "the people." At the end of his memo Madison asked himself: Is there any motive that would restrain one of the interests, especially when it became a majority? He lists three possibilities.

The first of the possible restraining motives is "a prudent regard to their own good as involved in the general and permanent good of the Community." But this prudent regard for one's own share in the common good "is found by experience too often unheeded." Madison had learned that in a contest between a big, immediate advantage for oneself and a long-term good of the community, the former very often wins out.

Second, there is "respect for character," meaning one's own reputation for probity. One cares what people think of one's "character." That, too, is "very insufficient to restrain [powerful interests] from injustice."

The third of these possible restraints on injustice, which Madison put in a separate category from the first two, is "religion." Did James Madison think we need more religion to restrain group interest and to solve the problems of politics? Not necessarily. "When indeed Religion is kindled into enthusiasm, its force like that of other passions, is increased by the sympathy of a multitude. . . . Besides as religion in its coolest state, is not infallible, it may become a motive to oppression as well as a restraint from injustice."

Madison noted that these possible restraints—moral restraints, as we may call them—insufficient in person-to-person encounters, become even less effectual when large groups clash. Of "respect for character," Madison wrote: "In a multitude its efficacy is diminished in proportion to the number which is to share the praise or the blame."

Large groups (e.g., nations), to put it another way, have very limited "conscience" or capacity for self-criticism, or sensitivity to the moral appraisal of others.

The generality of the population, Madison observed, will not care very much what outside opinion may be: "Is it to be imagined that an ordinary citizen or even an assembly-man of R. Island in estimating the policy of paper money, ever considered or cared in what light the measure would be viewed in France or Holland; or even in Massts or Connect.? It was a sufficient temptation to both that it was for their interest: it was a sufficient sanction to the latter that it was popular in the State; to the former that it was so in the neighborhood."

The point about the moral limitations of groups applies to religion: "Will Religion . . . be a sufficient restraint? It is not pretended to be such on men individually considered. Will its effect be greater on them considered in an aggregate view? quite the reverse. The conduct of every popular assembly acting on oath, the strongest of religious Ties, proves that individuals join without remorse in acts, against which their consciences would revolt if proposed to them under the like sanction, separately in their closets."

In other words, religion can make matters worse, by associating partial views and collective egotisms with the sanction of heaven.

Further along in the memo he gave an illustration of a basic political point: "Place three individuals in a situation wherein the interest of each depends on the voice of the others, and give to two of them an interest opposed to the rights of the third. Will the latter be secure? The prudence of every man would shun the danger. The rules & forms of justice suppose & guard against it."

Madison then enlarged the situation to ask what it will be with groups: "Will two thousand in a like situation be less likely to encroach on the rights of one thousand?"

No, they will be even more likely to encroach on the rights of the minority, as the numbers increase. So how then may the consequent injustice be dealt with? How can a republic—which includes majority rule—function justly?

Four

In the months that followed Madison would work out his answer. It included protections against that human inclination to neglect the public good, and to prefer private advantage, that he had observed in his years in politics and recorded in his memos; but it also presumed a capacity for human beings, to a degree and under the right restraints, to serve justice and the common good. The point of Madison's form of republican government was to arrange institutions so as to encourage that capacity, in part exactly by restraining that inclination.

Madison's view of human nature was not identical with that of the great pessimists and "realists," and the political position he came to was not like theirs either—not conservative. Madison put the realistic insights and perspectives usually more characteristic of conservatives (the awareness of power, self-interest, and disorder) at the service of a progressive politics—republicanism. And his view of human nature was not identical with that of the great conservative pessimists, who on the basis of a dark view of humankind supported rule by centralized authority. Madison's view of humankind was not uniformly pessimistic but mixed.

Madison came to a realistic view of human nature that may have differed somewhat from the outlook of his great friend and collaborator Thomas Jefferson. But it differed more widely from the kinds of "realism" that can be found in many times in the history of political thinking. If you take a page or two of this memo, or of the *Federalist* pieces that Madison would write a year later, and put them alongside a page or two of the central part of Machiavelli's *Prince*, or the early part of Hobbes's *Leviathan*, you may see what I mean. Madison's realism is placed in service of the moral purpose of government in a way that is very different from the outlook of Machiavelli or Hobbes or the defenders of Realpolitik or of reductionist modern philosophies.

To take just one great name for contrast, there is a luxuriancy—to borrow that new word from Madison—of interpretations of Machiavelli. Machiavelli is variously said to be a devoted republican and an Italian patriot and the father of political science and many other worthy and un-Machiavellian things. He may well have been all those and more, but it certainly seems as you read the central chapters of *The Prince* that he must have been a vastly different sort of republican from James Madison. The practices on the part of political leaders that James Madison in his memos was conceding but implicitly *deploring* had been, three hundred years earlier, not deplored but *recommended* to the Prince, with a kind of relish, by Machiavelli. "Morality" is something the Prince uses, or does not use, as may serve his purpose. When he talks about morality, Machiavelli seems to be talking about a public relations strategy rather than a program of worthy human conduct.

Machiavelli has been much praised for a willingness to look clear-eyed and unillusioned at the way states and princes really do behave—praised by, among others, himself. James Madison, three hundred years later, also wanted to "go to the real truth of the matter," but he did not swagger about it in Machiavelli's way.

Machiavelli's repute rests also in his single-minded insistence that first of all the Prince had to stay in power—had to protect the state and its security and interests. That's first. Without that, without keeping the ship afloat (and this particular captain?) then nothing else can be done, no other value served. And, to be sure, Renaissance Florence, where Machiavelli was writing, seems to have been a brutal place, where the raw nerve of politics—the "coercion" that Madison had talked about in item seven of his memo—was exposed. But it was not altogether hidden in the American republics under the Articles that Madison dealt with three hundred years later. And did not James Madison know the importance of political success, of political survival, of keeping the ship afloat? One of his notable attributes, in this pivotal thinking, was his concentration exactly on that matter: how to build a republican regime that will *last,* that will *survive,* that will not collapse and fall a part as the republics and confederacies of the past have done. That is why he focused so insistently on these vices. In a sense he was very much concerned with the Machiavellian question: survival, persisting, keeping the polity going, keeping an order. But for him the issue was the survival, not just of a Prince (a particular regime), or of *any* order whatever independent of its content, but of a *republican* order. And for him—for all these original Americans—a republican form of government had a moral content, a cluster of values, a defining deposit of human goods.

Behind the scrupulous observer of the vices of the new American states and of the selfishness, narrowness, and power-grabbing of human beings everywhere in politics (not least in the Continental Congress in which he was serving) there was the conscientious student in Dr. Witherspoon's classes in moral philosophy at the College of New Jersey, and the "child of the Revolution" and its ideals, trying to find a way to form a republican government that would serve justice and the public good, and keep on doing so through the centuries.

That Madison does not believe that ambition and self-interest, despite their prevalence, need be the whole story of political leadership is evident at the effective end of the memorandum. Rather abruptly he put down this paragraph: "An auxiliary desideratum for the melioration of the Republican form is such a process of elections as will most certainly extract from the mass of the Society the purest and noblest characters which it contains; such as will at once feel most strongly the proper motives to pursue the end of their appointment, and be most capable to devise the proper means of attaining it."

It is not a paragraph that Machiavelli, or anyone with a trace of cynicism, would be likely to write.

Madison did hope that the election process might "extract" "the purest and noblest characters." But that was an "auxiliary" desideratum; it was not the expectation and necessity upon which republican government should rest.

Five

Madison certainly would get a lot of mileage out of his memos. He drew heavily upon them in his speeches in the Federal Convention in Philadelphia. He gave his first major speech speech on June 6, when the ostensible topic was the election of representatives to the lower house (either by the state legislatures or—as Madison preferred—the people). The delegates in Philadelphia would range far from the ostensible topic, especially in the early weeks of the convention, and Madison, having the floor, used the occasion for his earliest and most fundamental laying down of philosophical underpinnings, and these were largely taken from his memorandums. He would draw particularly on point eleven from his memo on the vices in which he dealt with the question Why are there unjust laws in a republic? He presented his analysis of the groups, powers, and interests that compose any people, and proposed his republican solution—enlarge the sphere and thereby divide the community into so many interests and parties as to make it unlikely that any can become overbearing. His analysis of, and insistence upon, the inevitable divisions and differences among human beings appeared, slightly elaborated, in this June 6 speech pretty much as it had in the memorandum on the vices; in the convention notes (his notes) the memo appears often almost verbatim.

He included, in that presentation of these ideas, as examples of the kinds of oppression that could be built upon human differences, "verified from the History of every country, antient and modern"—Greece, Rome, Carthage, the United States and Great Britain. But he also included in his June 6 speech a sentence on a kind of human difference and oppression that had barely appeared in his memos and would not appear at all in *Federalist* 10. It appears as a single complete sentence in his notes on his own speech: "We have seen the mere distinction of colour made in the most enlightened period of time, a ground of the most oppressive dominion ever exercised by man over man."

Once again there is a brief lightning flash of recognition of a tragic dimension—the dimension of racial dominion—beyond anything his usual analysis reached; once again, having glanced at it, referred to it briefly, he said no more.

Even after the convention Madison continued to make use of his memorandums. He folded whole pieces of them into that long letter, already mentioned, that he wrote to Thomas Jefferson on October 24, telling him about the convention. And finally, in the following November, he pulled them out of the drawer (as we might imagine) and borrowed from them when he composed his entries in the *Federalist* papers. As we have said, he used the material from ancient and modern republics in *Federalist* 18, 19, and 20; and he used the reflections on the vices particularly in the first and greatest essay he wrote, *Federalist* 10. At last, one might say, this material would find a publisher.

3

Beginning the World Anew,
to a Certain Extent

One

SOMETIMES THE TELLING OF THE STORY of the American Constitution
moves so swiftly and so deeply into controversies about the machinery
(especially the dispute over the basis of representation and other disagree-
ments between the large states and the small) as to miss the still larger
points. One is that the American colonies had come to be committed to
republican government, whatever they might mean by that. Others are
that a key group, with the initiative, had come to believe that there should
be a new constitution, not a patchwork on the old Articles; that the new
national government should have supreme power; and that the inaugu-
rating of this new governmental undertaking should come not by negotiating with, or grant from, some preexisting power (a king) but should
arise from the whole people through the instrument of the constitutional
convention.

None of these points was original with, or distinctive to, James Madison; they were convictions widely held, though in some cases controversial. Alexander Hamilton held at least as strongly as Madison to the need
for a strong and new government of all the colonies, and had held so since
early experiences with the frustrations of the army dealing with Congress
in the war, in 1777. Many others did too, George Washington chief
among them. But Madison is one of those who gave persistent active intelligent voice to these convictions, pointing toward giving them practical
effect in Philadelphia.

While writing his second memorandum in New York in the late winter and spring of 1787, Madison wrote letters working out these ideas to Jefferson in Paris on March 19; to Edmund Randolph (then the governor of Virginia, who would be the leader of the Virginia delegation in Philadelphia) on April 8; and on April 16 to George Washington. These letters have been said to contain "the first shoot" of the key ideas of the Virginia Plan, the Constitution, and the *Federalist* papers; they contain many of the same ideas as the memorandums often in almost identical language.

And they develop the idea of a constitutional convention—an idea that does not seem radical, or perhaps even notable, to us today, but that was both in its time.

Two

How do "the people" institute governments? How do you get new governments *started?* It is all very well to speak of beginning the world anew (as Tom Paine had done, back in 1776), but how do you do it?

Paine's enormously influential pamphlet *Common Sense* had given the negative answer to that question—you do not start with a king. But it remained for others to give the positive answer.

It is difficult for a modern American now to reenter the mental atmosphere of the ages of monarchy, when the essence of rightful government was thought and felt to be already and always present, existing before our thinking about it in the timeless royal prerogative. The king was the great fiction of social order—the king's courts, the king's men, the king's peace, in the name of the king, the royal governor, the royal grant, the original royal priority, of which then the king's loyal subjects asked the grant of gracious favors. Magna Carta: Please, Mr. King, give us a charter guaranteeing our liberties. To this day one can get a flavor of that ancient monarchical attitude when one hears a true tory drink a toast to, or otherwise invoke, the name of the queen. Partly it's ritual, and partly it's the felt foundation of society—the shared symbol or fiction for the social order in which one lives.

That it was still powerful among these American colonials, raised as British subjects, is shown by an interesting passage, a digression answering an anticipated argument, in an important little document that John Adams wrote, a letter in answer to a request that he put on paper his ideas about the form of government appropriate to the newly independent states, which he had been urging to create new governments. This was in 1776, at about the time Paine was writing, for a much bigger audience, his *Common Sense.* Adams's paper came to be called *Thoughts on Government.* In it he wrote:

But must not all commissions run in the name of a king? No. Why may they not as well run thus; "the colony of ——— to A.B. greeting," and be tested by the governor?

Why may not writs, instead of running in the name of the king, run thus, "the colony of ——— to the sheriff, etc., and be tested by the chief justice?

Why may not indictments conclude, "against the peace of the colony of ——— and the dignity of the same"?

Why not, indeed? That Adams felt the need to raise and answer this question in his short paper tells a lot about the attitudes he knew he was dealing with. It must have sounded a little flat, to ears accustomed to the ringing phrase "In the name of the King!" to hear instead "In the name of the people of Massachusetts." That would take some getting used to.

Up to the beginning of the year 1776 most of these deferential English colonials still accepted the great royal myth they had grown up with. They had framed their "humble petitions" and they had preserved the fiction that the king himself was simply misled by bad advisors and could be appealed to—his gracious majesty—against the bad advice and bad policy that was the responsibility of others. Tom Paine in his pamphlet cut through all that, in a shocking, radical way, and blamed the king himself and spoke of him disparagingly. Paine called the king, among many other uncomplimentary names, the "hardened, sullen-Tempered Pharaoh of England" and "the royal brute of England." (Benjamin Franklin was among those credited by rumor with writing the anonymous *Common Sense*; when a British lady reproached him for writing in that pamphlet that the king was "the royal brute of England," Franklin responded that he had not written *Common Sense* and that, furthermore, he would never have so dishonored the brute creation.)

In addition to slurs on the current incumbent Paine attacked the very principle of monarchy itself: "Of more worth is one honest man to society, and in the sight of God, than all the crowned ruffians that ever lived."

Paine not only attacked kings but also lords and nobles and aristocrats—the heredity principle anywhere. We don't need any Lords this and Lords that. Paine thus attacked two of three pillars—the monarchy and the aristocracy—of "the British Constitution." Paine said: rescue the only sound part of that constitution, the only republican part, the House of Commons, and make that the whole government. In an appendix to later editions of *Common Sense* Paine wrote that if America could attain independence, "we have the opportunity and every encouragement before us to form the noblest, purest constitution on the face of the earth. We have it in our power to begin the world over again."

The Americans had then defeated—with the help of the French—the armed might of the British Empire; had signed a treaty and won independence; had set up new state governments; and had arranged a kind of union under the Articles of Confederation. But perhaps neither the state governments nor the Articles had quite represented "the noblest, purest constitution on the face of the earth," and perhaps the Americans after all had not quite yet begun the world over again.

One of the state constitutions, that in Pennsylvania, had conformed to ideas Paine had about constitution-making—keep it simple, make it "democratic," avoid all those complicated balances—but the others had not. Massachusetts in particular had not. And complicated questions had arisen about what republican governments should be, and, for that matter, how begun.

It was all very well to be independent of the king, but if the king be gone how then does "a people" get its government started? Some of the new Americans, especially in Massachusetts, were to work out a novel answer to that question, in a process of constitution-making in which John Adams played a large role. The answer was: by a constitutional convention independent of the regular legislature, which convention would be derived directly from the people and would produce a constitution that would be sent back to be ratified by the people, the onetime convention having meanwhile dissolved. Its members would not necessarily themselves expect to be part of the ongoing government they proposed; that would be the result of another shuffle and dealing of the people's cards, under different rules. (The French, who would get many of things they would borrow from the Americans a little wrong, or a lot wrong, would *prohibit* members of the constitution-writing convention from service in the subsequent legislature; that was carrying the point too far, as the French in general had an inclination to do.)

There would be a onetime constitutional convention, and a ratification of its product by "the people." Behind that process there would be the idea of, as a historian of these matters has put it, "the People as Constituent Power." "The formula, *We the people ordain and establish,* expressing the developed theory of the people as constituent power, was used for the first time in the Massachusetts constitution of 1780, whence it passed into the preamble of the United States constitution of 1787." This was the answer to the question How do you get a political system started, once you have dispensed with a king? "The people" do it; this constitutional convention is the institution by which they do it.

Now, in early 1787 the Americans were getting ready to use that method, employed seven years before by Massachusetts, for the *union.* Tom Paine had mentioned in passing, long before Madison's busy years, the possibility of calling a "continental Conference" "to frame a continental Charter, or Charter of the United Colonies," a suggestion that was ahead of its time. But now in a very different climate a segment of American opinion was moving toward such a "conference" and some were applying to it the idea of the people as the originating power (through the device of a onetime convention). Prominent among them was James Madison. He argued for that idea in the letters that he wrote to Jefferson, Randolph, and Washington.

Madison argued for a constitutional convention drawn from the people, whose product is ratified by the people. He explained one reason for this method to Jefferson: "I think myself that it will be expedient in the first place to lay the foundation of the new system in such a ratification by the people themselves of the several states as will render it clearly paramount to their Legislative authorities." He put the same point with other nuances this way to George Washington a month later: "To give a new System its proper validity and energy, a ratification must be obtained from the people, and not merely from the ordinary authority of the Legislatures. This will be the more essential as inroads on the *existing Constitutions* of the States will be unavoidable."

Madison was writing plainly to Washington, a month before the delegates would gather in Philadelphia, about "a new system"—not simply about amending the Articles of Confederation. To Edmund Randolph, on the other hand, a different kind of correspondent perhaps from the bolder thinkers Jefferson and Washington, Madison was writing at about the same time in a slightly more cautious way, at least at the beginning of the discussion. There is one paragraph in his letter to Randolph (too long to quote) in which Madison began by seeming to agree with him: "I think with you that it will be well to retain as much as possible of the old Confederation," but then immediately in effect takes it back: "tho' I doubt whether it may not be best to work the valuable articles into the new System, instead of engrafting the latter on the former." He begins his next sentence as though they were in accord all the way: "I am also perfectly of your opinion that in framing a system, no material sacrifices ought to be made to local or temporary prejudices." That is safe enough, and very much in accord with Madison's strong nationalistic leanings; but his introducing it with "I am also perfectly of your opinion . . ." is not without its guile. Madison proceeded gently to reject Randolph's idea that the proposed reforms could be presented to the states piecemeal and concludes; "In truth my ideas of a reform strike so deeply at the old Confederation, and lead to such a systematic change, that they scarcely admit of the expedient [that is, of piecemeal submission]." In other words Madison was pretty thoroughly disagreeing with the endlessly wavering Randolph, while not saying so bluntly.

Three

That was the large picture: a *new* system, ratified by the people. A new government, cut off from and supplanting the Articles, designed by a federal convention, and ratified by state conventions chosen by the people independent of the state legislatures. It sounds simple enough now, but it was momentous and original in its time. Most new beginnings are not new beginnings and, to be sure, neither was this one, completely. But in place of accident, inertia, usurpation, or force—beginning by the fiat of a few, or by default and accident without thought—here is a beginning in deliberation, with the people judging.

There was also the large essential idea, the core reason for the whole project—a central government stronger than the state governments. Madison anticipated a strong central government in his letters of the spring of 1787. Thus he wrote to Washington: "Conceiving that an individual independence of the States is utterly irreconcilable with their aggregate sovereignty; and that a consolidation of the whole into one simple republic would be as inexpedient as it is unattainable, I have sought for some middle ground, which may at once support a due supremacy of the national authority, and not exclude the local authorities wherever they can be subordinately useful."

In this so-called middle ground, however, there was no doubt that the central government would have "due supremacy" and that the states would be "subordinately" useful; without that subordination, in Madison's view, the new government would be pitched into the sea of vices his memorandums detailed. Madison also wrote to Washington (there are very similar notes in his letters to the others), "I would propose . . . that in addition to the present federal powers, the national Government should be armed with positive and compleat authority in all cases which require uniformity," some of which he goes on to specify. In this period of his life, negatively impressed by the weakness of the Confederation, further impressed by his studies of what had happened to confederations of the past, he knew that there had to be a "federal" government stronger than the governments of the states.

One form this conviction took was the idea that Madison presented to each of his three correspondents in the spring of 1787, that the "federal head" should be given a "negative" (a veto) over the acts of the state legislatures "in all cases whatsoever" (the phrase used by Parliament in the Declaratory Act, out of long British usage) "as hitherto exercised by the kingly perogative." He held this to be "absolutely necessary" to the strength at the center that he sought; "without this defensive power, every positive power that can be given on paper will be evaded & defeated. The States will continue to invade the national jurisdiction, to violate treaties and the law of nations & harass each other with rival and spiteful measures dictated by mistaken views of interest." Madison was to fight hard for this provision in Philadelphia, and to be much disappointed in his failure to achieve its inclusion in the Constitution. Madison, at that point, held no very high view of the behavior of the state governments—not without reasons. He added that such a "negative" would protect the rights of individuals and minorities against the "aggressions of interested majorities"; at that point, in other words, he saw the prime danger to liberty residing in the states, with the federal government a protector. His proposed "negative" by the federal government against any action by the state legislatures was a drastic proposal. That he failed is sometimes counted among the points in the argument that he was not, after all, the "Father of the Constitution"; what it shows instead is that he thought boldly and was fully convinced that the new government should have strength at the center.

In his letters of the spring of 1787 Madison expressed another idea, more successful than that of the "negative" on the states, and more distinctive to himself than the idea of the constitutional convention and strong central government. This was an answer to the quite widespread and persistent idea that republics by their nature had to be small.

How did one respond to the ancient and almost unanimous belief, with the prestige of Montesquieu behind it, that a republic could exist only in a small society? That by its nature a social order in which "the majority were the guardians both of the public good and of private rights"—to borrow the phrase from Madison himself—had to be *small?* Partly on the basis of his reading, Madison worked out in these same months a famous answer to that question. He also developed theories of humankind and of group relations that would undergird and justify that answer. He was developing the idea of the "extended" or "compound" republic, and of the balancing of factions—or "pluralism" as we have come to call it—that he would present in Philadelphia and then in most memorable form in *The Federalist.*

Four

The American Revolution had been different from what the French would be. We Americans did not have any Paris mobs partly because we did not have any Paris. We did not chop the heads off any kings and nobles partly because we did not have available any kings and nobles to attend to in that way. We were able to move directly into stable local self-government partly because we had already had such government, more or less, for almost a century and a half. It is certainly easier to move to republican government if you already have it. (The French did not even claim a republic in the first stages of their revolution in '89—not until '92.)

We Americans did not have to cope with the solid old reactionary opposition that combined monarchy and aristocracy with established religious authority and defended the Old Regimes against republicanism. We had neatly left that sort of thing behind three times: first, when the Protestant reformers broke with Rome; second, when the Dissenters in England and elsewhere broke with the established churches; and third, when the Puritans left Anglican England and put an ocean between themselves and the evils of Europe. And we took care of any remaining ties with European reaction by having our tories, such as they were, leave— go back to England, or to Canada—and, unlike the émigrés in France, never come back.

And despite some early strictures about behavior and piety and virtue, our revolution did not try to reach down to the roots of culture and prescribe dress and family life and schooling and a new week and new months and a new calendar with screwy new names—a new religion.

So our revolution had some advantages from the start. Nevertheless, our revolution was not a minor matter, to be disparaged by comparison to later revolutions that ripped things up more dramatically. Neither should it be regarded as the inevitable outcome of historical forces. We should not let slip what is distinctly worthy in the ideas and values department. The heirs of revolutions that feature, right at the center, the idea of *Liberty* surely cannot ignore the finest product of liberty—the ideas and values by which a people live.

The American revolutionaries had not been bashful about what they were constructing: A NEW ORDER FOR THE AGES, they said, in Latin— *nouve orda seclorum*—on the Great Seal and hence today on the back of the dollar bill. We have it in our power to begin the world anew. But then as the months and years had gone by, and the Americans had written state constitutions and fought a war with the British and tried to raise money and troops and govern themselves under a loose Confederation, starting the world anew and constructing a new order for the ages had proved to be rather a larger project than it had seemed in the first flush of defiance. If you were to try to build the world anew, the first thing you would want to understand is that you cannot do it. The world will not be as new as you thought it would be. And if you know that, you may make it somewhat newer, and somewhat better, after all, as the Americans in fact did.

To do so you need in the end not Tom Paine (who by '87 had gone on

41

to try to start the world anew someplace else) or any of those French fellows, but John Adams, reading his books on English republicanism and drawing on his long experience in the Massachusetts law courts and the endless committees of Continental Congress to write some *Thoughts on Government* to guide the writers of state constitutions back in 1776 and '77. You need Thomas Jefferson, a sufficient world-renewer himself, hurrying home after drafting great words for a declaration in order to be in Virginia for the really important work, rewriting the law code to give his state a truly republican government. You need (although you must be careful to balance him with others) Alexander Hamilton, writing with incredible speed brilliant defenses of a new constitution he did not in private altogether approve of, and insisting that governments, republican or whatever, need energy at the center. You absolutely need—for a different reason and indispensably—the hero who was to preside at the Constitutional Convention and who would be the first president under its constitution, so that all your efforts will not end in Napoleon. George Washington had planted in him so deeply a self-restraining republican version of the old aristocratic virtue of honor that he had already by '87 repeatedly rejected any such role—formed his "character" (that is, his reputation) in great part out of his rejecting of that role in all its variations. He declined to be Caesar, he declined to be king, and he not only declined to be the leader of a military intervention in government but in a moving moment at Newburgh—in 1783—he had stood alone against his restless, angry, unpaid officers in resisting it. Thomas Jefferson later interpreted what this episode meant: "The moderation and virtue of a single character probably prevented this Revolution from being closed, as most others have been, by a subversion of that liberty it was intended to establish."

And if you want to construct a continent-sized government of liberty that lasts (for, say, two hundred years)—you need James Madison. A Madison may take up into himself enough of a sense of the uncontrollable, of the only partial nature of any new beginnings, to persist and think the matter through and make distinctions and careful points that the Tom Paines don't have the patience to make. In the end, in compromise and collaboration with others, a Madison may make something that will not satisfy the Tom Paines of this world but may be rather new after all.

4

The Great Seminar in Print
or
Founding Scribblers

One

IT HAS BEEN WRITTEN that in the two decades before the meeting of the Constitutional Convention, "American political discourse was an ongoing public forum on the meaning of liberty." It has been written, in addition, that "the great debate over liberty and order which took place in America from 1763 to 1789 was also a debate about the nature of man." It has been written, further, that "America, in the era when democratic thought was being formulated, conducted one of the most informed public debates on the nature of free institutions ever to grace the annals of any nation." It could still further have been written—perhaps it has been—that in those years the Americans conducted a great clinic on the nature and purposes of government. (One could read the most famous paragraph in *Federalist* 51 as having said that.)

At the end of this continent-sized seminar, forum, debate, and clinic, carried on for over a quarter of a century, dealing with the great questions of liberty and government and human nature, there stood the striking result—the United States of America, a new nation, assuming among the powers of the earth, as the Americans were to declare, the separate and equal station to which the laws of nature and nature's God entitle it.

In this extraordinary debate the principles upon which human society rests were examined clear to the bottom. The examination was, however, not an exercise in speculation only but an integral aspect of the making of an actual state.

One part of those seminars, public forums, debates, and clinics was carried on by the popular orators; Patrick Henry's ringing phrases made him the most popular politician in Virginia throughout the Revolutionary period. His reputation has come down through the generations, the stuff of legend. Richard Henry Lee was sometimes ranked with Henry; as we will see in a later chapter, at the Virginia conventions of the Revolutionary period each side could field its squad of famous orators. Although the greatest of the founders were not primarily orators—you did not have to be Cicero to be a great founder of the United States—John Adams, the "Atlas of Independence," did make some memorable speeches, notably in the closing moments of the struggle for a vote for independence in Philadelphia in the spring of 1776. The same is true of Alexander Hamilton, who is said to have made a great speech at the New York State ratifying convention in 1788, and certainly made a long one a year earlier in the Federal Convention in Philadelphia.

Another part of the great colloquy took place in sermons in the churches. In fast day and election sermons, and at other times as well, the preachers in New England and elsewhere, the leading authorities and learned men in most of the communities of the new nation, held forth on "the sacred cause of liberty."

Much of the most important argument took place in all of those congresses and conventions and councils and committees, those gatherings within the states and then among the states, by which the Americans argued themselves into existence as a people. Charles Francis Adams said in his biography of his grandfather John Adams that the older Adams served on ninety-five committees in the Continental Congresses; the editors of the Adams Papers today suggest that that may have been an undercount.

Presumably a most important part of the great seminar of those years was carried on in the tavern and the square and the parlor, in the informal conversation of the people whose new continental government this was to be.

But the most distinctive part of these grand seminars, public forums, debates, and clinics, by which the United States was formed, was carried on in another way, feeding, forming, reflecting, and improving these others: by the printing press. The great seminar was conducted in an enormous outpouring of pamphlets, newspaper articles, broadsides, printed sermons, and other short publications. The historian Gordon Wood quotes a comment from the time: "Almost every American pen was at work." Bernard Bailyn, setting out to collect the pamphlet literature of the American Revolution, found there to be not—as he had expected—a dozen and a half or so but over 400 of these by 1776, and 1,500 by 1783.

In his introduction to the resulting collection he wrote: "Whatever deficiencies the leaders of the American Revolution may have had, reticence, fortunately, was not one of them. They wrote easily and amply, and turned out in the space of scarcely a decade and a half from a small number of presses a rich literature of theory, argument, opinion, and polemic."

The characteristics of the original American institutions are linked to their having been formed not in an oral culture or a script culture (writing but not printing) but in the world of the printing press. The concept of the United States was prepared in three hundred years of printing on paper; the nation was scribbled into existence on a piece of paper; the new republic was shaped and defended out of arguments carried on, on pieces of paper.

It was an opportune moment. By the late eighteenth century print, and the movements it encouraged, had had time to dominate and shape the culture. At the same time the new uses and misuses of the mass press had not yet emerged, nor had the photograph, the moving picture, or the electronic disasters that were to come.

Print made it possible to do what the small-scale democracies of Athens and Rome had done, chiefly by the human voice, now by pamphlets, broadsides, articles in newspapers. Whereas the exchange of ideas in the republics of Greece and Rome took place largely by the human voice, with the climactic movements in large face-to-face meetings in Areopagus and the Forum, with Demosthenes and Isocrates and Cicero and the like playing the central role with their tradition of oratorical eloquence, the modern republics that James Madison studied (in print) and the new one he helped to come into being (largely by print) had a much different cultural shape, and for one important reason: the means of presenting and arguing and preserving and spreading ideas had undergone a radical change. The great political moments that are most important to the making of America—the Puritan revolution and the Glorious Revolution in England and the American Revolution and constitution-making—were all inundated with furious hailstorms of print.

This argument by scribbling was conducted in an atmosphere of great excitement and intellectual stimulation. The American colonies came to be aware that they were participating in something of world-historical significance; the energy and vitality that ran through their resolves and memorials and petitions and declarations, all that pamphlet-writing and speech-making and political preaching, reflected that awareness.

Something of the same thing had happened over a century before, after 1640, in England, another great age of government-making, pamphlet-writing, and political dispute. Historians write summaries about that earlier time that are very much like what will also be said about the period of the American Revolution. For example, here is what one historian wrote about pamphlets and printing: "The years after 1641 were unique in that they saw cheap newspapers published of every political colour. In 1645 there were 722 of them. There was also a fantastic outpouring of pamphlets on every subject under the sun, at an average rate of three a day for twenty years, though much faster between 1642 and 1649."

In both of these periods—England in the 1640s, America in the 1770s and 1780s—there was a heady combination (of which the political pamphlet is an expression) between an immediate political dispute on the one hand and the perennial questions of political and moral philosophy on the other hand.

Tom Paine's *Common Sense*, published in Philadelphia in January of 1776, was one of the sensations of publishing in the English language, perhaps in any language; it could reach with his reverberating argument on the printed page, in a few months, virtually the entire population of the American colonies.

The great American founders, and most of the lesser ones, too, were men of print. Benjamin Franklin and Thomas Jefferson both first made their reputations, across colonial lines, and across the Atlantic, with products of their pens. Jefferson's first publication was the proposed instruction for the Virginia delegation to the Continental Congress called the *Summary View*—which then was printed in Williamsburg and reprinted not only in Boston but also in London, all within 1774. It was printed anonymously (by "A Native, and a Member of the House of Burgesses") but despite the anonymity, and despite the fact that the Virginians did not adopt it as their instructions, it made Jefferson known. When he took one of the Virginia seats in the Second Continental Congress in the following year he had already a reputation, according to Massachusetts representative John Adams, for having a "happy talent for composition." That talent was put to work by the Congress in that year, 1775, in the composing of responses and declarations in the endgame of the dispute between London and the colonies; and then in the following year, when the climax was reached, he was named the chairman of the committee of five to draft a declaration of independence, and although there were at least two members of that committee who at that time had larger general reputations than he—Benjamin Franklin, the most renowned of all, and John Adams—Jefferson, partly because of his "peculiar felicity of expression," nevertheless was asked to do the drafting, and, as is widely known, did. Jefferson's talent as a writer would run all the way through his immense career, for fifty years thereafter; a reader of these lines, anywhere in the world, two centuries later, almost certainly will find, in a nearby shelf of books, set in print, some sentences of his.

In Franklin's case the importance of print really does mean—*printing*. Benjamin Franklin, like Jefferson, was so many-sided that one's mind goes numb reading through the long string of his identities and occupations and accomplishments, but "printer" nevertheless stands at the top. When Franklin was twenty-two years old and ill, he composed for himself a famous epitaph that begins "The body of B. Franklin Printer . . ." His will, written sixty years later, at an age more appropriate for the composition of epitaphs, does not contradict the earlier designation: "I, Benjamin Franklin of Philadelphia, printer, late Minister Plenipotentiary for the United States of America to the Court of France, and President of the State of Pennsylvania . . ."

Benjamin Franklin created a persona, as the interpreters of later ages would call it, or several personae, not by public speaking but with his pen. Franklin invented himself as a figure upon the world stage through an endless stream of writings and printings.

In one of the more extraordinary cases a young man from a Caribbean island, whom one may not particularly think of as a writer, made his way to the mainland colonies by means of his pen. A prose poem that Alexander Hamilton wrote in his early teens, describing a hurricane in the West Indies, sent as a letter to the *Royal Danish American Gazette,* was so impressive a piece of writing that the local Presbyterian minister helped Hamilton to get to the mainland and to college. At Columbia, at age nineteen, Hamilton published a pamphlet defending the action of the Boston patriots at the Tea Party, and in 1781 he composed a series of seven essays, signing them "The Continentalist" in the *New-York Packet and General Advertiser,* answering a series that had an un-Continental inclination, in Hamilton's opinion. He went on writing steadily throughout his career in American government—including some of the essays that define what American government is, in a project, in print, that he initiated—*The Federalist*. In his retirement, Hamilton founded the *New York Evening Post*—first issue on November 16, 1801—which is sometimes in journalism histories said to be the only survivor of early American daily journalism today.

One common form of discourse was the pamphlet or essay or series of newspaper articles answering a previous one; as in the case of Hamilton's Continentalist, a large number of the pamphlets come, like senators who want to miss a floor vote, paired. When John Adams came home between the First and Second Congresses, in late 1774 and early 1775, and read in *The Boston Post Boy* an ably written series of articles of a tory inclination, full of arguments and ideas, signed "Massachusetten-sis," which he mistakenly thought to have been written by an old friend of his named Jonathan Sewell, who was a loyalist, Adams did not proceed to the Areopagus or Hyde Park to answer him with a speech, or grab a club and hit him over the head, or seek an invitation on a talk show or issue a press release, or arrange with a direct mail specialist to do a mail-ing (MASSACHUSETTENSIS' IDEAS WOULD REDUCE YOU TO SLAVERY! Send money in the enclosed envelope TODAY); instead he sat down and wrote an answering series of articles, also full of arguments and ideas, signed "Novanglus" (New England), in the *Boston Gazette*.

John Adams, an heir to the Puritans, read and wrote all the time, it seems, even though he did a great deal else, too—journals, diaries, and letters, but also drafts of public papers, laws, and constitutions, and also anonymous contributions to the public prints and pseudonymous polem-ical pamphlets—and also again an ambitious production on political phi-losophy, his long (three volumes) *Defense of the American Constitutions*, written in London while Adams was the first United States minister to Great Britain. Clear back at the start of things, at the time of the Stamp Act crisis, in 1765, he had produced for a discussion group of Boston lawyers, and then published anonymously in a newspaper, a *Dissertation on Canon and Feudal Law*. Despite the formidable title this was really a tract for the times, arguing for the application of the history of liberty, particularly as it developed in England, to the American colonies. It was reprinted in a liberal journal in London, although attributed to the wrong author. And, like the other founders, he kept on writing all his life.

Two

Print means, in the first place, that there are a great many more copies of pieces of writing a great deal cheaper, making for a much wider access to any particular written word; the citizen in Charleston and Williamsburg and New Haven could sit in the tavern and read in the *Gazette* the great arguments of those years. Young James Madison in the rather remote setting of Orange County in the Virginia Piedmont could participate in, and contribute to, the argument. Writing allows a closer argument, and a more sustained argument, than oral presentation allows; it allows that more careful and sustained argument to be referred to again and again; it does not pass away with the dying sound. Print allows that written argu-ment to be spread, and repeated, and responded to, in ways that hand-writing could not.

The changes introduced by the printing press, as over against the older means of communication, are not simply that there are a great many more copies of pieces of writing a great deal cheaper, making for a much wider access to any particular work, although that is important. But to understand more fully what these changes mean we have to multiply and to extend, and to see in our mind's eye, not one reader but thousands, and not one edition of a paper but hundreds, and not one occasion of reading but another and another and another throughout a lifetime, and see the multiple readers of multiple printed pieces thinking about them, and checking them against each other—easy to do in print, not in script, impossible to do with evanescent electronics or film—and then conversing about them, and writing to each other about them, and perhaps producing still more paper for the printer in response to them.

But then after we have done that imagining we have not gone far enough; we must imagine not just this widespreadness—this external diffusion in all directions—but the internal effect of living in a culture in which such diffusion, such availability, is the norm, and people have been shaped by it.

And we must imagine not only the pamphlet, written for the moment but also the book, lasting across the decades, and perhaps, the centuries. That gave another dimension to the great conversation, across time.

And the efficiency of print as compared to script made it possible for one scholar sitting in his study in a remote plantation in Orange County, Virginia, far from cities, libraries, universities, or circles of other scholars, nevertheless to have a desk full of books, from many hands, many years, many places. Print made it possible not only to have in Orange County books that were written in Paris or Edinburgh—but to have simultaneously books that were written in both places, and many others as well. Trunks full, bought in Paris. Because books were designed and expected to last, and were printed in large numbers—enormous numbers, compared to the precious manuscripts produced by hand—these books extended their influence across the barriers of nations and of geography. A writer in Paris or in an English country house or in Edinburgh alone at his desk wrote something that was printed as a book in many copies, and sent here and there, and then after he was dead what he wrote would light a fire in the mind of someone he had never seen in a place he had never been.

The reader in Orange County could spread his table with those twenty-one books, to study the ancient and modern confederations. Or the reader could look up for himself what Harrington said, when Cato's Letter refers to him, and what the commentators on Aristotle said, and how all of that relates to something he had read another day in John Locke. And these multiple comparative readings that could produce, in the brain of the lonely scholar, intellectual explosions.

These reading republicans had the opportunity not only to apply to this developing new world the ideas of others but also to shape and revise and refine those ideas—to think, and to apply what they thought. The object of their thought was society and government. They could seek in all those printed pages for universals—"science," in an eighteenth-century sense—on which to ground their work.

Jefferson collected libraries all his life—three personal libraries, one after the other as the early ones were destroyed, and left the last to be the nucleus of the Library of Congress. When you take a tour of Monticello they show you the chair and reading stand in the dining room, where Jefferson would keep on reading while waiting for the household to gather for dinner.

And James Madison was in some ways the most concentratedly bookish of them all. One of the moving moments, as it were, of the American story, we have already mentioned—when these two young Virginians—in their thirties then, Jefferson eight years the elder—made that deal about mutual services while he was in Paris as the representative of the fledgling nation. Madison would keep an eye on Jefferson's nephews; Jefferson would buy, for Madison, in Paris those boxes of books.

Three

Madison brought to his studies not only native intelligence but also a good college education. He had been well educated in Virginia by his tutors, but still it was important that he encountered at Princeton an intellectual outburst.

He might have been expected to have gone, as the sons of Virginia squires generally did, to William and Mary, but that Anglican college for the Virginia gentry had gone downhill since Thomas Jefferson had studied there eight years earlier—had gone downhill mainly because William Small (the only one of the seven professors whom Jefferson thought was particularly able, yet another Scotsman and representative of the Scottish Enlightenment) had left and returned to England. The sleepy Anglican Virginia college was not a center of intellectual excitement, or of the religious or political issues of the day. In an attack on John Witherspoon a couple of years after Madison's day, the tory Virginia Anglican preacher Jonathan Boucher would recommend that students go to William and Mary or King's College (both Anglican) and stay away from Princeton. Princeton had the wrong politico-religious affiliations, for that tory. James Madison's parents got the opposite advice from a second of his tutors, another clergyman, this one named Alexander Martin, who was not a tory. Martin told the Madisons what a worthy college the College of New Jersey was, for an able young man like their son James, Jr. And it now had this new president, Witherspoon, just imported from Scotland. So the Virginia Madisons sent their intellectually gifted son up there to New Jersey.

Witherspoon was a Scottish pastor of some learning and much personal force, and a controversialist on both sides of the Atlantic; he also proved to be a good administrator and certainly a good teacher. People from Princeton to this day will tell you that Princeton produced more signers of the Declaration of Independence, including Witherspoon himself, and more of the framers of the Constitution, including Madison, than any of the other five colleges in the American colonies. Witherspoon himself was active in politics, a vigorous supporter of the whig-patriot side. On arriving in the United States from Scotland he had become, perhaps rather surprisingly, almost an instant American patriot.

Witherspoon's reading and conviction and the scars of battle from Scotland made him an opponent of what he called "sacerdotal tyranny," and he comprehended in one cause civil and religious liberty. His orthodoxy—his moderate Calvinism, for want of a better term—in religious matters should not lead a modern reader to the mistaken conclusion that such a man would be conservative in politics; there is an old tradition, important to the Protestant beginnings of America, that combines Reformed Christian belief with republican (which then meant progressive) politics.

Witherspoon was in addition a mediator of the significant intellectual currents in Scotland from which he had come. As there was to be in the American colonies twenty years later a print-based explosion of high-level practical political thinking, so there had been in Scotland in this earlier period—the second quarter and the middle of the eighteenth century—a print-based explosion of pure moral philosophy, and allied subjects.

Scottish professors and writers like Adam Ferguson, Lord Kames, Thomas Reid, Hugh Blair, and a number of others represented an unusual concentration of intellect; the members of the group best known today are Adam Smith and David Hume. Although Witherspoon fought the leaders of this Scottish Enlightenment in the battles over ecclesiastical control, and opposed them on issues about religion, and rejected the ideas of most of them in moral philosophy, he nevertheless read them, and absorbed a lot from them and from the atmosphere. Perhaps ironically, this man who had been their opponent in Scotland was to become an effective carrier of the ideas and books of the leaders of the Scottish Enlightenment to the American continent.

Witherspoon reserved to himself as president of the college, as a sort

51

of a flagship course required of all seniors, significantly, not a course in Christian doctrine but rather a course called "Lectures on Moral Philosophy." That term then covered a great deal wider territory than it would today—almost all of the studying of society ("the proper study of mankind!") that would today be covered by the social sciences, although to be sure in a different way. It might almost be said that one of the social sciences as we know them today—economics—was invented by one of those Scottish professors, Adam Smith, in his lectures as a professor of moral philosophy, and in this period; *The Wealth of Nations* was published in 1776. Professorial designations and "fields" were not as rigid then as now; most of these Scots roamed; "moral philosophy" was often the name given to what they did. Frances Hutcheson, who was perhaps the most influential of them all in the United States of the late eighteenth and early nineteenth centuries—had taught and written moral philosophy, too, and so had Thomas Reid. Reid had developed a variant of the commonsense school of ethics, as against Hutcheson, to which Witherspoon had been converted just before he left Scotland.

Witherspoon was a forceful and able person, but he was not an original or a creative mind, despite some ventures into imaginative literature in satire. In his new post across the water in New Jersey this energetic pastor and ecclesiastical controversialist had to develop lectures, which he had not done before. One wonders how he got his lectures together. Perhaps he did a good deal of what other beginning lecturers have been known to do—borrowing.

Both as to the subjects he discussed and in the foundation in commonsense realism (as against what philosophers call idealism) from which he dealt with them, Witherspoon followed the outlook of the "Authors in Scotland" with whom he had quarreled on other topics in other places. Henry May, quoting some of these lecture notes about the commonsense philosophy of those authors in Scotland, wrote: "Copying these words faithfully, the students ranged in front of 'The Old Doctor' in Nassau Hall may not have realized that they were listening to the first promulgation of the principles that were to rule American college teaching for almost a century. . . . Witherspoon began the long American career of Scottish Common Sense." His teaching of that school gained strength, May wrote, from being coupled with the maxims of whig political tradition, which means those names that the founders—John Adams, for example—were continually citing, like Harrington, Locke, Milton, and Sydney—the forefathers of our forefathers.

Among those who absorbed that mixture, of an intelligent modified Calvinism, Scottish Common Sense, and radical whig politics, was no doubt the young man from Orange County, Virginia, who sat in one of

Witherspoon's first classes and who stayed on to take extra work with the Old Doctor. And that principle of exposing his students to all sorts of reading had led Witherspoon to put on his list of readings, along with Adam Smith's *Theory of Moral Sentiments,* and works of Hutcheson and Reid and various others of the Scots, the essays of David Hume, even though Hume was the object of President Witherspoon's particular scorn as the "infidel Hume" and, in addition to being an "infidel," had "industriously endeavored to shake the certainty of our belief upon cause and effect."

But one cannot know where one's teaching will lead. It may even help you with students if you can get their professors to attack you. Sixteen years after leaving Princeton, James Madison had occasion to look again at David Hume's essays—not to settle the great questions of "infidelity" or of cause and effect, but as a help in thinking about the modeling of an actual republican commonwealth.

Four

Which brings us back to early 1787, when (we may assume) James Madison was sitting in his rooms in New York with a printed copy of David Hume's essays in his hand.

David Hume was a Scot two generations older, as Thomas Jefferson would reckon the generations, than James Madison. Hume was born in 1711; Madison in 1751. Hume died in 1776, just as the portentous new commonwealth with which James Madison was to be associated was getting under way across the Atlantic. Print allowed him, nevertheless, to speak to Madison, from the grave as it were and across the Atlantic, on a particular point of government-making.

When Hume was young and determined to make a name for himself, he had published *A Treatise on Human Nature,* but, as he said in one of the best-known comments ever made by a writer about the fate of his book, it *"fell deadborn from the press,* without reaching such distinction, as even to excite a murmur among the zealots." He decided that it had failed not because of its *matter* but because of its *manner,* and trained himself to be a more careful and a better writer, and he succeeded thereupon in exciting many murmurs among the zealots. Of a subsequent publication he wrote: "Answers by Reverends and Right Reverends came out two and three in a year."

Hume developed when very young a skepticism not only on religious topics but about evidence and proof on other topics, too; his *Dialogues on Natural Religion,* which he worked on for twenty-seven years and left to be published posthumously, was such a hot potato that his friend

Adam Smith declined to see it through the press. It was his writings on these topics that led the Old Doctor in Nassau Hall to refer to him as the Infidel Hume (while assigning him to his students nevertheless).

Hume did not pursue pure philosophical topics much after his early productions, and turned out instead essays on moral, political, and literary topics, which went through many editions and enlargements and combinations. One of those he drew upon for political ideas was the seventeenth-century English republican political writer James Harrington, who, in this conversation in print across the generations and across the Atlantic, was important also to—among others—John Adams. Hume found Harrington's book *Oceana* to be "the only valuable model of a commonwealth that has yet been offered to the public," because it was realistic, closer to the ground of actual human conduct. Hume made a comment that may be taken to reflect Madison's view also: "All plans of government, which suppose great reformation in the manners of mankind, are plainly imaginary." Hume named Plato's *Republic* and Thomas More's *Utopia* as examples of this useless imaginary kind. For all John Witherspoon's denunciation of Hume on religious questions and matters of moral theory, when he got around to political matters—he had to cover a very wide territory—Witherspoon in his lectures at the College of New Jersey made exactly the same point that Hume had made—and used as his negative examples exactly the same two, Plato and More, that Hume had done.

Hume's writings on politics and history were not at all of the institution-overthrowing, order-destroying, tradition-repudiating sort that might in other contexts be associated with atheism—indeed, with one who carefully rejected all the traditional arguments not only for the existence of God but also for natural religion and for a moral order. In other settings one might expect such a person to be carrying the eighteenth-century equivalent of an assault rifle on the eighteenth-century equivalent of the barricades. Although his skeptical knife cut the rational underpinnings of established institutions, Hume had a deep opposition to popular uprisings; his skeptical knife cut their rational underpinnings, too, and he found guidance in sentiment, history, custom—which led him to a politics of moderation tinged with conservatism.

Henry F. May wrote in his book *The Enlightenment in America*: "His horrified opponents could find in Hume no snap and crackle of infernal fire such as those they easily detected in Voltaire; he refused to give off an odor of brimstone, and insisted on being a kind, decent, genial good citizen."

Despite his "infidelity," May went on to say, Hume played his role in the kirk: "His relations with the moderate faction of the Scottish Church were excellent; at one point as assistant secretary of state he found himself disposing (conscientiously of course) of Church offices."

That's a picture: the infidel Hume helping to give out assignments of Presbyterian pastors to their parishes.

Hume's writing on political, moral, and literary subjects, after he turned aside from more abstract topics and sought to improve his manner, took the form of short essays gathered without rigorous sorting by subject or any necessary order. One must skip around a good deal from essay to essay, to put the parts of his thought together, or to guess how Madison put them together.

Five

When James Madison in New York in the spring of 1787 read or reread the last part of Hume's essay "On the Idea of a Perfect Commonwealth," after having read many other authorities—Montesquieu and many others—who insisted that republics had to be small, there must have been one of those abrupt illuminations that can take place when the words on the printed page strike the right spot in the reader's brain.

Or at least—to carry the conversation in print down nearer to our own time—when a mid-twentieth-century American historian named Douglass Adair read the last part of that essay of Hume's and put it alongside Madison's notes on the vices of the American states, he—Adair—certainly did have such an illumination.

And when Adair put the brief passage from Hume alongside the speech that Madison would give in the Federal Convention on June 6 and Madison's letter to Thomas Jefferson of October 24 and—above all—Madison's *Federalist* 10, and looked elsewhere in Hume's essays, he found further evidence for his point. Madison clearly drew on Hume, and probably had a copy of Hume's essays before him when he wrote his notes or his first *Federalist* paper (*Federalist* 10 is the first one he wrote). So it seemed to Adair, and so it seems to most who now read Adair's article about the matter.

Adair quotes sentences from several other essays of Hume's, in addition to the one about the ideal commonwealth, as possible sources of ideas for James Madison. Hume suggested, in an essay "On Parties in General," for example, that it was not necessarily the case that a large nation required a single great leader, or that a great original leader would seek imperial, or one-man, rule. If instead of seeking personal glory and dominion some future leader would "suppress his personal ambition and found a free state in a large territory" then "if modelled with masterly skill" that free state—that republic—might last and prosper after all.

Adair, reading those words of Hume's more than a century and a half after they had been written, knew of a leader who had suppressed personal ambition and had founded a free state, just as Hume had suggested as a possibility. "In 1776," wrote Adair, "the year that Hume died, a provincial notable named George Washington was starting on the career that was to justify Hume's penetrating analysis of the unifying role of the great man in a large and variegated empire." Hume was right: "All great men who consolidated empires did not necessarily desire crowns."

And then Adair also saw who in fact it was that had the "masterly skill" Hume had anticipated, who might carry on the undertaking and design the large-scale republic that Hume had argued was a possibility— James Madison.

Adair found scattered among Hume's essays other comments and analyses that paralleled or anticipated ideas of Madison's; reading through Hume we may find more. Hume's comments on the "nature of man," for example, are calmly realistic, but not fiercely pessimistic. He will write in an echo or anticipation of a theme, in another context, of his great friend Adam Smith: "A republican and free government would be an obvious absurdity, if the particular checks and controls, provided by the Constitution, had really no influence, and made it not the interest, even of bad men, to act for the public good."

Much of this cool Scottish social thinking holds that human beings in the large cannot be expected to be consistently virtuous; and that therefore there must be an arrangement of institutions that makes it the interest of persons, even if not virtuous, to act for the public good. Hume, in another essay, "On the Independency of Parliament," made these remarks along the same lines:

> Political writers have established it as a maxim, that, in contriving any system of government, and fixing the several checks and controls of the constitution, every man ought to be supposed a knave, and to have no other end, in all his actions, than private interest. By this interest we must govern him, and, by means of it, make him, notwithstanding his insatiable avarice and ambition, co-operate to public good. Without this, say they, we shall in vain boast of the advantages of any constitution, and shall find, in the end, that we have no security for our liberties or possessions, except the good-will of our rulers; that is, we shall have no security at all.
>
> It is, therefore, a just *political* maxim, *that every man must be supposed a knave:* Though at the same time, it appears somewhat strange, that a maxim should be true in *politics,* which is false in fact.

This then will be followed by a contrast, found as we have seen in Madison's memorandum on the vices, between the greater possibility of virtue in individual life, and the lesser in group life:

But to satisfy us on this head, we may consider, that men are generally more honest in their private than in their public capacity, and will go greater lengths to serve a party, than when their own private interest is alone concerned. Honour is a great check upon mankind: But where a considerable body of men act together, this check is, in a great measure, removed; since a man is sure to be approved of by his own party, for what promotes the common interest; and he soon learns to despise the clamours of adversaries.

Hume did not hold to a relentless view of human egotism or systematic and unequivocal self-seeking. In fact he had yet another essay in his collections, "Of the Dignity and Meanness of Human Nature," in which he argues against the extremes of egotistical and systematically hedonistic conceptions of humankind. He begins by, in effect, asking about the whole question: Compared to what? Those who deprecate human nature make "a secret comparison with a perfection which it is one of the excellencies of man that he can imagine." And, he goes on to say:

There is much dispute of words in all this controversy. When a man denies the sincerity of all public spirit or affection to a country and community, I am at a loss what to think of him. Perhaps he never felt this in so clear and distinct a manner as to remove all his doubts concerning its force and reality. But when he proceeds afterwards to reject all private friendship, if no interest or self-love intermix itself, I am then confident that he abuses terms, and confounds the ideas of things; since it is impossible for any one to be so selfish, or rather so stupid, as to make no difference between one man and another . . . Impossible: He does not know himself: He has forgotten the movements of his heart; or rather he makes use of a different language from the rest of his countrymen, and calls not things by their proper names.

Hume was not, as his fellow thinkers of that period in the universities of Scotland also were not—varied though they were from each other—a systematic egotist, a cynic, one of those who insists that human beings never do anything except from self-interest. Hume wrote, to repeat the good phrase, that one who claims to hold to such a relentlessly cynical position "has forgotten the movements of his heart . . . and calls not things by their proper names."

Hume not only anticipated Madison's theory of the compound, or extended, republic; he also anticipated the theory of factions that is tied in with it. In the essay called "Of Parties in General" Hume analyzed and categorized the kinds of parties—factions—into which political humankind divides itself, with illustrations: personal factions and real factions; among the real ones, parties of interest, of affection, and of principle. This discussion, much longer than the one Madison will produce in *Federalist* 10, nevertheless has such parallels to and anticipations of what

Madison would write as to cause Adair to claim that Madison drew heavily upon it.

There are sage comments, of the sort Madison will also make: "Nothing is more usual than to see parties, which have begun upon a real difference, continue even after that difference is lost."

There is a striking contrast in what the two men would say about differences of race. Hume wrote: "The civil wars which arose some few years ago in MOROCCO, between the *blacks* and *whites,* merely on account of their complexion, are founded on a pleasant difference. We laugh at them." Madison, on the other hand, the Virginia slaveholder, does not laugh. On one occasion only—*not* in *Federalist* 10, but when he went through the causes of faction in his speech on June 6 at the Federal Convention in Philadelphia, with the intransigeant South Carolina slaveholders in the room—he included the item we have already quoted, rather different in tone, perforce, from Hume's statement: "We have seen," said Madison, "the mere distinction of colour made in the most enlightened period of time, a ground of the most oppressive dominion ever exercised by man over man."

Given that human beings incline (though not exclusively or automatically) to serve their own short-run interests, especially when they are gathered in groups, and that they divide this way and that way and the other way into factions (Hume does not make as much of economic divisions as Madison would), and that these characteristics are not going to go away—that one will not as the utopians do assume a great reformation in the manners of men—then what does an ideal commonwealth look like?

Madison did not take over the specific details of what Hume said the ideal commonwealth might look like. Madison put forward his own ideas in the Virginia delegation to the Federal Convention, and those ideas heavily influenced the Virginia Plan the delegation then presented to the convention, and that plan would be much modified by the ideas and interests of others, and would emerge not as an ideal commonwealth but as a real one.

Many years later, in 1830, the seventy-nine-year-old James Madison, the "last of the fathers," an established framer of this successful constitution in the real world, would then look back and make a disparaging comment to a young follower (Nicholas Trist) about eighteenth-century European proposals for ideal commonwealths—including that of David Hume. "Hume," he would write, "was among these bungling lawgivers." Madison's point to Trist was that the Americans "at the commencement of the contest with G. Britain" had understood "the doctrines of self-government" better than young Trist had implied; Madison cited the pamphlets the Americans wrote at the time, and the Virginia Declaration of Rights, as evidence of the early American grasp of these principles. Then the elderly Madison, looking back, would make an interesting generalization about the Americans' accomplishment (one in which, although to be sure he does not say so, he was a major contributor): "The merit of the founders of our Republic lies in the more accurate views and the practical application of the doctrines. The rights of man as the foundations of just government had been long understood; but the superstructures projected had been sadly defective." Madison named Hume as among the European bunglers who projected defective superstructures on those sound foundations—superstructures that the Americans were to improve, with their more accurate views and more practical application of the shared doctrines of human rights.

The Humean superstructure that the elderly Madison was dismissing appears in Hume's essay "On the Ideal Commonwealth," from other parts of which the younger Madison benefited. Having praised Harrington's *Oceana,* Hume specified the defects, as he saw it, of Harrington's scheme (each of these commonwealth-builders improving on the last). We may summarize by saying that Hume wanted to fine-tune some of the checks and balances in Harrington's scheme. Then Hume went forward with an elaborate governmental scheme of his own: divide a country into 100 counties and each county into 100 parishes; let all the freeholders meet annually in the parish church (!) and choose a representative; let all the hundred parish representatives in county chose a Senator . . . it all gets much too complicated to reproduce. But there is running through it, as there was through Harrington's complex scheme, too, the elements of an outlook that may have influenced Madison even before he got to the key sentences that electrified Douglass Adair (because he was persuaded they had electrified Madison). Hume's pyramid of indirect elections reflected the combination of trust with institutionalized distrust in the people that runs through these republican schemes. Why have a secret ballot, as Harrington recommended? Why the written constitution? Why these two houses, and multiple layers? Harrington and Hume both constructed on paper in their libraries schemes of republican government that a lawgiver working in real political assemblies may call "bungling" even while learning from them. The complexity of all these schemes may be offensive to devotees of simplicity in governmental form, whether totalitarian, populist, monarchical, anarchist, or direct democratic, whether Tom Paine, or the modern proponent of public polls by pushing buttons. But the complexity had a reason: to refine and restrain the contending layers and elements of the whole people, to find the institutional means to bring out their best and restrain their worst and protect liberty while enabling government to govern. *Representative* government is such a means. The legislative body—government by debating society, by the effort of mutual persuasion—is such a means. The separation of powers, defended in particular by Montesquieu in a passage well known to delegates getting ready to gather in Philadelphia, is such a means.

And Madison, reading Hume, and ruminating on these matters, saw another means, fitted to the Americans' situation: extend the sphere beyond the city-state, the small republic, and create the extended republic that may have, Montesquieu to the contrary notwithstanding, a better chance of lasting than the small one.

What Hume wrote near the end of his essay was this:

> We shall conclude this subject, with observing the falsehood of the common opinion, that no large state, such as FRANCE or GREAT BRITAIN, could ever be modelled into a commonwealth, but that such a form of government can only take place in a city or small territory. The contrary seems probable. Though it is more difficult to form a republican government in an extensive country than in a city; there is more facility, when once it is formed, of preserving it steady and uniform, without tumult and faction. . . .
>
> In a large government, which is modelled with masterly skill, there is compass and room enough to refine the democracy, from the lower people, who may be admitted into the first elections of first concoction of the commonwealth, to the higher magistrates, who direct all the movements. At the same time, the parts are so distant and remote, that it is very difficult, either by intrigue, prejudice, or passion, to hurry them into any measures against the public interest.

Madison in his memo on the vices wrote:

> The notorious factions & oppressions . . . take place in corporate towns . . . and in little republics when uncontrolled by apprehensions of external danger. If an enlargement of the sphere is found to lessen the insecurity of private rights, it is not because the impulse of a common interest or passion is less predominant in this case with the majority; but because a common interest or passion is less apt to be felt and the requisite combinations less easy to be formed by a great than by a small number. The Society becomes broken into a greater variety of interests, of pursuits, of passions, which check each other, whilst those who may feel a common sentiment have less opportunity of communication and concert. It may be inferred that the inconveniences of popular States contrary to the prevailing Theory, are in proportion not to the extent, but to the narrowness of their limits.

Madison would carry this insight further in speeches at the convention to come, and in his letter to Jefferson in October, and then give it lasting expression in *Federalist* 10 in November. Perhaps one could say the results of his reading were to be given lasting expression in the continentwide government of the United States.

5

The Business of
May Next

ᘓᘒᗧ

One

On May 2, 1787, his studies behind him now, James Madison left
New York and on May 5 he arrived in Philadelphia, the first delegate to
arrive. The memos had been the solitary work of his study; the "first
shoot" letters had been private one-to-one exchanges with a few friends;
now his reflections were no longer to be solitary but part of a great collaborative effort, with many revisions, improvements, and compromises
from the work of others.

From May 14 to May 24, after the other Virginians had also arrived,
he participated in the informal meetings of the Virginia delegation out of
which came the Virginia Plan. George Washington, the nation's first great
hero, soon to be president of this convention, was fifty-five years old;
George Mason, the respected chief author of the formative Virginia Declaration of Rights and the Virginia constitution, the first of the written
constitutions, was sixty-two; George Wythe, the first law professor in
America and Jefferson's teacher, the "Socrates of Virginia," was sixty-
one; and all of them were members of the Virginia group, meeting in a
Philadelphia inn to discuss the great matter before them. But James Madison, age thirty-six and not imposing, was nevertheless the intellectual
leader of the gathering.

On May 27 there were delegates from enough of the other states to
begin the convention. The fifty-five delegates who would attend at one
time or another included many able people but not Thomas Jefferson or

John Adams, who were abroad on missions for the new country. Alexander Hamilton came, gave one long early speech and left, to return at the end only when much of the essential debating and compromising and deciding were completed. Benjamin Franklin, at eighty-one, was the oldest and next to Washington the most respected of the delegates; but because of his age, and perhaps because close political institution-making was not his forte, his influence was slight; his interventions seem to have been treated, as Madison in his notes said explicitly about one of them, more from respect for the proposer than for the thing proposed. George Washington played his indispensable role as president of the convention in dignified silence. Of the six greatest founders only one was a full-time, articulate, continually influential participant in the convention that wrote the nation's Constitution: James Madison.

Well-known figures from '76 were not there—Patrick Henry, who smelled a rat and stayed home; the other great Virginia orator Richard Henry Lee; the great pamphleteer Tom Paine, the "Citizen of the World," had gone on to pamphleteer in another part of that world; Sam Adams, the marvelous political organizer. This was not to be a meeting for orators, pamphleteers, or political organizers; it was to be a meeting for—Americans and others would be inclined to use rather grand words—statesmen. Lawgivers. Reflective students of political institutions. Jefferson even used the word *demigods*. The delegates who were chosen must have had about as many encomiums written about them as any such body in human experience.

One delegate whose encomiums have not reached the broader public was James Wilson of Pennsylvania. The neglect of Wilson, the unsungest of unsung heroes, in the subsequent collective memory of Americans is regularly deplored in the retellings of the events of the American beginnings—so regularly that one might almost say that in the select world of books his unsungness is sung. Although Madison is neglected and underrated, too, by the American public, Wilson outstrips him in the unsungness department.

Wilson knew the world of the Scottish Enlightenment at first hand. Madison spoke French with a Scottish accent because he had learned it from his Scottish tutor, Donald Robertson; Wilson spoke English with a Scottish accent because he learned it at his mother's knee. James Madison did not acquire his dose of Presbyterianism until he was a student at the College of New Jersey; James Wilson acquired his at birth, in a poor Scottish family devoted to the kirk and intending their brilliant son for the ministry. The other American political intellectuals read the books of the great professors in the universities in Scotland, and heard lectures about them by their own professors, William Small (Jefferson's professor at William and Mary) or John Witherspoon; but Wilson was himself born in Scotland and educated by the real thing at the high period of the Scottish intellectual explosion. He studied at Saint Andrews; he was a student at Glasgow when Adam Smith was rector, and he studied at Edinburgh with one of the greatest of the professors in the Scottish Renaissance, Adam Ferguson. Scotland had intellectual connections with the Continent, particularly with France, where for example David Hume would be given much honor after his essays made him a world figure. By studying in Scotland at this time—the middle of the eighteenth century—Wilson was directly in touch with the liveliest intellectual currents in the world on historical, moral, political, and legal subjects.

Wilson was an immigrant to the United States from Scotland at age twenty-four, in 1765, just as the sequence of events that led to American independence was beginning. He turned himself into a lawyer (these founders were overwhelmingly lawyers) and into a philosopher of law and politics; some have said he was the leading legal theorist in the American states; he has been called "possibly the profoundest theorist of the Revolution." In the flurry of pamphleteering in 1774, when Thomas Jefferson published his *Summary View* and John Adams published his *Novanglus,* Wilson published a pamphlet that some say was better than those, though of a different persuasion (Wilson, like Pennsylvania's leaders of the time in general, was a conciliator, and developed a theory very much like today's British Commonwealth). During the Second Continental Congress in 1775, when Abigail Adams had asked about "Dr. Franklin," John Adams had answered that he wished all the Philadelphia delegates were like him, especially one (he meant John Dickinson) who was famous but had been "found wanting" (Dickinson was the leading conciliator, proposer of the "olive branch"; Adams was on the other side). Adams then volunteered this point, about another Pennsylvanian: "There is a young gentleman from Pennsylvania named Wilson whose Fortitude, Rectitude, and Abilities too, greatly outshine his Masters" (by which presumably Adams meant primarily Dickinson, who had in fact been a law teacher to Wilson). On the great question of the ends of government—on which the Americans were conducting this immense continent-sized seminar, 1763–91—Wilson would perceive in government (social ordering) an object other than, higher than, property or "happiness." On July 13, responding, in the climactic days of debate over representation solely on the basis of *number* (which he and Madison were fighting for) to proposals to take account also of "wealth," Wilson said that "he could not agree that property was the sole or the primary object of Governt & society. The cultivation & improvement of the human mind was the most noble object."

Wilson was a defender of the intellectual position that stands at the core of the new American understanding, that "all government originates with the people, that all powers of government are derived from them, that all power which they have not disposed of still continues theirs." That sounds obvious enough, perhaps platitudinous, two centuries later, and it was familiar enough then—propositions about power coming from the people have a long history—but large familiar propositions like this depend on their political and intellectual context, and on their clarity and priority and consistency. This insistence that the people were the fountain of all power was set over against the various notions that cluster around that rather mysterious term of political theorists, *sovereignty*. Theorists of law and government get the term set up, like a great Platonic idea, *existing* somewhere, and sometimes they say it is indivisible, and then they ask, Where *is* it located? It has to be somewhere. So they say. And the disputation about this somewhat hypostatized term gets tangled, of course, with social habits, intellectual grooves settling into traditional social grooves. Think of the root of the word *sovereignty*. The king, of course; there has to be a king, or a king-principle, somewhere.

The Americans began to see that government originates not with a king with whom the people make a contract—with some principle of sovereignty antecedent to themselves—but rather solely with a people, who make a covenant among themselves, and a grant of power to government, which is merely their servant. The ancient habits of thought, which ran very deep, saw *two* entities, the governors (the king) and the governed (the people), and saw the protection of rights and liberties as the result of a negotiation, a compact, between the two; that was the shape of the Magna Carta, and of a long history of rights-declaring and government-forming in England. But the Americans were coming to see that the people have no antecedent power over against themselves with whom to negotiate—no king, no government—but only themselves, as both ruler and ruled.

And as the sovereign had no existence prior to the grant from the people, so also—more to the point in Philadelphia in 1787—*states* had no such prior existence. In the early disputes over proportional representation or equality of states in the legislature, Wilson said (on June 30), "Can we forget for whom we are forming a Government? Is it for *men,* or for the imaginary beings called *States?*" Wilson used the metaphor of a pyramid, with the people as the broad base, and he regularly sought to rest the new government on that base: popular election of the House of Representatives, representation in the Senate proportionate to population, popular election of the president, ratification of the Constitution by conventions newly chosen by the people rather than by state legislatures.

Wilson was what is called a "nationalist" in writings about the convention; that is, he wanted a supreme and energetic national government; but he wanted it to be built on the right foundation. "Mr. Wilson. He wished for vigor in the Govt. but he wished that vigorous authority to flow immediately from the legitimate source of all authority. The Govt. ought to possess not only 1st. the *force* but 2ndly. the *mind or sense* of the people at large."

Wilson and Madison were the two most distinguished political thinkers at the convention, and they were on the same side, allies in the cause of a strong national government. Max Farrand, the great scholar of this convention, found Madison the most important of the framers but said: "Second to Madison, and almost on a par with him, was James Wilson." Between them, with the help and challenge and resistance of other delegates, they worked out the defining features of the American constitutional system.

Madison had made a decision, before the convention started, that he would keep a record of its work, of the sort that he had sought in vain for the formation of those confederacies and republics he had studied for his memos. He described his own decision and the way he carried it out, in an incomplete preface written many years later: "The curiosity I had felt during my researches into the History of the most distinguished Confederacies, particularly those of antiquity, and the deficiency I found in the means of satisfying it more especially in what related to the process, the principles, the reasons, & the anticipations, which prevailed in the formation of them, determined me to preserve as far as I could an exact account of what might pass in the Convention."

Therefore he took a seat front and center and noted in his own shorthand what was said. As soon as the session was over he wrote out his notes. It was an arduous task; later he told a secretary it almost killed him. He said he was never absent and missed at most "a casual fraction" of an hour, and not a single speech unless a very short one.

Why did he do it? To repeat: because when he started examining those confederacies back in 1786 he had wished *they* had kept detailed records of their process, principles, reasons, and anticipations. So—for the *next* James Madison—the James Madison of tomorrow—there would be a record. He was ill after August 23 and his notes fell off in quantity and he made some errors, but he kept at it. It was a remarkable performance. In the education of an American one hears about it, but rather takes it for granted. Madison took notes. (So, in much, much smaller ways, did eight other delegates.) What we know, we know mostly from James Madison.

The delegates, whose names have often been listed since, gathered in

Philadelphia. The story of what followed has been told many times, and will continue to be told as long as the nation it brought into being will live. There was that hot room in Independence Hall. There were the sealed windows and the pledge of secrecy. There was James Madison, determined to take good notes and keep a good record, taking a "seat in front of the presiding member, with the other members on my right and left hands." There was the unanimous election of George Washington as president. There was the presentation of the Virginia Plan and its apparent early acceptance—too easy. There was the formation of the body into a Committee of the Whole, with Nathaniel Gorham of Connecticut taking the chair and George Washington stepping down among the delegates—the same people, changing their parliamentary identity. There was the defeat within the committee, despite Madison's arguments for it, of that federal negative on state laws that he had brought with him in his mind and in his memos, a bad moment for him with more coming on the same point. There was after two weeks the favorable report—the delegates as committee reporting to themselves as convention, with Washington resuming the chair—of the somewhat enlarged version of the Virginia Plan. There came meanwhile the gathering objection by the small states, and a counterplan, presented by William Paterson of New Jersey, modeled on the existing Articles of Confederation. (In the high school history notes of how many millions of young Americans in generations to come there would appear, ready to be reproduced on final exams, mysterious references to a Virginia Plan and then a New Jersey Plan, to the large states' and then the small states' objections.) There was the long speech by Madison giving an extended criticism of this New Jersey Plan, fighting off that return to the terrible weakness he had itemized in his memos.

There came the defeat, in a sense, of the New Jersey Plan, but there then came the report of the Committee of the Whole—the convention as committee reporting to itself as convention—which contained an expanded version of that Virginia Plan, and presented its opponents—small-state people mostly—with another opportunity to resist it.

The parliamentary procedure allowed everything to come up twice or three times or more—first in the committee and then in the convention, perhaps again in the Committee of Detail, or another committee, and its report. The proceedings of this convention may have been glorious but they were not simple; they had that complexity that is exasperating to devotees of simplicity in high public affairs. This may have been the most wonderful committee meeting of all time, but it was still a committee meeting. Nothing was settled finally the first time, even though there might have been a vote, and nothing was tidy.

After anticipatory battles there came then in late June and the first half of July a crunch of disagreement in which the convention almost fell apart.

Two

The early days of the convention had spun along deceptively well, from Madison's point of view, but then there came some bumps and grumbles, and worse, as the small-state delegates gathered their objections. They had signaled right at the start that *state* identity, *state* equality must be preserved. The puny state of Delaware had explained, on the very first day back in May when the credentials of the delegates were read, that its delegates were prohibited by their instructions from supporting any change in the equality of votes among the states that prevailed under the Articles.

Already on May 30, on the first day of consideration in the Committee of the Whole, after Governor Randolph had presented the Virginia Plan, Madison joined the issue by moving "that the equality of suffrage established by the articles of Confederation ought not to prevail in the national Legislature, and that an equitable ratio of representation ought to be substituted."

This is one of the points in Madison's notes at which one reminds oneself that these are Madison's notes. He tried to keep an objective record—but he was engaged. One can sometimes find peeping through the words some human feeling. Madison writes, about the fate of his own key motion: "This was 2ded by Mr Govr MORRIS, and being generally relished, would have been agreed to; when . . ."

That un-record-like phrase "being generally relished" and the observation "would have been agreed to" carry a certain wistfulness, when you know how badly Madison wanted to win this point.

Madison's notes themselves break off, like a child's tale, with that anticipatory "when . . ." shifting to a new paragraph. The entry after the dramatic "when" is a speech by Mr. Read of Delaware moving to postpone the issue, reminding the convention of Delaware's instructions, and threatening to "retire from the convention" if a change contrary to those instructions were "fixed on." It was the first of many sharp exchanges on the issue. Madison made the first of his many speeches arguing the other side and suggested appointing a committee, but—Madison's notes say—"This however did not appear to satisfy Mr. Read."

The delegates did agree relatively easily that there should be *two* houses of the new national legislature, although Benjamin Franklin and perhaps one or two others favored a unicameral legislature (Pennsylvania's radical and interesting constitution of 1776, not much given to checks and balances, had provided for a unicameral legislature). By agreeing to two houses the delegates in 1787 unintentionally laid the groundwork for the compromise that would eventually be arranged. The idea of two houses, representing two different governing principles, had come to be a standard item in the republican convictions of the American patriots. James Harrington, for example, had defended the idea, and John Adams, who took a great deal from Harrington, strongly defended bicameralism in the big book that he had written in London, the first volume of which arrived in the American states just before the convention. The colonies had often had something approaching two houses (appointive governor's councils alongside elected legislatures, like Virginia's House of Burgesses) and the new state constitutions after 1776 generally included two houses (except in Pennsylvania and Georgia). The Virginia Plan had proposed two houses, the second being chosen *by the first,* and therefore, perhaps, representing, from the filtration, greater wisdom? Jefferson had had the same arrangement in the first constitution he proposed (unsuccessfully) for Virginia in 1776. The two-house idea was supposed to provide a balance and a check—it was closely associated with the idea of "balanced government"—and to represent two differing social bases and principles. One house of course was "popular," a commons, larger in membership, perhaps more often elected; the other house, by contrast, represented— what? Not for the Americans any longer "the few." At least it could not be a real House of Lords. Any idea of a hereditary aristocracy had been pretty well swept away in the colonial experience and the revolutionary ideology. Americans were making their way by a combination of thought and experience to an understanding of government that wiped away all the old categorical divisions of society that claimed an automatic, given place in government—kings, nobles, priests, "estates," orders, Lords Spiritual and Lords Temporal—and were beginning to rest the whole of the government (not just part of it) on the people. So what did the second house represent? Property? Wealth? Wisdom? The answer to the question about what the Senate represents would finally be none of these, but rather geography.

In the Committee of the Whole, and in the convention after it reported, the delegates kicked around many other matters—including the issues about the executive, which they would not resolve until nearly the end of the summer—but the issue of equality of states versus representation by population hung over everything. When one reads through Madison's notes one finds it striking how tenacious the two sides were. They did not give up. The defenders of the equality of states dug in their heels, right from that first day, and threatened bluntly to leave and not to join the union if that principle—state equality—were violated. From Madison's point of view, they did not listen to reason; they kept conceiving the issue in big-state, small-state terms, whereas for him, and for Wilson, it was an issue of clear-cut republican principle. "As all authority was derived from the people, equal numbers of people ought to have an equal no. of representatives, and different numbers of people different numbers of representatives. . . . Are not the citizens of Pena. equal to those of N. Jersey? does it require 150 of the former to balance 50 of the latter?"

So Wilson on June 9. But Brearly of New Jersey had said on the same day: "There will be 3. large states and 10 small ones. The large states by which he meant Massts. Pena. & Virga. will carry every thing before them."

And Paterson of New Jersey, the small-state leader, still on June 9, issued the kind of ultimatum that was not rare: "N. Jersey will never confederate on the plan before the Committee. She would be swallowed up. He had rather submit to a monarch, to a despot, than to such a fate. He would not only oppose the plan here but on his return home do everything in his power to defeat it there."

But then Wilson in his speech in response had an ultimatum, too: "If the small states will not confederate on this plan, Pena. & he presumed some other States, would not confederate on any other."

In the latter part of June and in early July there were repeated, and often tense, debates, and votes, on that issue—perhaps a little hard for Americans two hundred years later to comprehend. It came to a first sharp clash on June 30; it hovered over the first week in July, and over the Fourth of July weekend. There were votes and comments that showed already the way the convention was going. Two of the old experienced delegates—Roger Sherman of Connecticut and John Dickinson of Delaware—had suggested, fairly early, the obvious compromise. Some big-state people—Benjamin Franklin and George Mason—were inclined to compromise. There had floated up over the discussion, once it was clear that the convention would support a bicameral legislature, the obvious compromise: one house proportional, one house by states. And when a "grand committee"—one member from every state—was chosen, its membership told the story: Neither Madison nor Wilson was on it; Mason and Franklin represented their states, on a committee dominated by compromisers, localists, and small-state people. The outcome was becoming plain. But Madison and Wilson argued on, right through to the middle of July.

This long battle was not exactly a struggle over the strength of the central government, as one might at first glance think, but rather a struggle over the role and distribution of state power *within* the central government—not the same thing. You might well be for a stronger or a weaker central government, depending upon who has the power in that government. If you have little or no control over it, then you may seek a weakened central government, and many protections against its power. If on the other hand you can control it, or have a big say in it, then you may suddenly find great merit in a strong central government. This is a tendency one may discover elsewhere in human affairs, and it has not been unknown in the subsequent history of these U. States.

The struggle in Philadelphia on this point had to do with the representation of the *states* in the house or houses of the new legislature, whether by population (or property or some other principle) on the one hand, or by state equality (one state, one vote) on the other. The smaller states sought "state equality" in whatever legislature the convention would propose, right from the second motion in the whole summer's deliberation; the principle of state equality had its antecedent in the Articles. From Madison's point of view, that showed what was wrong with it. James Wilson explained that back in 1777–81, when government under the Articles had been formulated, it was a compromise, an expedient, not grounded in principle but in necessity. But *now*—Madison and Wilson would say—now that we are building a government to last *forever,* and on *principle*—let's do it right. Moreover, the Articles *was* a compact among states, a league; but this new government about to be born was to be something different, not a league, and therefore should rest properly on different principles. Madison and Wilson and the strong nationalists rejected the principle of state equality and insisted that the states be represented in proportion to their populations. The American states in 1787 were not equal in population or resources or territory; three years later in the first census, Virginia, the most populous state, had roughly ten times the population of the least populous, Delaware, 740,000 to 74,000, counting slaves, or 440,000 to 46,000 free whites, and the proportion was thought to be roughly the same in 1787. Not very much earlier Georgia would have been even more lightly populated than Delaware. The three most populous states, Virginia, Pennsylvania, and Massachusetts, had a combined population that equaled that of the six next.

And the differences were not confined to population. There was territory. There was wealth. There was history. There was distinction. A contemporary reader must remind himself that at the time states mattered a great deal more than they do today. Your state was really almost your country. In the days of the colonies the colonial allegiances had competed with and supplanted loyalty to England; under the Articles they had been the apex of most citizens' loyalty, and if this convention failed they would continue to be. The attitudes might be closer to our feelings of national than of state rivalry. And there were tremendous stakes in the shaping of power.

The big states were also the most prestigious and, in the case of Massachusetts and Virginia, the oldest. The other states were vales of humility (New Jersey, North Carolina) crushed between mountains of conceit (the big-state people might say, anticipating Churchill's remark about Clement Atlee's modesty, that New Jersey and North Carolina had a lot to be humble *about*). They were pieces chopped off or grown out of the great states, as Delaware and New Jersey came from Pennsylvania, and Virginia's vast original grant contained what had become Maryland and the Carolinas, as well as what would one day become Kentucky and West Virginia; all the New England states were outgrowths, one way or another, from their origins in Massachusetts Bay, cut off from these origins. To proud big-state people it was unconscionable that states like that little sparsely populated Delaware, a nothing over there on the Peninsula, or scarcely credible little Rhode Island, that could not even get itself together enough to send delegates to this convention, or Georgia, that sprinkling of ex-convicts spread throughout the woods way down south and "west," should have as many votes in any legislature as would *Pennsylvania, Massachusetts, Virginia*. For a proud Virginian in 1787 that was a little bit like a xenophobic and ungenerous American in 1990 watching his great country outvoted in the United Nations by a coalition of scrawny Third World countries of no distinction that just came into existence last Tuesday.

The delegations from Delaware and from New Jersey, and from Connecticut and from Maryland and from small states generally, understandably believed otherwise. They were frightened of domination by the big states. Madison argued, cogently, that the big states, differing by region and by economic base, and having therefore different interests, would not make common cause; bigness alone was no unifying principle. It was much more likely, he said, that the states would combine by *region*, as North versus South. He even did say—touching briefly but presciently on this most sensitive subject—that the more likely divisions would be between slave and nonslave, rather than big and little states. He was certainly right about that one. He and Wilson kept trying to get the small-state people to stop thinking in terms of states, of state egos. But these arguments were to no avail. The small states wanted their own power base and had their own fears and collective egotisms. They had by now their own histories and identities, and they had their own ambitions and leaders with power and careers at stake in their continuation and strength.

There were as always in such cases some ingredients in the battle that did not have to do with high principle or even straight territorial collective ego, but with state and personal interests in the most immediate and narrow sense—land, and lots of it, and soon. All the large states, and particularly Virginia, had claims on great swatches of that vast territory to the west, across the Alleghenies; and their speculators, including some delegates and statesmen at this very convention not excluding its president, were exploiting those possibilities. Small-state people did not want to be cut of from those acres and acres of possibility.

Not all of the arguing was altogether grounded in cool reason, free of power plays. Nor was it always perfectly polite. Some small-state people had suggested, right at the start that they would not federate if they were denied equal voting by states, and they continued to make that threat. Sometimes they did it in the ways negotiating representatives do in such a situation: they said their hands were tied. Their instructions *required* them to reject anything except state equality. Or: their constituents would not *allow* them to accept anything less. Madison and Wilson, although in my view (not everybody's) arguing from a larger ingredient of rational conception and a lesser ingredient of interest than the small states, nevertheless also made threats, implied or even explicit, that the big states—or rather those who accepted sound principles—might just set up their own union. At one point a small-state delegate had called Madison's abstract intellectual bluff, as he might have viewed the matter, about the abstract principle of basing all representation strictly on population, one man, one vote: all right, then, why not throw all the states back into the "hotchpot" and redraw lines for the voting districts, to make them all more equitable? In other words: take the Old Dominion and all the others and pitch them all into one common pot and redraw the lines. Madison had to scramble to explain why that could not be done.

On June 27, when the extended discussion of this issue really began (after preliminary skirmishes on May 30 and June 9 and 11), Luther Martin of Maryland gave a long and rambling ("upwards of three hours," wrote Yates) defense of the small-state position, and to the despair of all continued for hours the next day; both delegates and historians hint that he was drunk. On June 30 Gunning Bedford of Delaware, in a blunt speech ("Are not the large States evidently seeking to aggrandize themselves at the expense of the small? They think no doubt that they have right on their side, but interest had blinded their eyes") ended by suggesting—threatening?—that the small states if denied might seek foreign alliances. Here is Madison's report:

The little States are willing to observe their engagements, but will meet the large ones on no ground but that of the Confederation. We have been told (with a dictatorial air) that this is the last moment for a fair trial in favor of a good Governmt. It will be the last indeed if the propositions reported from the Committee go forth to the people. He was under no apprehensions. The Large States dare not dissolve the confederation. If they do the small ones will find some foreign ally of more honor and good faith, who will take them by the hand and do them justice.

Bedford was reproved.

After the small states' victory, or quasi victory—after the vote that finally settled the matter, on July 16—Edmund Randolph (who was far from being, in general, a solid supporter of Madison and Wilson but who was all big-state at this moment) exploded with what seemed to be a proposal that the convention just adjourn—call it all off. Paterson of New Jersey responded in kind: all right, let's *do* adjourn, and let the people know you big-state guys, the first time you lost, just wanted to pick up your marbles and go home. There, for the moment, were our "demigods" confronting each other as in the playground. Cooler heads prevailed.

Throughout the long argument on this issue there was an underlying pattern familiar in politics as it nears the extremes: a threat and counterthreat not unlike a game of "chicken" (as it has been described, at a still more rudimentary level, in the writings about nuclear deterrence) in which each side must measure the other's determination and true intentions. In this case both sides, or all sides and parties here represented, wanted a union—a stronger union than the Articles—and wanted it rather badly. Both or all sides feared the consequences of failure, of disunion: that the American states should fall into a cluster of confederacies, contending with each other and making foreign alliances.

So that common commitment and fear gave the convention a shared purpose, but also gave each side in a struggle the lever of a threat to withdraw, to hold out, not to join. And each side did use that threat; in Madison's and Wilson's views the small states' case consisted of little else. Both sides, for their differing reasons, cared enough about this issue to test the other severely, and to bring the convention to the brink of dissolution. (It is part of the tragedy of early American history that no comparable test of wills was made on the issues about slavery.) One side used the threat to withdraw, and all the other weapons. The other side—did not.

Madison had strong objections to state equality in the legislature on the basis of the principles he had been working out. The states would bring all their vices now straight into the core of the new federal government. To him, and to James Wilson, the republican principle was equality of *individuals,* not equality of states. Madison, the experienced politician who knew that these political forms *mattered,* and the sometime student of moral philosophy with John Witherspoon, and no doubt one must add the native Virginian, appealed regularly to an implicit moral standard when he claimed, as he did throughout this debate, that it was "unjust and unrepublican" that the vote of a citizen of Virginia should count for *less* than that of a citizen of Delaware or New Jersey ... because of course the small states' position did mean that, because equality of *states* meant *inequality* of citizens. State equality (Delaware equals Virginia) would create "rotten boroughs" of the sort that had disfigured British politics—boroughs that some lord could keep in his vest pocket because they had no people in them. One of the radical whigs whom the colonials had read, a man named James Burgh, another Scotsman in the circle of the great Scottish professors, had written vigorously against the rottenness of rotten boroughs in England. And perhaps Madison and Wilson were not entirely wrong to apply that whig horror at rotten boroughs to what might develop in this new land. What would one say, for example— to move ahead in history and to names that Madison had never heard of—about the overrepresentation of rural areas as compared with the growing urban areas both within the states—downstate Illinois versus Chicago, upstate New York against New York City, the rest of Michigan against Wayne County—and between the states—Wyoming and Nevada and Utah each in the passage of time to have as many senators as New York and Pennsylvania—with an enormous spread of consequences in American politics and government and politics to flow therefrom. Madison was not mistaken in believing the issue was important.

It meant, to Madison, bringing all those vices of state governments under the Articles that he had itemized and deplored in his memos straight into the core of the new national government. It is to be remembered that at the moment in the convention that our forefathers were having this portentous argument—late June and early July 1787—they assumed that the legislature of the new national government would be the whole, or almost the whole, of the government. They had not yet settled what the executive would be, though they had discussed the matter. They certainly had no notion of the modern presidency and "executive branch," let alone the modern bureaucracy. Under the Articles, the only continental government they had experienced, Congress was all there was. In the new state constitutions, written in the revolutionary enthusiasm after John Adams's resolutions in 1776 and 1777, and in reaction to the evil deeds of royal governors, the governors were characteristically weak; the legislature was the great center of power in government. Moreover, at this time it was expected, as far as the discussion had gone, that the representatives in the upper house would be chosen by the state legislatures. And it would then have been expected that state delegations in this new national legislative body would vote as a unit— Virginia one vote, Delaware one vote (when later in the summer, after this decision was taken, this matter was faced, Madison certainly supported the proposal that prevailed, that each of the two senators from a state should vote individually, but that was yet to come). So the picture that Madison had, on the evening of the discouraging day July 16, 1787, was that those squabbling state legislatures of the states, where most of those vices and unjust laws he had listed and deplored and fought against were concentrated, would now be choosing delegations to the more powerful of the two houses of the new continental government. And in that legislative body each state would vote as a unit so that state power would be enhanced. And the small states, where the vices were particularly vicious, would have more votes than the large states (the small Rhode Islands and Delawares and Georgias had somewhat more of the vices for reasons not unlike those he had presented in his letters and speeches and memos and would present in *Federalist* papers, having to do with the correcting effect of larger size on the factions that liberty produces in a republic—the little states had less of that). And so these small states, with a smaller total population—no majority—and with their narrowness and vices at their base back home in the legislatures, would nevertheless be able, in this central organ in the new government, to outvote the big states, including Virginia—as indeed they were to do on that very July 16 on that very issue in that very convention.

The vote taken that day was illustrative of the problem, as Madison would see it, not only in its outcome but in its composition. New York was no longer present. Its two representatives, who had participated almost entirely to protect New York's interests, and who had regularly outvoted Hamilton (one of the reasons he left the convention), had now, seeing the way the wind was blowing, themselves departed. So New York now had no delegation and no vote. New Hampshire had not yet arrived. Rhode Island never showed up. So ten states made the decision. But Massachusetts' four votes were split, so its vote was canceled. Thus we are down to nine states to decide this enormous issue. The Madison-Wilson side lost, 5–4.

In much of the early going Madison the politician had counted on Georgia and the Carolinas to vote with the big states because, although small in population now, they were growing fast or thought they were; they had the territory to accommodate people and had expectations of becoming big states. There had been a kind of implicit alliance between the three biggest states—Virginia, Pennsylvania, and Massachusetts, and the three Deep South states, which expected to be big. But on this vote North Carolina voted with Delaware, Connecticut, Maryland, and New Jersey, perhaps because of some deal—Madison was not the only politician in the room. After this fateful vote Madison went through one of those exercises one does in such a situation: if only this vote had changed, if only that vote, the outcome would have been different. The outcome was the Great Compromise that was to be enshrined in the history class notes of millions of young American scholars.

Three

On the next morning after that vote, July 17, the big-state representatives had a meeting before the general session. There were also a few small-state people attending, through whatever agency, so that this curious meeting was not quite a caucus of the big-state people, or of the opponents of state equality, but almost.

What do we do now? For the first time the Madison-Wilson forces had lost a significant vote, and this was an immensely important one.

And from whom do we learn about this meeting, gathering in sorrow after James Madison's hopes had been crushed? From James Madison himself, of course. Even though it was not an official meeting of the convention.

To comprehend the rare and curious form of this accomplishment, one must enter into Madison's own very strong convictions about the Constitution, on the one side, and then survey the thoroughness of his reporting, on the other. One place this combination becomes particularly poignant is in the report of this meeting on the morning of July 17.

Madison included a record of this meeting, held, as he said, by a number of members of the larger states in consequence of the vote in favor of an "equal Representation in the 2nd branch, and the apparent inflexibility of the smaller states on that point." Of course, there were other views about who was inflexible, but that was Madison's. This is one of the points at which if you are sympathetic to him you feel a certain poignancy. "The time was wasted," he wrote, "in vague conversation on the subject, without any specific proposition or agreement." Not the most neutral and objective reporting in the world. Then he described two positions among the large-state delegates. One was for yielding to them, and for joining in the convention's agreement "however imperfect & exceptionable . . . tho' decided by a bare majority of the states and a minority of the people of the U. States." Madison cannot stop himself from getting in those digs, these continuing arguments, right in his record of the gathering. And what was the other view? "Several of [the large-state delegates] supposing that no good Governm*t* could or would be built on that foundation, and that a division of the Convention into two opinions was unavoidable; it would be better that the side comprising the principal States, and a majority of the people of America, should propose a scheme of Govt. to the States."

That is twice in one short (reporter's!) note that Madison has appealed (like the American politicians to come) to the association of his position with a *majority* of the people of America.

More important—what is it that is here being said? That the big states should go their own way, make their own proposal of a government, and leave those small states to do whatever they would, in their small-state way. In other words, that the big states should pull out of this convention and have their own.

Was Madison the one who proposed that action? The editors of Madison's Papers infer that he was. Delegates from small states had made their threats—that they would pull out, even that they would seek alliance with foreign powers. Now some delegates from large states, in their turn, were on the point of pulling out.

But Madison—if it was he—or whoever presented this position could not carry the caucus with him. This almost-caucus of the big-state delegates included a few small-state people, however they may have come to be there. (Maybe they just walked in; the caucus was held, before the hour of beginning, in the convention's meeting room in the Pennsylvania State House. Or maybe someone tipped them or invited them. Scholars speculate.) The last sentence of Madison's note about this gathering refers, either sourly or resignedly or sadly, depending upon how you read it, to these small-state delegates. One pictures a deeply disappointed Madison seeing a certain smugness on the faces of the small-state delegates (there are no names in this note) who knew they had the votes, and maybe also a deal. In any case this is what Madison wrote, in conclusion. Notice the word *whatever*. "It is probable that the result of this consultation satisfied the smaller States that they had nothing to apprehend from a union of the larger, in any plan whatever ag*st* the equality of votes in the 2d branch."

The Great Compromise was secure. To James Madison, however, it was not a great compromise but a great mistake.

6

The Inadvertent Origins
of the American Presidency

One

SO ON THE EVENINGS OF JULY 16 AND JULY 17, 1787, James Madison must have felt that the convention, for which he had had such high hopes, was a failure. Two months later he was still writing letters that almost said so. Nevertheless, he kept on attending the convention and speaking and arguing—and taking notes. He certainly did not quit.

What happened in the remainder of the convention is instructive, and reveals something of the nature of a deliberative body as a human institution. Once certain decisions are taken, the terms for others are changed, sometimes radically. A deliberative body like a parliament, or this unique convention, is not a static encounter of fixed positions that win or lose without affecting each other, but is rather a process of interaction in which positions and alliances, and options and sometimes even minds, are continually changing. And the Great Compromise was a very big decision, in the minds, and the politics, of these delegates. Once the structure of power *within* the new government was determined (that there would be an equality of states—little Delaware would count for as much as big Virginia—in one house of the legislature), terms for all the other decisions—about what powers to give that government, and what shape it should take—were shifted. Delegates, and state delegations, altered their positions. The small states shifted dramatically, coming to favor strengthening the central government, and Madison and Wilson shifted significantly, coming to favor strengthening the branches of government *other* than the legislature . . . especially the executive. One might say, although the politics of this is enormously complicated, that the constitutional base for our modern three branches of the federal government, and for the full-fledged doctrine and fact of the separation of powers, and in particular for the strong presidency, came out of these two shifts of position in Philadelphia, after the Great Compromise.

Before these decisions in the middle of July the convention's work, although it roamed widely, had focused overwhelmingly on the legislature, with the implicit expectation that that body would be the great center of power and decision in the new government. There was some republican doctrine that it *ought* to be so—the people, through the people's representatives, being the superior power—ruling. So it had been under the Articles, in which Congress was the sole organ of government, and so it was ordinarily in the states under those new constitutions they wrote after John Adams's May 10 and 15 resolutions in '76: the governors were characteristically weak appendages to a legislature, which was the center of power. The Virginia Plan had proposed a weak and vague executive, ineligible to serve beyond one term, chosen by, and therefore dependent upon, the national two-branch legislature. There was provision for a national judiciary in the Virginia Plan, but it also was to be chosen by the legislature. The New Jersey Plan—the collection of points the small states put forward to stall the Virginia Plan and to defend state equality—built as it was fundamentally around strengthening rather than replacing the Articles—also proposed that power in the new government be centered overwhelmingly in the legislature. Even though these plans had rudimentary provisions for an executive and a judiciary, they did not yet have the three branches, or the separation of powers, as we have come to know them in American history. These branches, and the developed doctrines of their independence and reciprocal balancing, were to come in the subsequent work of the convention, in part as a result of the shiftings of position I have mentioned.

The small states, having obtained the reassuring protection of state equality in the Senate, now accepted and even proposed strengthenings of the central government. William Paterson, the New Jersey delegate who had been their first spokesman with the New Jersey Plan, now supported a strong national government, and was for the rest of his life a thoroughgoing "federalist." The small states, as Madison had predicted, became now ardent supporters of a central government upon which they were more dependent than their big and powerful neighbors. When the time came to ratify this Constitution, it sailed quickly and unanimously through Delaware, giving it the claim to be the first state on its license plates, and also through other small states—New Jersey and Georgia—

in both cases also quickly and unanimously. The potent opposition to this nationalizing Constitution was to come not in the small states but in the big ones.

And if his erstwhile opponents from the small states shifted their position, so too did James Madison. In the last half of July 1787, Madison, we may surmise, gathered himself together and tried to make what he could of this new government, flawed at its base fundamentally though he thought it to be. And I believe it would be accurate to say that he gradually discovered that the new government need not be quite so bad as he feared. Let us guess that one part of him was making that discovery, through the rest of July and August and early September, while there was still lodged in his belly a stone of disappointment about the defeat on the core issue of state equality in the second house. (We have to remember that other human beings on this earth are like ourselves, and that this extends to big figures in the past, like the celebrated founding fathers. We have simultaneous layers of diverse emotions and convictions. In a very complex negotiating-legislating body like this convention, filled with the excitement of an enormously heightened expectation, where there are lots of balls in the air, one could be operating simultaneously at several levels: disappointed, or worse, at one; fighting on, and gaining victories, and glimpsing new possibilities, at another.) Madison began to see a separation of powers, in which the other two powers—branches—had a new strength and independence. In discussing one abortive proposal put forward by Wilson (the participation of the judiciary with the executive in a "revisionary council" that would check the legislature), Madison said (on July 21), "Experience in all the States had evinced a powerful tendency in the Legislature to absorb all power into its vortex. This was the real source of danger to the American Constitutions; & suggested the necessity of giving every defensive authority to the other departments that was consistent with republican principles." So he, and Wilson, and others proceeded to give the other departments every republican "defensive authority" they could.

On the precise point of *state* presence in the legislature—in the Senate—Madison and Wilson's point of view won a quite sizable victory, without much resistance, on July 23, when the convention voted that the representation in the Senate should consist of two members from each state (the alternative of three was voted down, as leading eventually to too large a body) and that these two *should vote "per capita"* (each one individually) rather than by state. Only Luther Martin, the articulate dipsomaniacal small-state defender from Maryland, spoke against this proposal, and only Maryland voted against it, but it was a big decision, a big qualification on the small states' victory (to put it that way) in the Great

Compromise. Now *states* as such—as Luther Martin said—would not be voting in the Senate, as they did in Congress under the Articles, and as they did in this very convention (Madison's recordings of the votes go by states: Pa, ay; Ga, no; Va, ay.) Having each Senator vote *individually* meant, among other things, a sharp diminution of *state* power within the national legislature. A century and a quarter years later the Seventeenth Amendment to the Constitution would provide that these individually voting senators, instead of being chosen by the state legislatures, would be chosen by the people. The United States government after two hundred years has many kinks and defects and maybe even vices, but the domination of the national government by the state legislatures that Madison feared is not one of them.

The defect in the power base of the national legislature—as Madison and Wilson saw it—was further mitigated as the convention decided the shape of the other branches of government. It was widely accepted that there should be the three, and that they should be in some measure separated; the celebrated Montesquieu had said it should be so, and colonial experience had moved in that direction. Justice and republican principle indicated that those who *make* law should not also *apply* it and *execute* it, and that neither should be the *judges* of cases under it; this separating was an expression of that larger principle of checking and balancing power that ran through the whole American founding. The delegates had a rudimentary idea of three branches and separated powers from their state governments and colonial experience. The Virginia Plan had proposed "that a *national* Government [ought to be established] consisting of a *supreme* Legislative, Executive & Judiciary," and the expectation of that threeness ran through the convention. But the shape and power of the two branches other than the legislature was not yet clear—particularly, their *independence* from the legislature, standing over against it (and yet working with it) as independent branches. Neither was it clear at the outset that these three branches could *all* rest, in the end, on the whole public—that none need represent any class, or vocation, or "estate," as in the received ideas from political thinkers. John Adams, out of touch with the latest rounds in this constitution-making because he was over in London as the American minister, still had in his head the idea that "balanced government" should mean a balance within government of units representing different orders in the society. But in Philadelphia the delegates were moving beyond that idea—James Wilson had already moved beyond it. For him the whole pyramid could rest on that one undivided broad base, the people. And others came to see that, too: that the executive and the judiciary could represent the people as much as the legislature did, but simply in a different mode. It wasn't that the legislature represented the people and the executive and judiciary represented—something or someone else. It was that in the end they all rested on the people, serving them in different *functions*. And they could still check and balance each other, as contrasting functions, without representing different pieces or parts of the social order.

Two

But what shape now should the executive take? Not a king. Not a royal governor. But not a *weak* governor like those the states generally had constructed, in reaction against the royal governors.

The convention really did go up and down and around and sideways on this one: How should the executive be chosen? By the national legislature (a strong entry)? By the state legislatures? By the governors of the states? By the people? By "electors"? By lottery? How many of him should there be? One? Three? Seven? Thirty? Should he (these delegates would not have said "or she") be accompanied by a "council," a constitutionally based group of collaborators, a "revisionary council" as James Madison called it? (Madison at first favored this idea, and such a council was proposed in the Virginia Plan.) How long should the executive's term be? Four years? Seven years? "During good behavior"—that is, for life? Should an executive chosen for a term be eligible for reelection? And what should his powers be? Should Congress or the executive command the military? Should Congress or the executive appoint judges? Appoint ambassadors? Heads of departments? Should the executive have a veto of congressional legislation? The convention had set aside fairly early the proposals for anything other than a single person and they set aside, after a time, the idea of an accompanying council—a "revisionary council"—to be constitutional collaborator in the executive. But the questions about the powers to be given that single executive, and the length of his term, and the issue of his eligibility for reelection, and how to choose him, kept recurring in the convention, interwoven with other questions, now this way, now that way: if you changed one aspect—having the executive chosen by legislature, say, as Roger Sherman consistently wanted—then you altered delegates' opinion on another aspect—what the powers of the executive should be. There was a complicated interweave of considerations about the term of office, and eligibility for reelection, with these other considerations.

The debates about the executive were extremely confusing and repetitive; for good or ill they did not have the sharp, interest-based definition that the state equality debate had had. On this issue the delegates were venturing out into new territory, only very lightly fenced in by established interests and ideologies; they could give play to the penchant of some of them for applied political philosophy. James Madison admitted in his letter to George Washington in the spring that he had not yet formed much of an idea of the executive, and neither of his preparatory memos—on the ancient and modern confederations or on the vices of state governments—dealt explicitly with that subject. He developed his ideas under fire in the late summer of 1787. Madison was now particularly concerned to make this executive—given now the label "president"—as independent as could be of the national legislature, especially because this last was no longer as independent of the *state* legislatures as he had wanted.

The shaping of the presidency took place by fits and starts through the summer, and came to completion near the end. The Constitutional Convention in Philadelphia was like other such gatherings in this regard, that it started with high hopes and good temper and wide-ranging and thorough discussion, and came toward its end in a rush and a crunch and the assignment of many points to committees, and to a further touch or two of rancor and anger.

There were two committees of great importance to the decision about the executive, as well as other matters, in the last half of the Philadelphia Convention. The Committee of Detail, with John Rutledge of South Carolina as chairman, was the most important of all the committees to serve in the convention, and had significance on *all* subjects. The committee was potent on the subject of slavery; it was a grave setback, for any opponent of slavery, that John Rutledge was its chairman. James Wilson was a member of this important committee of five, but Madison was not. The Committee of Detail was given all the resolutions so far taken by the convention—twenty-three of them, representing the convention's revisions of, and additions to, the Virginia Plan, and also the Pinckney Plan and the New Jersey Plan, and was directed to make of them a draft constitution. The convention adjourned on July 26 to give them time to do this, and did not assemble again until August 6.

The Committee of Detail went well beyond mere compiling and drafting; on still disputed points they made decisions about what to propose that narrowed the options. They did so not only with respect to the executive branch but also about the legislative. The convention had been back and forth about whether Congress should have a broad unspecified power to act wherever the states were "incompetent", or be limited to specific powers that would be named—"enumerated." The second alternative represented a hedging of the power of the legislature, and Madison supported it, and so did this committee. They brought in a list of "enumerated" powers of Congress, most of which can now be found in Article I, section 8, of the Constitution. There was to be further dispute on this matter, but the Constitution as it emerged finally would include essentially the enumerated powers specified by the Committee of Detail.

Many of these powers were set forth in language borrowed from the Articles of Confederation. We have said that the framers were not starting de novo but were actually making a *second* try to frame an adequate continental government; there were not only some negative lessons, but also some contributions, from the first. The Committee of Detail borrowed also from state constitutions, and from other plans—the New Jersey one, and the offering by young Charles Pinckney of South Carolina on behalf of which he later tried to make large claims.

We do not know exactly what Madison did in these ten days of the convention's recess, while the Committee of Detail was doing its work, except that he wrote some letters home, but one may guess that he was keeping track of what was happening in the committee and working away on those notes.

On August 6 the Rutledge committee put before the reassembled delegates printed copies of the results of their work, twenty-three articles in sequence, a full draft constitution. From August 6 until September 10, essentially—although with some intervening committee reports—this draft was the basis of discussion, now in longer sessions, rounding into the home stretch. As always in such discussions, matters of great importance mingled with quibbles over language and minor matters. As always in such high-pressure convention settings, even among "demigods," there were mechanical errors: two articles were given the roman numeral VI and the numbering thereafter was thrown off.

What the Committee of Detail proposed about the executive was the *beginning* of the conclusion. The committee proposed, in its report on August 6, an executive who would be one person, whose "stile" shall be "the President of the United States of America" (and "title" "His Excellency"!), who shall give State of the Union messages and make appointments (*except* for Supreme Court judges and ambassadors—reserved to the Senate) and have power to grant pardons and adjourn congress when the two houses disagree. This president shall "take care that the laws of the United States be duly and faithfully executed," a clause that, like others in this committee's report, survived to go into the Constitution as we have it today. Most important, the committee said that this president shall be "Commander in chief of the Army and Navy of the United States, and of the Militia of the Several States." That is where that phrase, and power, comes from. This president could be impeached by the House. All of this survived. But the president proposed by this committee was to be elected by the legislature, was to hold office for seven years, was to be ineligible for reelection and if impeached, tried by the Supreme Court:

provisions that did not survive. That provision that he should be chosen by the legislature pitched the matter back into the big-state small-state wrangles. On the floor Wilson, who must have lost out on this matter in committee, tried again, with Madison's support, to have the president elected by the people, and the vote was only six to five against.

So the matter thus focused and aerated and begun was referred, along with other matters, to another "grand" committee (one member from each state: committee of eleven), the committee on "Unfinished Parts" (wonderful phrase), of which David Brearly of New Jersey was chairman. Madison was the Virginia member of this committee, which had an unusually able membership. On August 31 this committee took the matters still left undecided—including the method of choosing the president—and brought in a report on September 4 that included most of the elements of the constitutional presidency as it is known to American history. To repeat: the unique American office of the President emerged—almost—from this committee meeting from August 31 to September 4, 1787, with James Madison as the Virginia member and, we may surely infer, one of its most influential members. Surely he favored (among the available alternatives) the proposals of the committee with respect to the presidency.

The committee proposed that the president be chosen by that electoral college system that Wilson had long before suggested. Madison, in one of his typically analytical dissections of the possibilities, speaking on the floor of convention on July 25, had come down to the only acceptable alternatives, choice of a president by "Electors chosen by the people" and "immediate appointment by the people." At the end of the speech he said that this last, election by the people at large ("or rather by the qualified part of them"!), was "with all its imperfections" the best method. But in the meantime he had explained why choice by electors chosen by the people was the next best method—primarily because it disengaged that choice from any dependence on the state legislatures, which, he said, "had betrayed a strong propensity to a variety of pernicious measures," and from the national legislature, which might "be infected with a similar propensity."

The Committee on Unfinished Parts also proposed that the term of the president be four years, and that he be eligible for reelection—which, presumably, would make him more responsive to his constituents than a one-term president, ineligible to repeat, would be. And this committee shifted key appointment powers, lodged by the Committee of Detail with the Senate, now to the hands of the president: it bestowed upon the executive the power to appoint judges—a very big power, as history has shown—and ambassadors and other officials, subject only to the advice and consent of the Senate. If you ask yourself where in the Constitution does the power of this unique office rest, a principal answer will be, in these appointment powers, and in what can be inferred from them—for an important example, that the power to appoint ambassadors (and to receive them, and to "correspond with the supreme Executives" of other nations, for which the Committee of Detail had already provided) implies the power to conduct foreign policy.

On many of these points about the presidency Madison had changed his mind. The Virginia Plan, for example, had provided that the executive be chosen by both houses of the legislature, and Madison in early June had opposed giving the power to appoint judges to the executive branch, but after the Great Compromise lodged state equality in the one house of the legislature, he changed his position on both. Now the executive became for him the great repository of the national principle which he feared would not be protected by a legislature in which the states had so large a role, and presumably in that Committee on Unfinished Parts he helped design its restrained and independent strength.

When this committee reported, the delegates in convention added additional features that strengthened the executive office still further. The president was given the very important power to make treaties—but again with the concurrence of two-thirds of the Senate. James Wilson tried to eliminate the concurrence of the Senate, both on judicial appointments and on treaties, but—altering American history considerably—he was not successful. The powers and characteristics of the presidency fell into place, step by step, in the last stages of the Philadelphia Convention.

In the discussion of armies, war, and national defense the delegates kept the president as the "Commander in chief" as the Committee of Detail had proposed. Neither the Virginia Plan nor the New Jersey Plan had dealt with particular matters like armies and defense. This proposal of the Committee of Detail sailed on into the Constitution—on August 27, effectively—without debate precisely on that point, but with argument on another: Who could "make" or, as it came to be, "declare" war? The delegates wanted the civilian head of government to command the armed forces—but they wanted the war-making power strictly located in *Congress*. But whereas the Committee of Detail had said, among that body's enumerated powers, that it should have the power to "make" war, the objection that a legislative body is not an efficient body for that purpose in an invasion or emergency brought the change—suggested by Madison—to the phrase "*declare* war." And so the possibility, in a defensive emergency, of the commander in chief's making war before Congress "declared" it, or without Congress ever "declaring" it, slipped neatly between the phrases into history, where it was destined in the nation's second century to play a large role.

Three

Did the framers have a clear conception of the executive they were creating? One may doubt it. They came out of legislative government, not executive government. Many of the framers—including James Madison, James Wilson, and Alexander Hamilton—had served in the Continental Congress. That had been the government they knew. Under the Articles, Congress was all there was—the whole government. Committees of Congress would choose a secretary—as John Jay and Robert Livingston were secretaries of foreign affairs—or, before the Articles, a chairman—as John Adams was Chairman of the Committee on defense matters—but these were creatures of the Congress. There was no independent executive. Congress had been the union's whole government for seven years, under the Articles, and for thirteen years since the first Congress. The state governments that were instituted after 1776 were centered in the legislature, especially in the lower and more popular house. Characteristically they set up weak governors—like the very feeble governorship in Virginia that Thomas Jefferson filled for one unhappy war-torn term. The framers had *negative* models of executives—models of what they did not want. They did not want a royal governor, a Thomas Hutchinson or Lord Dunmore imposing a will outside the reach of the people. They did not want a British king. So what then was their model for an executive? For the legislature they had plenty of positive models: the "mother of parliaments" in that British government that many of them still, despite independence, held to be the best in the world; the colonial legislatures, in which they had begun a kind of de facto self-rule for a century and a half; the state legislatures in which they had served, the Continental Congress in which they had served, the diets and parliaments and assemblies of republics past and present.

Such a popularly elected representative body had been at the core of the kind of *republican* government they were bringing into being. But what then was their *executive* to be like, in this republican government? Where was the model for that? The only model was sitting there in front of them. He was sitting there in front of them, dignified, silent, universally admired and respected, above the battles of factions, impartial, honored for his selfless devotion to the common good, not intervening in, but presiding over, their councils—a presider, a *president*. The executive was to be—George Washington.

Madison, as we have said, had admitted before the convention that he had not thought out the nature of the executive in the proposed new constitution. The Virginia Plan's proposals were a very long way from the executive that was developed through the summer. The framers had to sort out the issue of the *number* of persons in the executive, settling on one person. They had to disengage him from any constitutionally grounded advisory council, of the sort that many state constitutions had set up (including Virginia's; James Madison's first major political office was on this council, and it was in that role that he came to be the friend of Thomas Jefferson. The Virginia Plan had proposed such a council; George Mason thought to the end that the new Constitution ought to provide for one, and made its absence one of his strong objections to the Constitution as it was finally written.) They had to sort out the length of term for this executive, and whether he would be eligible for reelection. The varying answers to those questions would change the answers to the other questions about this executive. It was a complicated and a shifting package; change this and we change our mind about that.

When Thomas Jefferson in Paris would read the proposed constitution, one of his two strongest objections would be to the perpetual reeligibility of this president: there's your king, he said. After George Washington is gone, and some less disinterested mortal holds that post, he will keep on being elected and elected and elected (To the tune "Always": "Not for just two terms; not for just three terms; not for just four terms but—Always." Republican satirical campaign song, 1944).

Though with respect to this branch of government, as not for the legislature, the framers were drawing more on imagination and philosophy than on experience, speculating in the dark, they did manage to compromise and settle these issues about the form of the executive: one person, no council, four years, eligible for reelection. But what then was he to *do*? For Congress in Article I of the Constitution they would make the long list, much of it taken over from the Articles of Confederation, of "enumerated powers." They had a debate—to repeat—about whether simply to make a general grant of power—that the federal legislature body should have power for those things in which the states were "incompetent"—or a specific grant, and decided on the latter, as more careful and more restrictive, and made the long list of enumerated powers that appears in Article I, section 8. But this executive, this "president," what was he to do? Make a speech "from time to time" on the state of the union. Grant pardons. Call special sessions of Congress. Receive ambassadors. There is really not much to it. To some extent the vague shape of this office was the residuum of debate on the more familiar ground of the legislature, and the filling in of Montesquieu's (and others') theories of three separated branches. Because it was thought to be improper for the legislature to execute the laws it makes, there should be this executive to execute the laws—to "take care that the laws are faithfully executed." And that sense of the need for the pieces and parts of government to be checked and balanced by each other—that old radical whig and new Madisonian doctrine—meant that this executive should be a check upon the legislature. He should have a "negative," as they put it back in those days, a veto as we would say later, on the acts of the legislature. But, after consideration, not an *absolute* negative; the legislature in its turn can balance the whims and arbitrariness of an executive, if it is strongly enough motivated to gather a two-thirds vote.

And this executive should do those things that we know from experience a legislature is not good at doing. A legislative body is not the place to look for the qualities—to use words often on the lips of Alexander Hamilton—energy and dispatch. If you need something done in the next hour and a half, don't ask a legislative body to do it: if there is an invasion to be countered, an insult by a foreign power to be responded to, an army to be moved from here to there, an economic crisis to be dealt with right now—you need an executive, not a legislature. That is a main reason for having a one-man executive, so that he can decide quickly and clearly.

And a legislative body is not a good organ for making appointments. The Continental Congress kept making ineffectual three-man and five-man appointments. When Jefferson and Adams and Franklin were appointed to go to Europe by the Congress, these appointments and instructions and their recall would be debated in Congress, one candidate against another, and then compromises made, perhaps three persons sent instead of one—not the way to do it. An executive—one centered will—should make appointments—but (second thought) not without some check in its turn. There should be "advice and consent" (a phrase of Madison's) by the Senate, as another check.

The powers at the core are, as it was regularly put in those days, the power of the purse and the power of the sword. Without those the nationalist, or federalist, group led by Madison would say, the union is no government but only a toothless alliance. The powers of the purse—to tax, and to appropriate money—must not be given to the executive but lodged in the lower house, the representative house closest to the people. The convention fought about that—whether the Senate (a kind of aristocratic body, a collection of the wise, chosen by the state legislature to represent the states) should have a role in "money bills." The republican tradition and ideology suggested that money bills should originate in the lower house. In any case, not with the executive.

But what then of the power of the sword? And of what later generations would call "foreign policy?" Although the danger of being weak in the international field, and of becoming a shuttlecock of European power politics, was an important motive making for union and strong government, the convention did not think of these matters in the central and continuous way we do today. Foreign affairs meant *treaties:* the treaties of Paris, the Spanish treaty, the treaties with the Indians, shortly after the government began, the extremely controversial Jay treaty. This executive was given the power to negotiate treaties—but again, not unrestrained. Not without a check. Only with the concurrence of two-thirds of Senate. They did not anticipate a day when a president would journey to Europe to participate in another great treaty of European settlement, only to come home and to find it rejected by a minority of senators, a "little group of willful men." In this treaty-making power, and in his role as commander in chief of the armed forces, the whole vast panoply of the American executive's involvement in the politics of superpowers will find its constitutional grounding. He is to be commander in chief; these republicans insist on civilian control of the armed services. Shall he the one to *make* war? Again, the careful pause to watch for unchecked power. No. Although the executive shall be the commander in chief, the direction of the effort of the armies set in combat, the decision to *engage* in combat shall *not* be lodged in the executive, lest he use perpetual war as the engine of tyranny—as the experience of the race told them might happen. So *Congress* shall have the power to "declare" war, a legislative function as it were, after which the executive shall wage the war so declared.

For the republican *legislature* there were many years and many varieties of experience from which to draw, many volumes of theory, and much thinking by the framers themselves. For the republican *executive* there was none of these. What this "president" was to be was filled in not by the framers but by history.

Four

The constitutional provisions for the presidential office, in Article II, were sparse compared to those for Congress, but they had latent possibilities, as history, particularly recent history, has shown. From these sparse provisions there has come, in the American executive's role in the great politics of the globe in the second half of the twentieth century—in the age of American world power, nuclear weapons, and the television set—one of the most powerful engines of human agency in the long story of the life of the species on this planet.

The office of the president was to a degree invented and made potentially strong as a counterweight to the excesses of legislative bodies. After two centuries it may be that the problem of counterweight has shifted sides.

In its origins it was a strong office—but hedged. The office was granted real power—but shared. The president would appoint judges and ambassadors and other officials—but with the advice and consent of Senate. The president could veto bills that Congress had passed—but Congress with a two-thirds vote could pass them over his veto. The president was commander in chief of the armed services—but the right to declare war was reserved to Congress. The president could command the militia of the states—but only when called into "actual Service of the United States." The president was already potentially powerful—but he could be impeached by the House, tried by the Senate.

This was a new office, not like the kings and governors they had known. Perhaps they were willing to make these grants of power—of appointments of judges and ambassadors, of treaty-making, of commanding the army, of granting pardons, of calling Congress into session—because they assumed that the first person to fill the office was a man whom they could trust and who rose above their differences to symbolize the nation as a whole, who was sitting there in the room presiding over their own deliberations, who they were sure would be the first to fill the office, George Washington.

The office the convention designed was hedged, as everything they built was hedged, but this was a large new grant of power, a new office, unlike anything before in republican government, an energetic single national executive, separated from the legislature.

The other branches were also hedged, partly by the executive branch and partly by each other. The legislature could not "execute" the laws, or carry on foreign policy or direct the war, as Congress had tried to do under the Articles. Its legislative acts were subject to veto by the president and to being declared void when unconstitutional by the courts. The courts, as Hamilton was to write, had no money and no army; they depended for efficacy on the other branches, and were appointed and confirmed and impeached by those other branches. The combination of a grant of great power with hedges upon it, applied not only to each of the three branches but to the new federal government they created, and to the whole system of which the states are parts.

The separation of powers within the governmental structure rested upon the larger theme of checks and balances, which in turn rested upon the prevailing doctrine of humankind, the framers' republican realism. This outlook, and the governmental structure that resulted, we may venture to say, differentiated these American revolutionaries from their European counterparts in the French and later revolutions.

Hannah Arendt has written: "What the men of the American Revolution counted among the greatest innovations of the new republican government, the application and elaboration of Montesquieu's theory of a division of powers within the body politic, played a very minor role in the thought of European revolutionists at all times; it was rejected at once, even before the French Revolution broke out, by Turgot, for considerations of national sovereignty, whose majesty . . . allegedly demanded undivided centralized power."

That the Americans did *not* think national majesty required undivided centralized power, and on the contrary wanted all of this hedging, this limiting, dividing, balancing, and restraining of power, may be said to rest upon their wary and realistic view of human propensities: no person is to be trusted with unrestrained power. As Madison in his notes quotes himself as having said in the convention on July 11, "The truth was that all men having power ought to be distrusted to a certain degree." Every person should submit his or her will, each group should submit its will, to the criticism and restraint and balance of others, other wills, other interests, other conceptions of the common good.

7

Supreme Law
Unfinished Parts

One

ENACTING LAW IS ALWAYS a serious undertaking, because one is affecting
the individual lives, and the common life, of many of one's fellow beings
on matters of consequence; if they were not matters of consequence they
would not be a proper subject of law. Because law is properly and by
definition, as the lawyers say, general and prospective, it necessarily affects large numbers of people—everyone, in the future, who fits a certain
definition. (Only in the future, and only in general: one of the many items
the delegates dealt with in the last weeks in Philadelphia was whether the
Constitution needed a specific prohibition against ex post facto laws—
laws that try to apply the sanction of law backwards, to something that
has already happened, or against bills of attainder—law directed against
a specific individual. Those who argued that the United States Constitution did not need these prohibitions—which appeared in some of the
state constitutions—said that any lawyer knew such laws were improper,
not law. But there in the Constitution is the prohibition against them any-
way in Article I, section 9, paragraph 3.)

Enacting the laws of a people is a serious matter also because in the
law coercion and reason, power and morality, meet. Law rests upon the
ultimate sanction of physical violence, "legitimate" physical force, represented by the policeman, the jail, the soldier; government, of which law
is the instrument, includes as a constituting element, in a famous definition, the "monopoly of legitimate violence." As James Madison had writ-

ten in his second memo, criticizing the weak confederacy under the articles, "A Sanction is essential to the idea of law, as coercion is to that of government." When you drive too far over the speed limit, an officer of the law can come up behind you with his blue light flashing and force you to stop; when your protest breaks through the barriers the law has arranged, and when you go limp and refuse to cooperate, or when you resist arrest, an officer of the law may use the necessary physical force to restrain or coerce you, and you may be confined, against your will, by the power of the law, in a room with bars, that you will not be allowed to leave. At the time of this writing the states of the American union, as is now rare in civilized countries, may even, although the community is troubled and divided about this, kill you. The implicit threat of these ultimate uses of force runs through the whole vast structure of the law: you must obey.

But the law does not properly rest simply upon this force or coercion and nothing else, nor is government *wholly* defined as the agency with a monopoly of legitimate violence (this famous phrase comes from Max Weber). In the traditions that formed the United States, in particular, but in the whole of Western history, and perhaps elsewhere as well, for law to be law it must guide and shape that use of force not by whim, chance, interest, favoritism, personal pique or arbitrary will, but by reason and conscience: by forming the law of the social order in accord with the law written in—what? Reason? A *higher* law? The moral order of the universe? The law written in the human heart, to which Antigone had appealed in Sophocles' tragedy? The Americans were more inclined than others to affirm or imply that beyond the written law there was a higher law that it should reflect. Otherwise "law" or "government" is sheer power and sheer interest, mine against yours, and human social life is a war, a jungle. A number of thinkers, and a number of human beings, have concluded, to be sure, that that is exactly what social life is. But not many Americans. And not many of the English and other sources upon which the Americans drew—the republican forefathers of our forefathers. The Americans by and large did not draw much upon the strand in human thought about politics that sees power and egotism as the only realities. The Americans drew upon many sources—scholars dispute the proportions and rankings—but certainly the mainstream of the English and Scottish Enlightenment and Reformed Protestant thought that had different configuration on this point from that of the continental reactionaries and proponents of realpolitik, or romantics, or later Marx and Lenin and a new sort of revolutionary. Law for the Americans did not begin at the barrel of the gun; it began where reason and conscience met and managed force. The Americans were trying—to borrow from Madison's memos again—to substitute for violence and disorder "the mild and salutary coercion of the magistracy."

Enacting such law is a serious human activity. How much more so, then, was this convention, making the government that would enact the law. Our legislatures deal in retail lawmaking; this was wholesale lawmaking. Economists find in modern advanced economies points at which there is a "multiplier"—where economic activity in the broad is narrowed, concentrated, and exaggerated—multiplied—as for example in a machine tool industry that makes tools for many factories in many industries, and therefore has wider swings of activity than the factories it makes tools for. A little upsurge, causing each of a hundred factories to order one more tool, causes a giant upsurge in the machine tool factory, which suddenly gets orders for a hundred; a small downturn has the same exaggerated effect—multiplied effect—in the other direction. This convention was the giant machine tool factory, the great multiplier and concentrate, the great original wholesale house, of American lawmaking—not merely the making of laws one by one but the making of the engine for making every law.

Or we might set aside these perhaps too revealing modern metaphors of machines and markets, wholesaling and retailing, tools, factories, and engines, and reach back instead to the more lasting and elegant metaphors that Thomas Paine eleven years earlier had drawn from nature—planting seeds, carving on trees—and applied in *Common Sense* to the opportunities provided by the American Revolutionary situation: "Now is the seed-time of Continental union, faith and honour. The least fracture now will be like a name engraved with the point of a pin on the tender rind of a young oak; the wound would enlarge with the tree, and posterity read in it full grown characters."

So it was now, more precisely than in Paine's moment, with what these delegates did in Philadelphia. A comma or a semicolon put in by Gouverneur Morris, or the exact location in a sequence of the phrase "general welfare," or the almost incidental inclusion of the phrase "necessary and proper," as a kind of residual or windup paragraph after a long list of itemized powers of Congress (now at the end of section 8 in Article I of the Constitution) would one day grow into full-grown characters with nation-shaping effects.

This last one, for example, became the foundation for the response of the United States government to the enormously changed world of machine tools and wholesale houses, of modern industry and technology. The framers, after debating back and forth whether to enumerate the specific powers of Congress or simply to make a general grant (that the national legislature could act wherever state legislatures were incompetent) decided in the end for the former, and took over half the enumerated powers from the Articles of Confederation and then debated many additions (Madison came in with lists of proposed additions; one of them—a continuing idea among the original American nationalists—was the power to create a national university, which was not accepted). But then after enumerating the powers—*limiting* the national lawmaking to specific items—they added then at the end the power "to make all Laws which shall be necessary and proper for carrying into Execution the foregoing Powers, and all other Powers vested by this Constitution in the Government." Well, of course, once that little phrase "necessary and proper" appeared, all it took was nimble lawyers to open the door to a very wide range of lawmaking powers on subjects these eighteenth-century gentlemen could not have imagined.

The framers came to underline the separation of powers, and checks upon the legislature, in the second half of the convention. They shaped the presidency. And they opened the window to a new role for the judiciary.

The convention did not quite articulate the distinct new doctrine of judicial review, but that idea was hovering over the proceedings, ready to be given authoritative formulation. Some state courts had already rather tentatively found actions void under the state constitutions. This convention did compose a written constitution, like those of the states, and it did specify in Article VI that the Constitution, and laws, and treaties of the United States are the "Supreme Law of the Land," and that judges in every state are bound thereby in spite of anything in state constitutions to the contrary.

But who was to decide when a state action, or an act of Congress, or any other action, violated the Constitution? The convention did not quite give the answer but it would soon be forthcoming: the courts. Convention delegate Alexander Hamilton, in the following March, writing as Publius an authoritative defense of the Constitution, gave that answer clearly in *Federalist* 78. He described the independent judiciary, appointed for life, as "one of the most valuable of the modern improvements in the practice of government." This judiciary "from the nature of its functions, will always be the least dangerous to the political rights of the Constitution; because it will be least in a capacity to annoy or injure them." This least dangerous branch "has no influence over either the sword or the purse; no direction either of the strength or of the wealth of the society, and can take no active resolution whatever. It may truly be said to have neither FORCE nor WILL but merely judgment."

But its judgment includes reviewing the constitutionality of legislation.

The interpretation of the laws is the proper and peculiar province of the courts. A constitution is, in fact, and must be regarded by the judges as, a fundamental law. It therefore belongs to them to ascertain its meaning as well as the meaning of any particular act proceeding from the legislative body. If there should happen to be an irreconcilable variance between the two, that which has the superior obligation and validity ought, of course, to be preferred; or, in other words, the Constitution ought to be preferred to the statute, the intention of the people to the intention of their agents.

Hamilton wrote of the courts of justice "whose duty it must be to declare all acts contrary to the manifest tenor of the Constitution void"; he spoke of "the rights of the courts to pronounce legislative acts void"; "no legislative act," Hamilton wrote, "contrary to the Constitution, can be valid."

When the first Congress assembled, in 1789, it had to fill in the Constitution's brief sentences about the federal courts. The Judiciary Act of 1789, the product of that first Congress, which essentially created our federal court system, was written chiefly by Oliver Ellsworth, who had been a Connecticut delegate to the Constitutional Convention, and was passed by the Congress in which a number of other delegates, including Madison, served. It made explicit the duty of the courts to measure the acts of legislative bodies against the Constitution. And then, in early years of the republic, the Supreme Court itself, especially in the opinions of Madison and Jefferson's fellow Virginian John Marshall (a fellow Virginian who was usually on the other side from them politically) and especially in the case of *Marbury v. Madison* in 1803, made explicit the doctrine of judicial review.

The law the framers wrote was an unusual kind of superior law, a onetime nation-making document, devised by a convention chosen by the people (in theory) and then ratified by the people, that establishes a supreme law of the land, superior to the particular laws that come and go.

And our relation to that Constitution is itself a curiosity of the inner history of Americans—not only the formal relationship to it as a law above the laws, which judges, and constitutional lawyers, chop and blend and squeeze and mince and brew and carve for us down to the present day, but also as an icon, a symbol to be celebrated and interpreted and reinterpreted in the culture. Hugo Black has his copy in one pocket and Sam Erwin his in another, like New Testaments in another subculture, and they whip them out and cite lines to each other. Poets and philosophers and some citizens, perhaps only in private, and foreigners freely in public, may express some bewilderment that a great people should find such unity and moral sustenance in a document which when they actually read it—Article I, section 3, "No Person shall be a Senator who shall not have attained to the Age of thirty Years. . . ." Article I, section 8, "The Congress shall have Power to lay and collect Taxes, Duties, Imposts, and Excises"—proves to have about as much lift and inspiration as a bill of lading. It may be like Matthew Arnold's stopping his reading of the Gettysburg Address in disgust when he came to the phrase "dedicated to the proposition": One cannot be "dedicated", he said, to a "proposition." Oh, but the Americans can—in a sense. To a proposition that all men are created equal and to a formal legal document—a constitution—in place of a king or a unity of blood. The Constitution is more than a legal document, as the founders are more than lawgivers. The Constitution is more than its provisions. It was to become the symbol of the way this people finds its unity and conducts its life.

Two

Throughout the days of August and early September, both before and after the work of the grand Committee on Unfinished Parts, the convention considered and decided and postponed and decided again a whole series of particular points that would give shape to the life of the new nation, some of them small, but others immense. They restricted the financial excesses of the states, of the sort that had made the behavior of state governments under the Articles a source of anguish and heartburn particularly to conscientious citizens like Madison. They prohibited the states from coining money. They required that each state give "full faith and credit" to the laws of another. They gave the national legislature— Congress—the power to regulate foreign commerce. They constructed the "Supreme Law of the Land" clause that made the Constitution and laws of the United States, and all treaties under their authority, supreme over the laws and also over the constitutions of the states, binding all judges—perhaps one could say the kernel of the Constitution and union, establishing their superiority over the states. Some of the delegates and states had come to the convention, and supported a stronger union, almost exclusively—as Oliver Ellsworth of Connecticut more than once said—for reasons of commerce. They wanted to end the chaos of the states each acting as a separate economic unit. They wanted to end the "injustice"—as Madison and most of these other relatively well-fixed delegates would see it—of paper money and laws that undercut the obligations of debt (the debtor class was not significantly represented). The convention made of the United States a common market, to the great advantage of its economic and therefore of its political and social development in the centuries to come.

They debated the militia and treaty-making and the eligibility of the foreign-born to hold office (Madison took the side of the more generous allowance. Wilson allowed himself a touch of autobiography. Madison's notes for August 9 report this speech: "Mr. Wilson said he rose with feelings which were perhaps peculiar; mentioning the Circumstance of his not being a native, and the possibility, if the ideas of some gentlemen should be pursued, of his being incapacitated from holding a place under the very Constitution, which he shared in the trust of making").

Of the greatest importance was the debate about how the Constitution was to be ratified and set in motion, and also how it could be amended, questions that came to be entwined with each other as many questions in this convention did. One of the many defects of government under the Articles had been that it could be amended only by *unanimous* decision of the states, which meant in practice that it could not be changed, one state's veto blocking all. Madison introduced the proposal for the methods of amending the Constitution that were in fact adopted, and Alexander Hamilton, back in Philadelphia in early September and soon jumping energetically into the fray, seconded his motion. This complex method or methods differed from the proposal made by the Committee of Detail decisively in granting a central role, and a possible initiative, on amendments to *Congress*. The Committee of Detail had left the initiating of amendments entirely to the state legislatures; Hamilton, speaking in behalf of an "easy mode" of amendment, argued that the state legislatures would not apply for alternatives but with a view to increase their own power. Madison's motion—the successful proposal— also provided, as one alternative, for ratification by state conventions called for the purpose, or as another alternative, by legislatures—three-quarters required in each case—instead of by one national convention. The provision in the Constitution for its own amendment distinguishes it not only from the Articles that went before but also from the French Revolutionary constitution that would follow, neither of which made provisions for amendment. The United States Constitution's provision for its own continuing adaptation and improvement is another indication of the framers' realism—an important one. There would continue to be "unfinished parts" as long as this Constitution would last. To those initial markings on the rind of the young oak there would be added many more; the full-grown characters of later years would reflect not the first markings alone but many later ones, too, and would never stop growing.

One of the issues resolved in late August, perhaps the third most controversial in the whole convention (after state equality and the method of electing the president)—was the matter of the originating of tax bills. Where should the power to tax be lodged? The issue, of course, evoked powerful echoes of the passions of the American Revolution itself, and of

99

English republicanism before that; much of the patriot ideology had turned upon what was thought to be illegitimate taxation by the English. No taxation except by direct representatives of the people themselves. In early July the grand committee dealing with the big struggle over state equality—the one that came up with the compromise—had sweetened the pot for the big states by proposing not only that all money bills should originate in the lower, popular house (which protected the big states, with their larger delegations in the house) but also that such money bills "shall not be altered or amended by the 2nd branch." In other words the Senate would have been denied any role whatever with respect to taxing and spending money. The grand committee of early July had nailed the point down by adding: "No money shall be drawn from the public Treasury but in pursuance of appropriations to be originated in the 1st branch." But then it had added the provision insisted upon by the small states to which Madison and Wilson had strongly objected: "In the 2nd branch each state shall have an equal vote." It had been a package deal: in return for granting that state equality, which the small states wanted, in one house of the legislature, the compromise proposal would strip that house of any role in money matters, and confine such matters entirely to the popular house, as presumably the larger states wanted, and as presumably ancient republican ideology dictated (money bills only from the Commons, from the representatives of the people).

In the back and forth of the convention after that early July report the restriction on the Senate had been removed, but in this convention anything could come unstuck and almost nothing was decided the first or even the second time: the issue came up again in the material shoved onto the docket of the Committee on Unfinished Parts.

The purest republicans (from big states) like Madison's Virginia colleagues George Mason and Edmund Randolph, and the volatile intermittent populist from Massachusetts Elbridge Gerry, beat the drums for their side of that grand committee bargain, and for ancient republican ideology: don't let that other house, that "aristocratic" Senate, touch the purse; only the direct representatives of the people should be allowed to "meddle with their purses." (So Gerry on August 13.) But Madison and Wilson did not take that line. This is one of the points at which one might discern the larger vision, the statesmanship, that despite all the political deals and contending interests and narrow outlooks is nevertheless a striking feature of this Philadelphia Convention. Madison and Wilson, as we have seen, had strongly opposed and deeply regretted that provision for state equality in one house ("rotten boroughs" right here in the founding of this new republic), in Madison's case at least almost to the point that he believed it vitiated the entire system. Nevertheless, they did not now propose to compound that wrong with another—to make this wrongly constituted Senate an unworkable body. In other words, they did not accept what was supposed to be concession to their "side" in the bargaining of the Great Compromise: they did not accept it, because it did not make sense. The localist-populists listed above *did* want and did accept the bargain. But Madison was more realistic. Wanting this government to work, he pointed out that all important legislation involved money in the end. Either the Senate would be an impotent appendage, or it would block other legislation to give itself some leverage on appropriations. In the states that had tried that money-discrimination provision it had *not* worked; taken over from an Old World history (Lords and Commons) it had not applied to the New, with no lords and a different history. Think anew. Promptly on the reconsideration of this matter in August, Wilson opposed the restriction of money bills absolutely to the House "on its merits without regard to the compromise" and Madison also opposed it "as of no advantage to the large states as fettering the government and as a source of injurious altercations between the two houses." It is to be noted that James Madison's second reason for opposing this restriction was that he opposed "fettering the Govt": he wanted a checked and balanced, but not a "fettered," government. That was on August 8. When the matter was finally settled, on August 13—these issues wove in and out of the discussion—Wilson and Madison reiterated and expanded their arguments. Wilson said he had opposed equality of the states in the Senate, but that "he wished not to multiply the vices of the system." Madison added the argument that the term *revenue* was full of ambiguities, as the disputes with England before the Revolution had shown, and that the terms *after* and *amend* were open to much fancy footwork by a foxy Senate: this restriction on the Senate would open a hornet's nest of contention. In the Constitution as it emerged—Article I, section 7—there is the provision that all revenue bills shall originate in the House, but then the additional clause removes its teeth, "but the Senate may propose or concur with Amendments as on other bills."

In the debate over money bills John Dickinson of Delaware made the observation, often quoted, that "experience must be our only guide. Reason may mislead us"; this, too, was on August 13. Dickinson, then from Pennsylvania, had been John Adams's old opponent in the Second Continental Congress, the one who offered the olive branch to the king at the last minute, whom Adams had compared unfavorably to the younger Wilson. He had moved to Delaware and now represented that little state in this great convention. By "experience" he did not mean the mere encounters of one lifetime; he meant the long experience of the race, as one learns about it exactly from books. This sentence of his is often and favorably quoted as some kind of epitome of the empirical wisdom of the convention as a whole. In context it is not so impressive. The best of the delegates were empirical—looking at the facts of their own experience and the experience of the past—but they were also reasoning about facts, and making reasoned judgments, which included some new departures. Wilson and Madison are more impressive than Dickinson, both in general and on this point. Dickinson appealed to chance discoveries in "the singular and admirable English constitution" like "the absurd mode of trial by Jury." "Absurd" was his word; he meant *absurd* "in the eye of those who are governed by reason." He was not attacking trial by jury; he was taking its worth for granted, and using its nonrational emergence as an example of the way very desirable institutions grow. "Accidents probably produced these discoveries," said Dickinson, "and experience has given a sanction to them." Dickinson was urging this curious theory of a sort of mindless Darwinian selection of republican institutions in favor of the long English "experience" that successfully confined money bills to the House of Commons against the short American "experience" of only eleven years, that tried the same thing, unsuccessfully.

Madison and Wilson and the best of the convention combined "experience" in both senses with reasoning, thinking afresh. For all that it may have arisen from some accident, one could certainly make a reasoned (republican!) defense of trial by jury. And a certain amount of thinking may have contributed to its development. If on these political matters there is danger in abstract intellection, uninformed by wide participation and observation in actual human living, there is also danger in a mindless traditionalism. The American framers built on "experience"; Madison's two memos represent a deliberate assembling of the lessons learned thereby. But they thought anew, also, as Madison in *Federalist* 37 would urge his countrymen to do.

Late in the month of August, in considering the provisions by the Committee of Detail dealing with navigation acts—with exporting and importing, all of which took place in those days by ship—the convention did deal, in a way, with the lurking, or overarching, subject of human slavery. That subject, though not very often mentioned, was in the background of many issues, and intertwined with their discussion and their outcome. The subject is so large, if not in the Constitutional Convention then in the moral history of the American people, that we postpone its consideration here in order to spread it out in another chapter.

The prospect of the new states that would one day surely wish to enter the union, especially from the territory to the west, was another immense topic, to some extent expressed in the convention but much more implicit, hovering in the background. It involved money and power:

who would make money from all that land? How would the power balances be, once new states came in from the West? Gouverneur Morris and others tried to protect the existing states, and the domination of the monied East, but Madison and others resisted. The debate revived the fundamental power struggles, and perhaps some conflicts of moral vision as well; Madison at one point said "the Western states neither would nor ought to submit to a union which degraded them from equal rank with other states." And happily that point of view won out.

The Committee of Style was appointed on September 8. Both Madison and Hamilton served on it but the most important member proved to be the imperious New York aristocrat Gouverneur Morris, the delegate whose many speeches as Madison records them exhibit the most flair and rhetorical imagination of any delegate. This committee at the end of the proceedings cast the document into the language of its final form—all of the innocent little phrases to which lawyers across two centuries have given the most intricate and wonderful, and consequential, meanings. Morris composed the graceful preamble, one flowing sentence setting forth six purposes of government logically ordered, a nugget of political philosophy, beginning as had the Massachusetts constitution with later generations' sometimes rather self-indulgent favorite constitutional phrase, "We, the people of the United States." The last phrase was in part a solution to the literary and political problem of the cumbersome predecessor in the report of the Committee of Detail: "We the People of the States of New Hampshire, Massachusetts, Rhode Island and Providence Plantations, Connecticut, New-York . . ." and so on through the list of thirteen states (only eleven of whom incidentally ever were simultaneously in attendance; Rhode Island never came; and New York left before New Hampshire arrived).

The now-resolved big issue in the eyes of this convention (state equality) made one last little appearance when Gouverneur Morris proposed that this proviso be added to the provision for amending the constitution: "that no State, without its consent shall be deprived of equal suffrage in the Senate." Occasionally in Madison's notes one becomes aware again that a human being is composing these sentences of reportage. He wrote, about Morris's proposal: "This motion being dictated by circulating murmurs of the small states was agreed to without debate, no one opposing it." The "circulating murmurs of the small states" . . . one of the stories of the convention. The unanimous murmur-driven adoption of this provision left it to the courses in constitutional law in the centuries ahead this puzzle: whether this prohibition against any amendment on this one point could *itself* ever be amended.

There were attempts to persuade the three unpersuaded delegates (Elbridge Gerry of Massachusetts and both Mason and Randolph among Madison's Virginia colleagues) that they should sign. Benjamin Franklin made a graceful appeal, but to no avail. The three explained why they could not sign (other opponents, like Luther Martin, had gone home).

There was the signing on September 17. There was the last homely observation by Dr. Franklin, one of the many appeals in these great events please to be reasonable and give up a little and don't expect perfection. And then there was the completed document to be circulated to the states, a completed document with which almost no one was satisfied, but a "miracle" nonetheless—called that not only by later encomiasts but, despite all of his reservations about it, in his long October 24 letter to Thomas Jefferson by Madison himself.

8

Sundays
Excepted

One

MADISON'S MOTHER, STILL ALIVE AT MONTPELIER during these adventures of her son, and for many years thereafter, was a devout Anglican. Madison himself acknowledged all his life, in extravagant terms, his debt to the Anglican clergymen who were his most important tutors. Madison had gone to college, as we have seen, to the institution founded by the New Side Presbyterians primarily to train pastors, of which college Jonathan Edwards had been very briefly president, and whose president when Madison went there, as we have seen, was the formidable Scotch Presbyterian pastor and teacher the Reverend John Witherspoon, "the good Doctor," as Madison and his friend Billey Bradford called him. Madison stayed on after graduation for some months of study with Witherspoon; his studies included "divinity." He had many friends from his Princeton days who were Presbyterian pastors; he himself briefly entertained the idea of going into "Divinity" himself, or at least commented on the worthiness of those who do, in his correspondence with Billey Bradford. He acquired, from the learned clergy who were his teachers, a sufficient knowledge of the church fathers and the Christian intellectual tradition to be able in his retirement to make a competent list of books on those subjects for the University of Virginia library. A historian editing the Madison Papers called him (by perhaps a not very exacting standard) "probably America's most theologically knowledgeable president." He had been baptized in the Church of England; he and Dolley were married (to the consternation of her Quaker relatives) by an Episcopal priest in an Episcopalian ceremony; he was buried, this Father of our American Constitution, in 1836, according to the Book of Common Prayer. We may add that during his political career he became a particular hero to the Baptists and other Dissenters in the Virginia fight over religious liberty. But, for all that, it is a little hard to say just what his mature religious views were.

One can certainly say that in his maturity politics and government, rather than religion proper, became his primary interest. And that the "religious" issue that stirred him most deeply was that of freedom—of religious liberty, freedom of conscience.

He did not write sentences like those of his friend Jefferson, exclaiming against the irrationality of the doctrine of the Trinity or the teachings of St. Paul. He was a product of the Enlightenment, but not of its sharply antireligious phase; he was a product of Christian teaching, but not of its insistent, explicit, evangelical phase. In his maturity he rather kept his mouth shut on these issues. And the great issue he cared most about was liberty. In this combination he was not unlike some others of the great founders, with their different mixtures: Benjamin Franklin, warning Tom Paine, with whom he essentially agreed on doctrinal matters, not to carry on so explicit an attack on orthodoxy in public; John Adams, who despite his Puritan background and religious interests saw his church become Unitarian and pretty much agreed with Jefferson on doctrine in the correspondence of their old age; George Washington, cagey enough that both popular disputants and scholars argue to this day about his religious views; and Jefferson himself, who though more explicit and antiorthodox than other Americans, did not go as far as his European counterparts in the worldwide fraternity of the Enlightened.

When it came time for the framers to draw a fundamental law for the new nation it contained mixtures and silences and freedoms and perhaps an implied background not unlike that of James Madison and other great founders.

In the body of the Federal Constitution, as it was hammered out by James Madison and the others in Philadelphia in the summer of 1787, we discover that the topic of religion is treated primarily, although not quite entirely, by negation, silence, exclusion, and inference. There is in this Constitution, in contradiction to claims made by pious citizens of a later time, no formal commitment to Christianity, or to belief in God, or to any religious belief whatsoever. The Constitution of the United States of America is not soaked in the explicit claims of Christian devotion, as, say, the constitution of Pakistan is soaked in the claims of Islam. The document that issued from the summer's work in Philadelphia made no religious affirmation, even of the conventional kind that was a commonplace in other documents written by the founders: no references to the Creator, or the Almighty, or Providence, or to that Supreme Being which the Supreme Court would later say the nation's institutions presuppose.

There was no appeal, as in the Declaration of Independence, to nature and nature's God; and no expression like these, from state constitutions written later: "The people of Connecticut, acknowledging with gratitude the good providence of God, do . . . (1818)." "We the people of the State of Arkansas, grateful to almighty God for the privilege of choosing our own form of government . . . (1874)."

Perhaps the most interesting contrast is to the Constitution of the Confederate States of America. The Confederate constitution would be drawn in 1861 from the United States Constitution; the secessionists thought that they were loyal to the Constitution in a way that the Unionists were not. The document they produced parallels the Federal Constitution throughout. It is therefore the more interesting to see those spots in which there are changes. The rebels' revised version of the preamble began thus: "We the people of the Confederate States, *each State acting in its sovereign and independent character* . . ." Although the purposes of government set forth in the rebels' preamble parallel those set down in the Preamble to the Federal Constitution, and are expressed in the phrases that Gouvernor Morris had written in Philadelphia, the purpose to "promote the general welfare" was pitched overboard. There would be no promoting of the general welfare by the Confederate States of America. And then in the last line there was this *addition:* "invoking the favor and guidance of almighty God."

But there had been no such invoking in the United States Constitution. When the New York State Board of Regents, designing a program for piety and virtue in the schools, in the 1950s, would refer to the belief in God reflected not only in the Declaration of Independence and the speeches of the founders and in other early documents but also in the United States Constitution, the skeptic might respond, to this last: "Where?"

The absence of any "acknowledgment of God" in the Constitution became an issue early in the nineteenth century when Timothy Dwight at Yale, condemning the absence of any such acknowledgment as a disgrace, mounted a movement to have that omission rectified. It was not successful, nor have the subsequent efforts to enact a "Christian amendment"— efforts that continue to this day—been successful either. The formal charter of our national being makes no substantive religious affirmation, no collective religious commitment on the nation's behalf. The United States was not to be a "confessing" state.

And then when we look at the Constitution again we find that there is also no provision for any church's support, protection, or participation in national life. There were to be, under this American Constitution, no bishops in the House of Lords. That was true partly, of course, because there was no House of Lords for there to be bishops in, but also because there were no bishops to be in it if there were one. No bishops in an Established Church sense—no bishops like the fictional Archdeacon Grantly in Anthony Trollope's novels, who waits anxiously upon the outcome of a parliamentary election to see whether he will be named a bishop, or like real William Temple, whom the still more real Winston Churchill, though holding his nose, could not avoid naming archbishop of Canterbury. It is significant that the new American nation was to have no Lords Temporal, but it is perhaps even more significant that it was to have no Lord Spiritual.

In the midst of a transatlantic discussion of the theme of "national purpose," in the 1950s, the British prime minister, criticized for a pragmatism inadequately rising to the scope of the big picture, made a response that then crossed the water to be told as though it were appropriate to the same discussion in the United States: "If the people want a sense of national purpose let them get it from their bishops!" Very funny. It was the kind of half-cynical deflationary comment loved by all journalists and most modern politicians. But in the United States the people *have* no bishops, to get a national purpose, or anything else, from. There are Episcopal bishops and Methodist bishops and Lutheran bishops and Catholic bishops—very much, recently, Catholic bishops, perhaps filling a kind of void—and AME bishops and AME Zion bishops, and many other kinds of bishops in this multireligion country, but no bishops of the whole people, no bishops who can express with any kind of authority, to be received with any kind of deference, a purpose for the whole nation.

Our forefathers of the Revolutionary period had indicated, indeed, how strongly they were opposed to any national, political, official bishops in the controversy just before the Revolution over the proposal to send a Church of England bishop to America. So strong was the "antiprelatical" bias of these Puritan-sectarian Americans that this "Great Fear of Episcopacy" was a major cause of the shift in American opinion toward Revolution and Independence, in a way that few Americans today even remotely understand and none can recapture.

That there were no bishops in the Constitution is an indication of the larger point, the absence of any formal provision whatsoever for any ecclesiastical institution. Usually now our American disengaging of church from state is found to rest in the First Amendment, but one may find it already in a negative way in the silence of the rest of the Constitution. These Americans, heirs of the long tradition of Christendom, and Englishmen who were born under an established church, assembled in all sobriety and thoughtfulness to construct from their reasoning and their compromises and their best understanding a new order of the ages, which would be written down on paper—and they said nothing whatsoever about the church or the churches that had figured large for fourteen hundred years in the formal makeup of the states of Christendom from which they had come.

It would have been difficult to have said or done anything on that topic, given the diversity of the religious makeup of the states, and the hostility of many toward any church-state connection. But in addition they were designing political institutions with a differing ground and beginning point from those of the past. They did not begin with an explicit and formal affirmation of the nation's theistic foundations, as in some sense the nations of the Old Order had done (the Dissenting Protestant Americans might say also a half-cynical and empty affirmation); but they also did not begin the state with the *repudiation* of that foundation, as revolutionary nations to come would do.

As we have already said, James Madison and his colleagues came to the position—a new one in the political thought of the West—that in this republic *all* of the parts and pieces of the complicated governmental machinery shall rest, in the end, upon the whole and undivided people. In other words, under this Constitution there will be no division of the realm into "estates," each of which shall be constitutionally recognized, and represented by a piece of the governmental machinery. Neither is there the arrangement stemming from more recent political theories— like those derived from the papal encyclical *Rerum Novarum*—that reserves places in the constitutional scheme for the mercantile and agricultural and seafaring interests, for lawyers and doctors, for each of the "industries and professions." There is no slicing of the body politic, of the whole people. The layers and divisions and hierarchies of feudalism are now altogether gone. All the parts of the government rest in the end on all the people. Even the Supreme Court, so many times in the American history condemned for its nonmajoritarian resistance to the opinion of the day, rests in the end upon appointments by a president, who was to be chosen by electors who were to be chosen by the whole people of a state; and this president's appointments are made with the advice and consent of the upper body of the federal Congress, the Senate, which in the beginning was to be chosen by the state legislatures, which then finally were chosen, again, by the whole people.

Among the "estates" and orders that were thus eliminated from any formal place or recognition, any preferred or distinct representation or role, the most venerable was the ecclesiastical institution. Among the "professions" that were denied any distinct constitutional place the most consequential was the clergy. When to that omission in the body of the Constitution the protections of freedom would be made explicit in the First Amendment, among the "opinions" (as Jefferson would call them) that would be left free for each person's voluntary acceptance or rejection, without any shared commitment by the whole people set down in fundamental law, the most significant would be "opinions" about religion. The church, the clergy, and Christian belief were all thrown out into the great sea of public discourse, to sink or swim altogether on their own, without any safety net whatsoever in the nation's fundamental law. Christianity was cut free from all formal collective support in a way that in Europe it had not known since the emperor Constantine raised the banner of the cross as the insignia of the Roman state.

That is not a small matter, in the history of Western Civilization—of "Christendom." There are those who find the separation of church and state, as it would one day come to be called, the most significant of all the departures and novelties in the arrangements of the new nation.

Two

No collective commitment, no state-supported church—and no religious test for public office. The one significant explicit reference to religion in the body of the Constitution is the provision at the end of Article VI that "no religious test shall ever be required as a Qualification to any Office or public Trust under the United States"—very important in its own time, forgotten in ours.

This provision, together with the rejection of all titles and nobility, was the reason that Isaac Backus, the most important of Separate Baptist clergymen—the pietists—could support the ratification of the Constitution in Massachusetts, and urge his fellow Baptists and other Dissenters to do likewise.

No religious test: no *requirement* that one profess any tenet of religion in order to be a legislator, a president, or even—as it will turn out—a notary public: no required religious profession in order to hold a public office and by extension to be a voter, a citizen, a member with equal standing to every other in the polity. Throughout Western history, including the experience of all the American colonies at one time or another, there had been such tests: excluding Jews from office virtually everywhere, excluding Catholics in Protestant states, excluding Protestants in Catholic states, excluding Quakers, excluding Unitarians, and of course excluding atheists, agnostics, and "free thinkers" everywhere; requiring a belief in the "Protestant Christian Religion" in the first South Carolina state constitution; requiring belief in the Trinity in tolerant Maryland; requiring a belief in God in more tolerant Pennsylvania. Reading in the history of colonial Virginia, one is startled to discover a requirement that the potential officeholders swear that they do *not* believe in transubstantiation in the mass . . . a specific searching-out of Catholics for exclusion. All of the colonies except Roger Williams's Rhode Island, and after the passage—with young James Madison as the legislative leader who got it passed—of Jefferson's statute, Virginia, had some sort of religious oath for officeholders still in the Revolutionary period. So the prohibition in Article VI was no small thing. It was part of the same Enlightenment and Dissenting project, to sweep away, at last, the history of state-enforced exclusions and preferentialisms and persecutions that had marked the fourteen-hundred-year history of state-supported Christianity.

Surely the actual and symbolic meaning of the prohibition against religious tests must have played a large role in the decisions made by millions of Europeans in the nineteenth and early part of the twentieth centuries—from Ireland, Italy, Poland, Russia, and every country of Europe—to make the arduous journey across the Atlantic to settle in this new "empire of Liberty." James Madison was no phrase-maker but even he bordered on eloquence when he had argued, back in 1784, in favor of, as he put it, "that generous policy, which, offering an Asylum to the persecuted and oppressed of every Nation and Religion, promised lustre to our country."

Back in 1787, in the Constitutional Convention, North Carolina's delegation opposed the provision prohibiting test oaths in Article VI, because it might allow "pagans and Roman Catholics" to hold office, as indeed it has.

Three

The overwhelmingly most important provision of the Constitution with respect to religion was still to come, when the thirty-nine founders present and willing to sign the Constitution affixed their signatures on September 17, 1787. Already at that moment there was grumbling because the document contained no bill of rights; George Mason, having failed in a last-minute effort to attach a bill of rights in Philadelphia, declined to sign, went grumpily home, and opposed ratification. Thomas Jefferson in Paris objected to the absence of a written bill of rights, and that objection was a prominent theme in the campaign of the Antifederalists against ratification. In contrast to the present time, when religious freedom—

something like "freedom to go to the church of your choice"—is a somewhat halfhearted and absent-minded addition to the list (rather far down the list) of freedoms the broad public cares about, long after economic freedom, and some kind of freedom of "expression"—the eighteenth-century Americans who wanted a written bill of rights cared most of all about religious liberty—freedom of "conscience," as they would put it. The "contagion of liberty" spread the fever of freedom to the struggle against state restrictions on religious beliefs and against established churches. The first clauses of what came to be the First Amendment would affirm religious liberty. The "Free Exercise" clause, as it would come to be called, picked up the phrase that the young James Madison had used in his amendment of the Virginia Declaration of Rights back in 1776. It was joined to and preceeded by the rather curious Establishment (or no-establishment) clause ("Congress shall make no law respecting an Establishment of religion") which waits there for courts and judges and constitutional lawyers much later to fill with meaning, the clause that has been taken to signify our tradition of separating church and state.

The prohibition against religious tests in Article VI had much importance in its own time, but has become much less so in our time; with the Establishment clause the situation is reversed. That clause has exploded in significance in the United States since the Supreme Court decisions of the late 1940s.

By then the nation's religious institutions and religious culture had long since changed shape. The state establishments still in existence at the time of the Constitution-writing were abolished, the last ones New Hampshire in 1817, Connecticut 1818, and Massachusetts 1833. As Tocqueville observed, the "voluntary way" in religion had so completely triumphed in the American mind that he could find nobody who disagreed with it.

Four

So the American Constitution reflected these great national negatives on the subject of religion: no common confession; no state recognized church; no required belief for holding office; no state interference with the freedom of opinion in matters of belief. In some quarters in Europe perhaps it was therefore concluded that the constituting of the new nation represented at least a liberating disengagement from, perhaps even a hostility to, the long Christian tradition of the West. Perhaps those European scholars and philosophers and literati who, in the ten years since it was written, had greeted Jefferson's bill for Establishing Religious Freedom with "infinite approbation" (Jefferson's own phrase), and "propagated" it with "enthusiasm," and translated it into French and Italian, and inserted it in the *Encyclopédie,* and other publications where America was mentioned, and circulated it in the courts of Europe (all these phrases from Jefferson's own enthusiastic letter about the reception of his bill in Europe)—perhaps these enlightened European folk had concluded that that thrilling document of Jefferson's had meant that across the Atlantic this new land, or these new lands (Virginia; Pennsylvania; the earlier Rhode Island) declaring their independence now from the European past, were going to realize what they, these enlightened Europeans, in their own countries, thought to be necessary: a repudiation of the Christian past, with all its superstitions and cruelties and restrictions on the freedom of the mind. Perhaps they would conclude that this Philadelphia Constitution, continuous with that great Virginia document from their friend Jefferson, represented, at last, in this new nation, what they sought in Europe: freedom from religion! Liberation from the "shackles" (Jefferson himself was a great one for the word *shackles*) on the mind, the obscurantism, the social oppression of the religious past. Perhaps they would have expected therefore that in this constituting of the first new nation, this making of a new order of the ages, there would be, as there was surely later to be, when they had their own continental European revolution, the other great revolution in this age of democratic revolutions, a new counting of the days of the week without any ancient Sabbaths, a new set of names for the months, even a new calendar for the counting of the years. When it came time for their revolution, the great revolution in France that would convulse the continent, the revolutionary rulers would, for a time, turn Notre Dame into a Temple of Reason, and institute a new weekly cycle, abolishing the Christian Sabbath and replacing it with a new festival every tenth day. And the French in 1791 would institute a new calendar dated not from the birth of Christ but from the autumnal equinox, the day after their republic was proclaimed.

Is that what their American predecessors had done a few years earlier in their Constitution? No, it was not. When the Americans provided, in the body of the document, for a counting of days for a presidential veto, they simply tossed in, in parentheses, taken for granted, an absentminded but significant phrase: "If any bill shall not be returned by the President with ten days (Sundays excepted)." But why except Sundays? Because Sunday was built into the law and custom and culture as the Sabbath. They certainly did not even consider constructing some new kind of a week.

In the same way, when in September of 1787 the framers came to the end of their Constitution, with its great implicit and explicit emancipating negatives with respect to religion, how did they give the date? "In the year of our Lord seventeen hundred and eighty-seven, and of the Independence of the United States the twelfth."

Exempting Sunday. In the year of our Lord. These customary items are minor, to be sure—these little differences between the French and American revolutions—and yet they are also major.

Although the American founders accomplished the Enlightenment and democratic goal of a full religious liberty to a degree unique in Christendom, at the same time, in sharp contrast to the other great revolution of the "Age of Democratic Revolutions," the other great overturning spawned by the Enlightenment, and in contrast to subsequent revolutionary events in Europe, the Americans did not regard their revolution as a repudiation of the Christian past. Their new order of the ages was not *that* new. They did not set the new republic over against the old Christianity. It was no part of the Americans' revolutionary purpose, in constructing this new nation, to break explicitly with the long history of Christendom. Within the Constitution itself the Americans did not repudiate, but rather absent-mindedly acknowledged and continued, the overwhelmingly Christian heritage out of which they had come.

The United States was unusual as measured by the European *past* in its provision of full religious liberty. It was to be unusual measured against the European *future* in the degree to which Christianity persisted and for a time penetrated the culture.

No confessing state—and "in the year of our Lord." No religious test-and a believing people. No established church—and a still somewhat Christian culture.

Although the Enlightenment, republicanism and Christianity, were often separated and even opposed to each other, as they join to form the United States they overlapped, interpenetrated, qualified, and in some measure endorsed each other. They were not as sharply hostile to each other as they were elsewhere. Although the Christian religion in Europe was often, and often seen to be, the great opponent of the modern age—of liberalism, of republicanism—in the United States it was no opponent but a friend.

When one picks up Michelet, the great sympathetic historian of the French Revolution, one finds him saying, of his revolution: "The Revolution continues Christianity, and it contradicts it. It is, at the same time, its heir and its adversary." It is not likely that anyone would write a history of the American Revolution which saw it to be a contradiction to, or an adversary of, Christianity.

There was, in America, to put it mildly, no consistent identification of religion, or of Christianity, with the feudal or monarchial or aristocratic resistance to a new republican government. We observed before that the part of the American colonial population that would make that connection—Loyalists, tories—had, in large part, left the United States at the time of the Revolution for England or Canada—and, in contrast to France, they did not come back. We observed before, also, that the original Americans, mostly Dissenting and Reformed Protestants, mostly Englishmen, with an ocean between themselves and Europe, had decisively cut away from the Old World's politically reactionary religious element. In the New World religion and liberty were not opposed to each other; not only were not opposed to each other but were for a great part of the population linked. They were joined for many Americans in the "sacred cause of liberty."

The radical, reformist, republican, revolutionary component of the colonial American populations did not see religion as a systematic enemy of the new order they were bringing into being. Although major leaders of the American founding can be said to have been a part of, or much influenced by, the Enlightenment—Thomas Jefferson, Benjamin Franklin, perhaps Jefferson's friend James Madison, and even the New Englander who was also a Puritan in many ways, John Adams—these American Enlightenment revolutionaries did not regard hanging the last king in the entrails of the last priest as part of their revolutionary program. Although an American leader, Thomas Jefferson, could regard the Revolution as a repudiation of the rule of kings, priests, and nobles, the kings, priests, and nobles to be repudiated were all conveniently elsewhere. Although the Revolution and the founding, in the atmosphere of the international Enlightenment, did generate a "religion of reason," a "republican religion," with a certain popular following, and some well-known leaders, the adherents of the republican religion fought in the Revolution and disputed in the ratification debates alongside New Light products of the Awakenings, Old Side Presbyterians, standing-order Congregationalists, Anglican gentlemen. And "republican religion" did not last very long, after the second great wave of revivals in the early nineteenth century.

For Americans in their civic capacity, religion was not perceived to be on the wrong side of the coming into being of the new nation; religion was not perceived to be opposed to republican government. For believing Americans in their religious capacity, liberty, republicanism, the new nation under the Constitution were not perceived to be inimical to the Christian church or Christian beliefs. Rather the opposite. For Madison's Baptist supporters in Virginia and elsewhere, the making of America was a Second Reformation—another religious triumph.

The United States would not divide politically or systematically along a religious faultline. As John Courtney Murray, the leading American Catholic thinker of the twentieth century, would observe, there were not to be two Americas, as there are two Frances, two Italys, and two Spains. In the United States religious conservatives were not antirepublican, and the political radicals were not necessarily antireligious. The Americans, unlike the Europeans, explicitly disentangled themselves from monarchy, and explicitly repudiated aristocracy and hierarchy, and implicitly repudiated priesthood, and set in place a new nation with liberty and equality at the center, without casting the Christian religion as an opponent.

The United States managed to come into being as a modern democratic state with the connection to the Christian past unbroken. Christianity, the great muddy Mississippi of Western civilization, was able almost uniquely in the American setting to flow unvexed to the sea of modern democratic life.

9

Other Persons

One

MADISON AND HIS GENERATION had come to adulthood in a moment of high human adventure, a revolution, in which they had repeatedly used, as a primary moral claim, the word *liberty,* and very often, too, as its negation and opposite, the words *slaves* and *slavery:* the British with their tax on tea, their Stamp Act, cannot make of us *slaves.* Madison himself, two and a half years before his study of constitutions, back in the early summer of 1784, had written in his great Memorial and Remonstrance: "People who submit to . . . laws made neither by themselves nor by an authority derived from them, are slaves." That was the language, the imagery, of the patriots. It was very much the language of the "commonwealthmen," the coffee house whigs like Trenchard and Gordon in their CATO letters, which were widely read and widely influential with the founders. *Slavery* was the condition to which submission to the British Parliament, finally to the British king, would reduce them. *Liberty* was the great central term, for these sons of liberty, and *slavery* was a central term, too.

As Jemmy Madison sat there in Montpelier pursuing his studies, somewhere else in the house, and out in the tobacco fields, and in the barn, and with the horses, there were people with black faces, preparing the meals, curing the tobacco, caring for the horses, bringing him his meals while he wrote his words in behalf of liberty, getting his horse ready for him to ride to meetings where the patriots would condemn the "slavery" to which the British proposed to reduce them. And so it was also with Thomas Jefferson, thirty miles to the south at Monticello, where the slave quarters are decorously hidden in the architecture; and up north at Gunston Hall, with George Mason, who had written the first of the great Declarations of Rights (all men free and equal); and so it was over on the hill overlooking a great bend in the Potomac, with the Father of his Country, at Mount Vernon. How did it sound to the ears of the black persons who served the tables while the sons of liberty grew furious with the British at the "slavery" to which they would reduce their fellows by a requirement of a stamp on paper, or of a threepenny tax on tea?

The first census of these United States, in 1790, was to count 3.9 million Americans, of whom 697,000 were bound in a perpetual and hereditary form of chattel slavery founded upon race. Thus the proportion of the founding generation of Americans who were black slaves was higher than the proportion of black citizens to white today (1 in 10, roughly) and higher than the proportion of slaves mentioned by Lincoln in the Second Inaugural (one-eighth of the population.) More than one in six of founding fathers and mothers was black. In the days of the precursors to the civil rights movement of the twentieth century, just at the end of World War II, one black man active in interracial protests claimed that he would in big mixed meetings in the multiethnic big shoulders city of Chicago sometimes ask everybody to stand, and then ask all those who had four, then three, two, just one grandparent born outside this country to sit down, and then he would start in on the greatgrandparents, and before long most of those who remained standing, with all-American ancestries, would be black.

All the best-known founders were troubled by the contradiction between their libertarian and egalitarian claims and the institution of human slavery in their midst. Among those much troubled were Thomas Jefferson, whose paragraph about slavery—I tremble when I remember God is Just—was often to be quoted; George Mason, owner of 200 slaves, who was an abolitionist; George Washington, who actually did better than the other Virginians when it came to manumitting his own slaves in his will; and James Madison, who opposed slavery all his life and when young tried to arrange his own livelihood so that he would not be dependent upon slavery.

But James Madison and the others did not travel to Philadelphia in May of 1787 to take up the moral issue of slavery. Slavery was not on the agenda. It was a topic, we may be sure, the framers wished as much as possible to avoid. The topic of their meeting was, overtly, reforming government under the Articles of Confederation and, not terribly covertly, supplanting it. The topic and occasion of their meeting was to form a more satisfactory government for the union of the American States—an extremely delicate and difficult undertaking, as events would prove, enough so that quite sober men were moved to attach to its successful completion the word *miracle*. And the states with which they were trying to carry off this enormously delicate and sensitive task had all once been, and were almost all still, slaveholding communities (even in the North, although that was rapidly changing.) And these slaveholding states were also "sovereign." Or claimed to be.

How much they were sovereign states and how much they were already a part of a union that antedated these states was to be a central theme of the politics of the early history of the republic, and was not to be resolved until a bloody civil war. It was necessary to negotiate with these sovereign slaveholding states as they presented themselves in the form of the delegates here in the room in the Pennsylvania State House, in order to get the votes (the votes of *states*) to produce a constitution, and it would be necessary to deal with them again in the form of delegates to the ratification conventions in the states (or the state legislatures— whatever mode of ratification was chosen would entail decisions state by state). So the delegates in Philadelphia who said they saw slavery to be a moral evil—as almost all of them who spoke about it said they did— faced a difficult situation. They were not there to consider slavery. They were there to try to form a government among a group of states that included two or three or four or five (South Carolina and Georgia certainly, and then how many others?) that insisted absolutely that no constitution could be ratified that contained a restriction on slavery. When James Madison wrote to Jefferson at the end of the following October, in the big summary letter I have quoted before, he included in all the many pages of his report only one brief paragraph touching on slavery, and that as an aspect of "the adjustment of the different interests of different parts of the Continent." This brief passage describes the conflict and compromise on trade and slaves, and concludes "S. Carolina and Georgia were inflexible on the point of slaves."

S. Carolina and Georgia were inflexible, we might say, and the rest of the nascent country was . . . flexible.

Two

Just what did the framers include in the United States Constitution on the subject of slavery? The three explicit passages reveal two interwoven characteristics: collective bad conscience and moral embarrassment, on the one hand, and a timid but definite effort to limit the concessions to the evil, on the other.

Although there is only a little evidence about the specific role of James Madison in the notes he himself kept and in the notes of others, that evidence is revealing. Madison, it appears, fully shared both aspects of the collective performance—the moral embarrassment and the desire to limit the concessions. He was a leader in the latter.

The first provision has been called "a masterpiece of circumlocution," a description that fits the other two as well. It provides for the notorious three-fifths ratio, and is to be found right there on the first page of your Constitution, in Article I, section 2, paragraph 3: "Representatives and direct Taxes shall be apportioned among the several States which may be included within this Union, according to their respective Numbers, which shall be determined by adding to the whole Number of free Persons, including those bound to Service for a Term of Years, and excluding Indians not taxed, three fifths of all other Persons."

And who are these "other Persons?" The passage first refers to "free Persons" and then later refers to . . . other persons. So there are some persons who are *not* free, implicitly recognized by the Constitution. Liberty and justice for all, except for . . . other persons. Notice also that persons bound to service for a term of years—indentured servants—are included within the whole number, distinguishing them implicitly from those who are "bound to service" without any term. But in order to distinguish from all others the unfree persons "bound to service" forever, without using the word *slave,* and without explicitly describing slavery, the drafters had to resort to this spectacular roundaboutness. This remaining carefully discriminated but very carefully unnamed group of persons is . . . slaves.

I suggested that these verbose provisions reveal a bad conscience. As with Thomas Jefferson writing his long and wordy charge against the king about the "cruel war against human nature" in the draft of the Declaration, so, in a quite different way, it may be here. A moral embarrassment, an inability from moral embarrassment to be quite straightforward, and perhaps also a moral confusion, produce a circling smoke of many words.

But one does discern also this point, through the smoke of the complicated locutions, that the delegates are struggling, at considerable stylistic cost, to keep the words *slave* and *slavery* out of the document. They may not be able to end slavery, in this free country. They may not be able even to end the slave *trade.* They may have to make deals allowing the counting of slaves to add to the power of slaveholders in Congress. They may even feel they have to agree to use the power of free states to return slaves to captivity. But at least they can keep the *words* slavery and slave out of the Constitution.

James Madison was one of those who was alert on this point. On August 25, for example, we read, in the account of a discussion about taxing the importation of slaves, the following: "Mr. Madison thought it wrong to admit in the Constitution the idea that there could be property in men . . . slaves are not like merchandise."

This scrupulosity was not without its historical effect: it contributed to Abraham Lincoln's argument that the founders only from necessity acquiesced in slavery, and in no way accepted or endorsed it.

This is the infamous three-fifths ratio, the "federal ratio" that came in this form out of compromises in late August in the Constitutional Convention, after having been worked out originally in the negotiations to shape the Articles of Confederation. It had first appeared, in the 1787 convention, in the discussion in early June of the potent matter of state representation, in which the major focus of course was on the small-state, large-state battle. The issue of the representation of slaves—either as part of the population, or as part of property—wove in and out of that discussion.

There was available in the short history of the United States an earlier compromise on a different issue involving the measurement of slaves. The issue had then been—back in 1781 when these newly independent states were just beginning to deal with each other in a kind of a government— how to assign states their fair share of the tax burden. By population. But how then should slaves count? The same as free persons? Not at all? In that earlier case the interests had been reversed from what they would be in the convention in 1787: for purposes of assessing states their taxes, the big slaveholding states wanted slaves to count as little as possible, and the states of the North, with few slaves, wanted them to count for as much as possible. A Virginian had back then proposed that slaves count only half what a free man counted, but New England had insisted they count 100 percent—for purposes of measuring a state's capacity to pay taxes. So then Congress under the Articles did what such bodies do: bargained, compromised, split the difference. Two-thirds was proposed, but lost; three-fifths was proposed, lost, then barely and finally won out. And it came to be agreed to by eleven states in the Articles of Confederation, given the name the "federal ratio," and embedded in the law of the new land.

That earlier decision by Congress contributed to the language that now appears in this clause in the Constitution. Congress under the Articles had said the rule for counting people in the states, for tax purposes, would be "the whole number of white and other free citizens and inhabitants of every age, sex & condition including those bound to servitude for a term of years and three fifths of all other persons not comprehended in the foregoing description, except Indians not paying taxes, in each State." So the complicated language had not started in 1787. This act by Congress in 1781 is notable, not only for its interesting reference to "every . . . sex," but also for its explicit racial reference: "white . . . citizens." It is very important to note that the Federal Convention of 1787 did take that out. The source they were using had a racial reference. As the Federal Convention avoided the word *slave,* so it also omitted the word *white.* But it *did* use the federal ratio, now for another purpose than the earlier one: not for appraising taxes (upon how much wealth a state should be taxed) but for assigning proper representation (how much power a state should have in Congress.)

That ratio appeared first on June 11, in the early stages of the convention when the delegates were meeting in the Committee of the Whole. But then in July it came up again and almost came unstuck. When the three-fifths ratio was attached to the census by which representation would be regulated, South Carolina decided to go the whole way and proposed that "blacks" count *equally* with whites, because slaves are equally productive. That would have meant a large increase in the relative power of the major slaveholding states. Northerners, perhaps stunned a little, resisted, and for the moment the ratio was voted down. But then out of the continuing argument over the counting of blacks in measuring a state's representation—southerners saying they wanted 100 percent, northerners resisting—there came a committee and a compromise, with that three-fifths ratio sitting there in precedent to provide it. The compromise consisted in resorting to that figure not only to apportion representation (which favored the South) but also now joined to it "direct taxes" (thus in theory to favor the North). But only the first mattered. For this unsavory bargain the delegates congratulated each other. And there it was for the Committee of Detail (which gave to slaveholding states almost everything they wanted), in late July and early August, and there it would be for discussion on the convention floor when after the recess that committee brought in its report on August 6, and there it would be in the United States Constitution.

It is sometimes said that this provision is demeaning to blacks (or to the blacks who were slaves) because it sees them as counting only three-fifths as much as white persons, but that charge contains a misunderstanding. The whole passage, and the entire situation of which it was a product, were indeed overwhelmingly demeaning, but not in quite the way that charge implies. The three-fifths "counting" does not have to do with any right or privilege or moral worth of the black person or the slave; it has only to do with the way the wealth (or the claim to representation) of states was to be measured. No one was proposing that slaves have three-fifths, or any other fraction, of the suffrage, or of any right, enjoyed by free persons. The ratio in that regard was not one to three-fifths but one to zero. The issue was rather how large, proportionately, each state's representation should be in the House of Representatives. The advantage of a higher ratio would go not to the slaves but to the slave-owners. As I have said, at one point in the convention the South Carolinians, perhaps sensing the weakness of any opposition and feeling greedy, proposed that the ratio be one to one—that a slave should for this purpose count the same as a white person. That did not represent any sudden conversion to racial egalitarianism on the part of General Pinckney, but rather a power play.

The real issue was the representation of states in the new Congress. How should it be determined? By population? Or by wealth? Or by some combination?

There was the large dispute over representation in the new government between state equality and some kind of *proportionate* representation of the states that culminated in the Great Compromise. There was *within* the group committed to *proportionate* representation a further division between those who wanted the proportionate representation to be based solely on *population* (Madison and Wilson) and those who wanted it based in whole or in part on *wealth*. And among these last there was the division between those northerners who meant by "wealth" all kinds of wealth and property, and those from South Carolina and Georgia who when they said "wealth" meant slaves.

But which were the slaves—part of the population or part of property? James Wilson made the logical distinction: "Are they . . . citizens? Then why are they not admitted on an equality with white citizens? Are they . . . property? Then why is not other property admitted into the computation?" Elbridge Gerry sharpened the point about the second alternative: if slaveowners got an added increment of power for their property in slaves, why did he not get the same for his property in horses?

But logic was not the master in this morally tortured and politically intense situation. What happened in the final compromise—though of course nobody put it this way—was that slaves were to count as an odd mixture of property and human being—to the advantage of the slave-holders.

The slaveholding states won for themselves a curious increment to their power in the House, by adding to the count of their free population this fraction of the slave population, not to any advantage of that population but rather the reverse, to the increase of their masters' power. And as a justification for this extraordinary outcome they would suddenly remember to say, momentarily and partially and for this purpose only (that is, to increase their own power in Congress), that though these slaves were fundamentally property, they were to some extent human beings also.

Three

The Committee of Detail, we have said, was an extremely important committee that went further than had been expected and provided the draft of an actual constitution. It had been chaired by John Rutledge of South Carolina, who was perhaps the ablest of the Deep South delegates. The other four members were James Wilson, and two of the New Englanders—Ellsworth of Connecticut and Gorham of Massachusetts— most given to intersectional compromise; the Virginia member was not Madison but Edmund Randolph. The committee brought in a report that gave the big slaveholding states everything they wanted: no prohibition of the slave trade—ever! And no taxes on slaves as "imports." And no special head tax, beyond the proportions of the census (southerners feared that antislavery elements might use a head tax to discourage slavery). And the three-fifths federal ratio for representation. If the draft brought in by the Rutledge Committee of Detail had become the Constitution of the United States, there would have been a perpetual, constitutionally protected slave trade continually augmenting (by the three-fifths ratio) the special power of the white populations of the slaveholding states in Congress. And there certainly would have been a very different United States of America. Fortunately, the proposals of the Committee of Detail did not go unchallenged or unamended.

There were in the Constitutional Convention four speeches of some length that included important material opposing the proposals of the Rutledge Committee of Detail on this subject, and making some substantive attack on the slave trade or slavery itself. These speeches did not necessarily come from the quarters from which they might have been expected, but then in the flow and exchange of republican politics you can never be sure from what quarter help will come, and sometimes you do not want to examine just why it did. The four speeches were by Rufus King and Gouverneur Morris on August 8, by Luther Martin on August 21, and by George Mason on August 22.

On August 8 Rufus King of Massachusetts intervened after a vote that reinstated that federal ratio with an objection to the way those Rutledge committee provisions on slavery and navigation acts worked against the North: "The admission of slaves was a most grating circumstance to his mind, & he believed would be so to a great part of the people of America. He had not made a strenuous opposition to it heretofore because he had hoped that his concession would have produced a readiness which had not been manifested, to strengthen the Genl. Govt. and to mark a full confidence in it. The Report under consideration had by the tenor of it, put an end to all these hopes. In two great points the hands of the Legislature were absolutely tied. The importation of slaves could not be prohibited—exports could not be taxed. Is this reasonable?" King's speech was not exactly a humane cry for justice to the slaves; it was a practical outburst against the imbalance against the North. King's conclusion shows the North-oriented practicality of his protest: "At all events, either slaves should not be represented, or exports should be taxable."

King (a follower of Hamilton and a nationalist promoter of a commercial future) was objecting on sectional grounds to an irrational extra representation for the slaveholding South (through the three-fifths clause) that would be continually augmented by a perpetual slave trade. Slaveholding states would now under the union be able to call on the resources of all to put down the slave insurrections they were thus fostering (this was a point also for Gouverneur Morris and other northerners: we will have to help pay the cost of putting down their slave insurrections). Moreover, we—the North—will be forestalled from using an export tax on those exports of tobacco and rice from the South to help pay the cost. What an unjust package! In Madison's notes on King's speech one can feel the moral indignation seeping through. But the primary injustice King is upset about is not the injustice to free blacks or to slaves or to Africans who will be captured and made slaves; it is the injustice to the *North*. Nevertheless, King's speech did have the effect of initiating a counterattack on the Committee of Detail's apparent capitulation to the slave states.

Gouverneur Morris shortly thereafter on the same day made what is sometimes described as the only abolitionist speech at the convention, but, in the end, also more sectional defense than antislavery. He did include a direct attack on slavery. He would never concur in upholding domestic slavery. It was a "nefarious institution," "the curse of heaven."

Morris began his speech with a motion to insert the word *free* before the word *inhabitants* in the clause on representation, to deny, as he said, any concurrence in domestic slavery. At the end of his speech the youngest delegate in the hall (younger than Charles Pinckney, who would claim to be the youngest), a twenty-six-year-old named Jonathan Dayton, from New Jersey, made one of his very few interventions in the deliberations, we may assume rather timidly: He seconded Morris's motion and explained that whatever should be the fate of the amendment, he spoke so that "his sentiments on the subject might appear," and so they do right down to the present moment, there on the page in Madison's notes.

When late in August the time came for compromising the complex of issues having to do with slavery, navigation acts, sectional relations, and commerce, it was Morris who proposed that a committee do the compromising. Although there were other important changes in others of the pro-slavery provisions of the Committee of Detail, the three-fifths ratio stayed and passed on into the United States Constitution, the charter of freedom providing this bizarre extra power to the institution of slavery.

Four

The document brought in by the Committee of Detail was a full draft of a constitution, twenty-three articles putting into full formal sentences not only the resolutions of the convention up to that point but some additional matters as well. The first discussion of the items that touched on slavery had come on August 8, after the challenge by King and Morris to the whole combination, including the three-fifths ratio. The second challenge came later in August and focused on the slave trade.

The first voice was that of Luther Martin, the belligerent, hard-drinking attorney general of Maryland. Madison's summary of Martin's speech is worth including in its entirety, to see the points he made in the language in which it was summarized at the time. The date was Tuesday, August 21, toward the end of the session.

> Mr L—— Martin, proposed to vary the sect: 4 art VII so as to allow a prohibition or tax on the importation of slaves. 1. As five slaves are to be counted as 3 free men in the apportionment of Representatives; such a clause wd. leave an encouragement to this trafic. 2 slaves weakened one part of the Union which the other parts were bound to protect: the privilege of importing them was therefore unreasonable—3. It was inconsistent with the principles of the revolution and dishonorable to the American character to have such a feature in the Constitution.

So it was said, at least, in the Federal Convention, that (point 3!) the slave trade was "inconsistent with the principles of the revolution" and that it was "dishonorable to the American character to have such a feature in the Constitution."

Mr. "Rutlidge" (as Madison usually misspelled his name) responded to Martin with a sweeping, and revealing, rejection of that third point, now cast in terms of the religious and moral presuppositions upon which it rested. "Rutlidge" reassured the northerners that slaveholding states felt they could take care of any insurrections without help from the North and then said, on the larger topic, that "Religion and humanity had nothing to do with this question—Interest alone is the governing principle with Nations—The true question at present is whether the southern States shall or shall not be parties to the Union."

The Deep South states repeatedly used the threat to withdraw or not join as a kind of blackmail on issues affecting slavery. Of course they were not alone in that kind of thing but their threat had a bluntness that the others could not match. Shortly after Rutledge spoke, Charles Pinckney said that "South Carolina can never receive the plan if it prohibits the slave trade."

On the next day George Mason gave his speech, quite different from those of his brothers to the South, deploring slavery and the slave trade with points that were much like the characteristic themes of his fellow Virginian Thomas Jefferson: the slave trade—the "infernal traffic"—had originated with "the avarice of British merchants" and the British government had repeatedly stopped Virginia's efforts to end it; some of our Eastern brethren had "from lust of gain" embarked on this "nefarious traffic"; the presence of slaves was a danger, especially in wartime; slavery had bad effects, including "the most pernicious effect on manners"; "every master of slaves is a born tyrant." Mason's speech was sandwiched between two New England shoulder-shrugs, after which the two Pinckneys gave vigorous defenses of slavery and protestations of impotence.

General Pinckney's was particularly sweeping: "General Pinckney declared it to be his firm opinion that if himself & all his colleagues were to sign the Constitution & use their personal influence, it would be of no avail towards obtaining the assent of their Constitutents. S. Carolina & Georgia cannot do without slaves."

Five

Now the other two provisions in the Constitution. First on the slave trade, Article I, section 9, paragraph 1: "The Migration or Importation of such Persons as any of the States now existing shall think proper to admit, shall not be prohibited by the Congress prior to the Year one thousand eight hundred and eight, but a Tax or duty may be imposed on such Importation, not exceeding ten dollars for each Person."

Here again there is the careful euphemism for slaves—"such Persons"—but now in the context of a stunning euphemism for the slave trade: "The Migration or Importation of such Persons as any of the States now existing shall think proper to admit." It surely takes gall to describe the commercial traffic in Africans in chains as a "Migration," and to use that word as a preliminary softening of the somewhat plainer word "Importation." A migration is a movement from place to place undertaken through the agency of the creature doing the moving, which was certainly not the case with the slaves imported by force from Africa. Then these "migrating" persons are going to be "admitted" to—certain states. These are such persons as certain states "think proper" to admit. That thinking proper, and by implication not thinking proper, on the part of states, is surely a curious concept in constitutional law. Gouverneur Morris had wanted to specify the thinking-proper states by name—North and South Carolina and Georgia—but out of deference to the tender feelings of those states that specificity was not accepted. By implication there are states that do *not* "think" it "proper" to "admit" such persons—as indeed, fortunately, there were.

The most significant phrase politically speaking, though, was none of these but the phrase "the States now existing." Was that intended to confine the protection of slaveholding from congressional prohibition to the then existing states? In other words could Congress immediately prohibit slave trading everywhere else—that is, into the new states that would soon be formed out of the territory to the west? If so that would give support to Abraham Lincoln's interpretation of the framers' position, that they merely acquiesced in its presence where it then existed, out of necessity, but confined it to those states in order that it be put on the road to its ultimate extinction.

This phase had *not* been included in the report of the Committee of Detail, whose proposals provided the foundation of the discussion on this subject. And neither had there been, in that report, *any* date after which Congress could prohibit the slave trade. It would have been protected forever.

There is much to lament in the Constitutional Convention's treatment (treatment and avoidance) of slavery. But as is so often true in human affairs the chief consolation is this: it could have been worse.

There was resistance to the report of the Committee of Detail on the slave trade, of which I will say more in a moment. The discussion was intertwined with a debate about trade—navigation acts—and led Morris and others to see the possibility of "a bargain among the Northern and Southern States." A grand committee was chosen; of this committee, in contrast to the Committee of Detail, James Madison was the Virginia member; William Livingston of New Jersey was chairman. The report of this committee was a marked improvement on the Committee of Detail— an improvement from a very low base—in that it now proposed to allow the government to prohibit the importation of slaves after 1800: the new nation *would* be able to stop the slave trade. And there could be taxes on the imported slaves (James Wilson at one point had said that if slaves were the *only* import exempt from taxes, that was in effect a bounty). In other parts of the intersectional deal it was proposed that *export* taxes, which the South feared, would be prohibited, but that other kinds of "navigation" acts would require only a simple majority. Why are we talking about such matters in the midst of a discussion of slavery? Because that is the way the convention dealt with the topic, as part of a complex intersectional deal.

It was this Livingston committee that inserted the phrase "the states now existing." The Livingston committee's report, as I say, considerably modified, for the better, the proposals of the Committee of Detail.

But then when they reported, on August 24, there was a step backwards, surely as the result of yet another deal behind the scenes. General Pinckney immediately rose and moved (without recorded explanation or argument) to strike out "1800" and insert "1808" as the date when Congress could first prohibit the slave trade. And—why this? Surely some prearrangement. Nathaniel Gorham of Massachusetts, also without argument or explanation, seconded the motion. They proposed to extend the slave trade for eight more years beyond the proposal of the Livingston committee, for a full twenty years from the time they were speaking.

Only one speaker opposed the motion—James Madison: "Twenty years will produce all the mischief that can be apprehended from the liberty to import slaves. So long a term will be more dishonorable to the National character than to say nothing about it in the Constitution."

But the motion *passed*—with New Hampshire, Connecticut, Massachusetts, and Maryland voting with the three Deep South states. Virginia voted no.

Forty thousand slaves were to be imported in the added years, the years between 1801 and 1808.

Six

The third provision of the Constitution directly dealing with slavery is the provision about fugitive slaves, which appears in the section toward the end of the Constitution dealing with the "privileges and immunities" that the citizen of one state shall be granted by another state. The South Carolinians and Georgians sought protection for their peculiar property, and after some interesting revisions in their proposal they achieved it, and it appears in Article IV, section 2, paragraph 3: "No Person held to Service or Labour in one State, under the Laws thereof, escaping into another, shall, in Consequence of any Law or Regulation therein, be discharged from such Service or Labour, but shall be delivered up on Claim of the Party to whom such Service or Labour may be due."

The delegates did have to struggle to find ways to indicate slavery without saying the word. Here a slave becomes a "Person held to Service or Labour." Such a person, so *held*—and *held* is certainly the right word—under the laws of one state, "escaping" (not "migrating" now, not moving or traveling—*escaping*) into another state shall not be "discharged" but shall be "delivered up on Claim" (one hears the whiplash in the words, delivered up! on claim!) of that party to whom the service and labor "may be due."

This fugitive law provision came up in late August, as the delegates were tired and eager to be done. It had no antecedent in the Articles, but it did have a new antecedent in the Northwest Ordinance, passed by Congress in New York during that same summer, in July, as part of still another of these bargains, this one as the price of keeping slavery out of the Northwest Territory. Now here it was in Philadelphia, going into the very Constitution of the new union. When the topic first came up, at the end of the session on August 28, Butler and Charles Pinckney put it in a rather crude form: "to require fugitive slaves and servants to be delivered up like criminals." But by the next day they had cleaned up their act. South Carolina's Pierce Butler, not long after a bouquet from General Pinckney to the "liberal" easterner that I will quote in a moment, and immediately after the vote of South Carolina against the two-thirds requirement for navigation acts (in other words, South Carolina voted the way the northerners wanted on that one), rose to propose this odious act, which without saying the word gave a kind of national sanction to slavery (because all states would be required to return escapees to slavery; in addition to giving slaves no haven, one consequence of the provision, as history would show, would be to place free blacks everywhere in jeopardy).

Butler's proposed version, which, like a modern paper conscious of feminism, called the escaping person "he or she," said in the last line that the escaping person should be delivered up to the person "justly claiming" their service or labor, and it passed that way in the convention. But that "justly" was too much for the Committee of Style, which committee took it out. We have to guess why, but surely it is not hard to guess: some members of the committee, of which James Madison was a member, and Alexander Hamilton, by then back in the convention, also a member, and Gouverneur Morris chairman, noted the word and did not want to let it be said in the Constitution of the United States that the holding of slaves was just. Moreover, that committee's substitute phrase for "justly claiming" was notable noncommittal: in place of the "person justly claiming their service or labor" there now appeared only "the Party to whom such

130

Service or Labour *may be due*"—I underline the softness of the claim of due-ness: *may* be due. And, back in the first clause, the committee made another change in the Butler proposal that the convention had passed; they inserted the word *legally* before the word *held* in the description of the slave: "No person *legally* held to service or labor." Again, one must guess at the meaning of the change; presumably it was done at the same time the "justly" claiming was dropped from the last line—thus eliminating any constitutional commitment to the justice of the claiming and the holding, but specifying only its (bare?) legality. That at least would be one reading. But then back again in the convention on September 15 there was still another narrowing of the Constitution's grant of legitimacy to the claim of ownership. The phrase from the Committee on Style, "No person legally held to service or labor in one state" was changed to the phrase that went into the Constitution: "No Person held to Service or labour in one State, under the Laws thereof." So it is not "legally" held, but just held under the laws of particular states. Madison in his notes gives a brief (hasty?) and somewhat confusing explanation of why this was done: "In compliance," he wrote, "with the views of those who thought the term [*legal*] equivocal and favoring the idea that slavery was legal in a moral view." Guessing in context, one may presume that it was the opponents of slavery like himself who instigated this further restrictive change, because they thought the phrase "legally held" might still, with the majesty of the law, imply some moral approbation to slavery, and therefore got the phrase whittled down just to the sheer fact of the laws of particular states. And one may guess that the South Carolinians and Georgians, and their supporters, may not have cared as much about these changes, because they are susceptible of more than one reading, and because for all that on the big main point they got what they wanted.

If we start with what the boldest defenders of slavery wanted, as revealed in what they tried at first to get in the convention, and what the Confederate constitution seventy-four years later would provide, one may perceive quite a net of restrictions that were constructed around the concessions to the institution. They wanted to call a slave a slave, and give slavery by name constitutional respectability; but no, the framers would not speak those words. They wanted a constitution that would say that fugitive slaves should be "delivered up like criminals"—but no, they themselves could sense that that last phrase would not pass. They wanted it specified that the labor of slaves was *justly* claimed—but although at first it passed that way the Committee of Style got that "justly" out of there. They wanted the "service or labor" the slave owed to his owner unequivocally affirmed (the Confederate constitution, with none of these moral hang-ups, would bluntly say that the fugitive slave "shall be delivered up on claim of the party to whom such slave belongs"). But no—the Committee on Style and then the convention and the Constitution would say only: "the party to whom the service or labor *may be* due." They wanted at least the standing of slavery in the law affirmed. But no; the framers would say only "held to Service or Labour in one State, under the Laws thereof"—the laws of one particular state. So you can say that the framers ended by being about as restrictive as they could be with respect to the moral standing of slavery—if they were going to make such a provision in the first place. And you can say that that became important in the 1850s, when there came a tremendous argument about the moral standing of American slavery, and what the founders intended, and in particular what the framers intended. But when you have said all that the still more important fact remains, that on the nubbin of the issue the framers yielded: they granted a place in the Constitution to the concept of fugitive slaves, and to their recovery, anywhere in the country.

In addition to the explicit provisions we have examined—the three-fifths clause, the fugitive slave clause, and the postponement for twenty years (or—the alternative interpretation, the granting after twenty years) of the constitutional possibility to end the slave trade there was in the Constitution another important feature not treating on slavery specifically but very important to its protection. This was the right to property, in which property in slaves was implicitly, from the facts of the time, included. (General Pinckney had said, on July 12, that "property in slaves should not be exposed to danger under a government instituted for the protection of property.") The right to property in slaves was apparently on the same footing with all the other rights protected by the Constitution—as much of a claim, paradoxically, as the right to liberty itself.

Seven

These provisions are not what James Madison or James Wilson or Benjamin Franklin or Gouverneur Morris or George Mason would have wanted them to be, different though these men may be from each other. They are also not quite what John Rutledge or Pierce Butler or the Pinckneys—the South Carolinians—would ideally have wanted either, although they got much of what they wanted; these defenders of slavery showed by their proposals that they would have made these provisions even worse than they are, if they could have.

And in some sense they are not what the leading New Englanders would have wanted, either, but therein lies an important part of the story of the convention on this topic. New England was not represented by as able or as imaginative a group at the Federal Convention of 1787 as it had been at the Continental Congresses. There was now no equivalent of John Adams, or perhaps even of Sam Adams. At those first Congresses the Massachusetts men, the New England men, had been the leaders, the spokesmen out in front with vision and energy. But not at this convention.

There was no one who represented the New England attitude on slavery of Abigail Adams or James Otis, or of Samuel Hopkins, the antislavery preacher in Newport, or of Jonathan Edwards, Jr., the preacher in New Haven (where Roger Sherman had once been mayor). What New England was represented by at this momentous convention was not the moral clarity and earnestness and vision of the New England Puritan in the Age of Enlightenment at his best, but more by the self-regarding shrewdness and commercial interest and cunning localism of the New England Yankee.

By New England here one means Connecticut and to some degree Massachusetts, because Rhode Island never showed up and New Hampshire did not arrive in time to figure large in these matters and Vermont did not yet exist. The larger role was played by the Connecticut delegates, who took the lead in the conventions' key compromises and deals. The leader was Roger Sherman, an older public figure whose career ran all the way through the Revolutionary period. When the high-living South Carolinians would meet with Roger Sherman in taverns, they would have to remind themselves that he would not meet on a Sunday, that he would not take a drink, and that he would want to say a blessing before the meal. But he would make a deal. These New Englanders regularly introduced their speeches, like white folks in civil rights discussions centuries later, with concessionary grants of general virtue to themselves before violating it in the present instance. What they did, generally speaking, was to make the New England–Deep South compromises.

Reading the notes and the histories of the framers' convention when it dealt with the subject of slavery, one asks, where was New England? Where was this community that shall be as a city on a hill, with the eyes of the world upon it? The answer is: New England was in the backrooms of the taverns making deals, and then on the floor of the convention prefacing its part in those deals by saying that of course it had never owned slaves and disapproved of the slave trade and knew slavery to be a moral evil.

If the reader should think that the words above about the role of the New Englanders on this issue are too harsh, he should read Madison's notes for August 21 and 22 on this subject: interwoven with statements from the South Carolinians and other Deep Southerners defending, often in blunt terms, the slave interest, are concurrences by delegates from Connecticut Roger Sherman and Oliver Ellsworth, often prefaced with personal statements of disapproval of slavery. At the outset of the discussion, for example, on August 21, after Luther Martin's speech and Rutledge's response, "Ellsworth" said "let every State import what it pleases. The morality or wisdom of slavery are considerations belonging to the States themselves." Not only that—hands off the slave trade. He even repeated one of the most pernicious of the southerners' arguments, that the North could profit from the continued slave trade, too: "What enriches a part enriches the whole, and the States are the best judges of their particular interest." Throughout these discussions one feels that New England delegates—especially these two from Connecticut, but sometimes some Massachusetts delegates, also—are making the slave states' case for them. There appears to have been a spider web of bargains and bargains within bargains at this gathering but especially there had come to be agreements of mutual interest between New England, especially Connecticut, and the Deep South, especially South Carolina, and the New England people certainly kept their side of it.

So what did New England and other northerners get, in return for accepting most of what the Deep South wanted on slavery? A concession on commercial matters—on trade, on what were called navigation acts. The Connecticut–South Carolina connection went back to the middle of the summer, and touched on many other issues, apparently, in complex bargaining, but now in the crunch on slavery there was the explicit deal. *Navigation acts* was a specific term that had a certain weight and negative meaning to the Americans, because of restrictions the British had placed on colonial trade in the past, and then because the independent states had quite different interests to some degree identifiable by region, on the subject of government regulation of trade. The South as a region was heavily dependent upon exports, and did not have its own shipping, and therefore did not want it to be easy for the central government to pass acts taxing exports or limiting shipping to American ships. Therefore they wanted to require a special majority—two thirds, presumably enough to give the South a veto—to pass navigation acts. Although it was complicated, much of the rest of the country had interests that were the reverse of these (not Connecticut, an exporting state—a reason for the Connecticut–South Carolina alliance). Many placed aid to commerce at the top of the list of reasons for union. There was a rough but important sectional difference on this weighty matter. So—illogical though it may seem to a modern reader—the section-dividing issues came to be treated by the convention in packages.

There is at the end of all the deliberations on this whole cluster of issues a little speech by General Pinckney, quite interesting in its sad way, a kind of valentine to the New Englanders (he calls them, as was then the geographical style, "Easterners"), as he acquiesces for his part in the bargain that had been struck. This is on August 29.

> Genl. Pinckney said it was the true interest of the S. States to have no regulation of commerce; but considering the loss brought on the commerce of the Eastern States by the revolution, their liberal conduct towards the views of South Carolina, and the interest the weak Southn. States had in being united with the strong Eastern States, he thought it proper that no fetters should be imposed on the power of making commercial regulations; and that his constituents though prejudiced against the Eastern States, would be reconciled to this liberality."

And then comes General Pinckney's bouquet. "He had himself, he said, prejudices agst the Eastern States before he came here, but would acknowledge that he had found them as liberal and candid as any men whatever."

It is significant that Madison himself added an explanatory footnote—something he rarely did—on the "views" of South Carolina about which these Easterners had been so liberal and so candid and so wonderful. "He [Genl. Pinckney] meant," wrote Madison, explaining, "the permission to import slaves. An understanding on the two subjects of *navigation* and *slavery,* had taken place between those parts of the Union, which explains the vote on the Motion depending, as well as the language of Genl. Pinckney & others." General Pinckney down in Charleston had heard that these New England "Easterners" were fierce and unreasonable on the subject of slavery, but now he had come to this meeting in Philadelphia and found them to be "as liberal and candid as any men whatever," veritable pussycats.

Eight

What are we to make of the way these heroes of our national founding, building a new society based on human liberty, coped, or did not cope, with the fact of human slavery in their midst? Did the framers distinguish themselves on this question? I think not. Does the story do them credit? I think not. Not the framers.

Perhaps it is a little too easy for us, living when and where we do, to answer swiftly that it does not. But that is a better answer than a simply celebrational one, that covers over the moral embarrassment with patriotic piety.

There is a doubleness in this story, and as in so many of the troubled areas of life it is important not to simplify in either direction. However one interprets the work of the founders with respect to slavery—whether emphasizing what they accomplished, or what they failed to accomplish—there is no doubt that they left to later generations an unstable combination. The founding generation bequeathed, we might say, a double doubleness; there were two claims, slavery and antislavery—and there were also, as their work concluded, two sections.

There is perhaps a stronger case in defense of the total work of the great founders, with respect to slavery, than of the work specifically of the Constitutional Convention. Those who make that case insist that we think our way back into the actual historical situation and recognize accomplishments that are so complete and so long ago that we now take them for granted. And one of the accomplishments of the founding generation which we are not likely now to recognize, but which was real and important nonetheless, was exactly the shrinking of the domain of slavery to one section of the country—the ending of slavery in the North.

When the quarrel with England started in the middle of the eighteenth century all of the colonies of British America had slaves. Slavery was a presence in all the colonies, and a more considerable presence in the North than we now realize. Historian William Freehling notes that "when the American Revolution began slavery was a national institution, thriving both north and south of the Mason-Dixon line." Slaves constituted 14 percent of the population of New York state, 8 percent of those in New Jersey, 6 percent even in the New England state of Rhode Island—not insignificant percentages. The zeal, and the ideals, of the American Revolution placed slavery on the defensive and began its demise in the states in which it was most vulnerable. The same thing happened with respect to the territories. In the Northwest Ordinance of 1787 slavery was excluded from the territory north of the Ohio—another significant accomplishment, not to be taken for granted. The result of these achievements was to isolate slavery in the South, as the peculiar institution of that region.

The worthy deeds of the founding generation include, in addition to the shrinking the national institution of slavery down to a sectional institution, the ending of its augmentation by the slave trade, the putting of slavery on the moral defensive by the spread of the nation's ideals, the denial to slavery of explicit recognition in the Constitution, and the provision of the instruments of government and free debate by which it would one day be ended forever. Not a small list.

And the framers did part of that. It was possible at the time to interpret the constitutional clause on the slave trade as antislavery, because it did allow Congress to end it—as, following the report of the Committee of Detail, it might not have done. The possibility that the slave trade might not have been ended—might have been given perennial constitutional protection—is so far from our present imaginings as to be almost impossible for us to credit. And yet there it was, a real possibility, on the floor of the Constitutional Convention, when the Committee of Detail brought in its report; much of that report did become constitutional law—but the protection forever of the slave trade did not. The framers did provide that the slave trade could constitutionally be ended—and Congress, on the initiative of President Jefferson, did end it promptly in 1808.

That was one worthy deed of the framers—enormously important. Then there was also another, symbolic and yet very real. There was that rather touching implicit appeal to future generations to do what the framers themselves were not able to do: the elaborate euphemistic and circumlocutionary avoidance of the word *slave* or *slavery*. On this matter Madison himself seems to have played a key role—keeping the Constitution from recognizing, as Madison put it, that there could be "property in men." They would not speak the word, not in this document. The historian Don Fehrenbacher minted a figure of speech to describe the framers' doubleness in particular with reference to this careful avoidance of the word *slave* while they accommodated it in fact: "It is as though the Framers were half-consciously trying to frame two Constitutions, one for their own time and the other for the ages, with slavery viewed bifocally—that is, plainly visible at their feet, but disappearing when they lifted their eyes."

Suppose they had not lifted their eyes. Suppose they had looked at slavery not bifocally but only through the plain lenses of the practical reality of the day: there it was, an entrenched fact, and they could not get rid of it. Suppose the proposals of the Committee of Detail had been enacted on this matter, as in fact it was on many others, and that the framers had not added to the ending of slavery in the North and the exclusion of slavery from the Northwest Territory, the constitutional provision allowing the ending of the slave trade? Suppose they had not been scrupulous to keep the word *slavery* out of the Constitution?

We may make more vivid how much worse the Constitution might have been by moving forward seventy-four years to look once more, as we did with respect to the invoking of the guidance of Almighty God while dropping the general welfare clause, at the blunt explicitness of the Confederate constitution. As we said before, that document was copied from the Federal Constitution almost verbatim—except for a few quite significant variations.

The confederates would use the words *slave* and *slavery* throughout. In the federal ratio clause, which they retained, they would say "three-fifths of all slaves." In their clause on fugitive slaves they would use no euphemisms or evasions: "No slave or other person held to service or labor in any State or Territory of the Confederate States" it begins, and it ends with the clause we have already quoted "shall be delivered up on claim of the party to whom such slave belongs." They also had no reluctance to use racial categories in their national instrument, as the framers, significantly, and in contrast to the Articles, avoided doing. In the slave trade provision, the rebels in 1861 would refer to "the importation of negroes of the African race," which was forbidden from any foreign country, "other than the slaveholding States or Territories of the United States of America," who thus had a monopoly.

Nor were the changes confined to the three sections that touched on slavery in the Federal Constitution. In the United States Constitution itself in Article I, section 9, paragraph 3, there is in the enumerating of the powers of Congress a little nubbin of a bill of rights which prohibits bills of attainder and ex post facto laws. The confederates chose that spot to added another quite striking additional civil right of their own, which I italicize: "No bill of attainder, *ex post facto* law, *or law denying or impairing the right of property in negro slaves,* shall be passed."

Here was *constitutional* protection against there *ever* being a law even "impairing the right of property in negro slaves."

Among the "privileges and immunities" of citizens of one state protected in another the confederates added these, to nail down the Dred Scott problem: "The right of transit and sojourn in any State of the Confederacy, with their slaves and other property; and the right of property in said slaves shall not be thereby impaired."

There were to be new territories: "In all such territory, the institution of negro slavery as it now exists in the Confederate States, shall be recognized and protected by Congress, and by the territorial government; and the inhabitants of the several Confederate States and Territories, shall have the right to take to such territory any slaves, lawfully held by them in any of the States or Territories of the Confederate States."

To be sure, invoking these passages from a much later document is unhistorical and anachronistic; the convictions and interests that would lead to those provisions had in 1787 not yet hardened into the rigidities that developed after 1830. But they were present already in embryo in Philadelphia, and in the states that sent their delegates to Philadelphia. If those views had carried the day, there would have been for the United States of America no role—or rather a regressive role—in the moral history of mankind. This might have been a unitary slave country, a South

Africa with pretensions, its institutions betraying and undercutting the ideals in which it began.

But if we may concede that it could have been worse, we may, on the other hand, still within the limits of realism, imagine the ways that it might have been radically better. It is not only unhistorical and anachronistic to make comparisons with the Confederate constitution; it argues both ways. Much historical water had flowed over the dam, in the years between the two constitutions, and the founders had done much to give direction to the flow. The conditions that made the Confederate constitution so blunt, explicit, and repugnant were themselves created in part out of failures of the framers and the founders—among others, the failure to confine slavery explicitly to the states that already had it. The decisions and nondecisions of the framers allowed there to be new slave states, beginning with Kentucky in 1792, and continuing almost contrapuntally with a slave state matching a free state until the Civil War. Slavery was not excluded by the founding generation from the entire territory of the nation—in the terrible near miss in 1784—but only from the Northwest, and so slave territories were formed, and then slave states. Those slave states were admitted to the union, transforming its politics, and those slave states—cotton plantation slave states like Alabama and Mississippi—were to have their power augmented by the three-fifths clause, and would make the nation far different from what it might have been. That difference would lead to the attitudes and interests that would write that Confederate constitution, and to the moral logjam that would end in the terrible scourge of war.

How big a difference these carvers on the rind of the young oak might have made! Did Make! Suppose that taking all possible steps to restrict the evil of slavery had been for more delegates a higher priority and more clear-cut and persistent moral commitment. Of course the forming of a union, a working republican union for the continent, had to be the highest priority—but suppose that restricting the evil of slavery had been second only to that. They could not have ended slavery. They could not have overcome, at a stroke, the new nation's racism—including their own. But it is not unrealistic to believe that they might have restricted the effects, in accord with the ideals they themselves professed. One writer asks: "Could slavery have been confined to states now existing? Could the rights of free Negroes have been defined and secured? Could the rights of owners who wished to emancipate their chattels have been established against state laws to the contrary?"

Surely, we may surmise, a resolute opposition could have retained the date of 1800 for the ending the slave trade; could the trade have been ended even sooner? On the slave trade there was possible an alliance of idealism with the bluntest kind of realism: Virginia had a surplus of slaves, and wanted the foreign slave trade ended to protect its own market.

Was it a political necessity that the fugitive slave provision be entered into the Constitution—so easily, so little examined or resisted?

The delegates yielded on these matters to the ultimatums of South Carolina and Georgia, need they have yielded so easily?

When in the interesting moment on August 21 John Rutledge said, in exasperation with the moral objections of some northerners, that "religion and humanity had nothing to do with this question—interest alone is the governing principle with Nations"—he exposed one aspect of the politics of this convention, especially on the issue of slavery. The states were almost like nations, and their negotiations were almost like those dealings in national interest and balance of power that characterize international politics. It was almost like Henry Kissinger dealing with Le Duc Tho, or Harry Truman with Stalin at Potsdam (not quite). It was to a degree like NATO or the Congress of Vienna in that the states were separate entities of power whose differing interests might, if pressed too hard, prove to be weightier than the thin threads of possible common action across state boundaries; although there was the Confederation under the Articles, that was not much more than an alliance—a League of States, as Madison said. It was exactly to overcome that condition that the delegates of those states were assembled in Philadelphia. But meanwhile, before they had overcome it, they had to deal with each other in major part as sovereign entities resembling nation-states. So there was that probing and power-balancing and testing of the strength of interests, like an international parlay. That does to a considerable degree explain and also justify the compromises the framers made on slavery.

But not entirely, because those who might have pressed hard, to test the will and interest of those "inflexible" slave states, with their threat not to join the union—did not make that test.

Those smaller states—South Carolina and Georgia—*needed* the union, needed the association with the big states and the continental union, for commercial and military reasons. They felt their need for the union, as their rapid ratification of the Constitution in the following winter and spring would attest. In the convention's balance of power, and challenge of wills, might they not have been opposed, and tested, and pushed?

There was, no doubt, a terrible heritage from the past, and tragic conflicts of value, which we should not glibly overlook. We can say that these passages in the Constitution reveal a tragic dimension in the otherwise apparently so fortunate founding of the United States; here are the delegates, making a *novus ordo seclorum,* starting over, building a new state in a new world, starting fresh with republican principles—but then they are caught, as human beings elsewhere are caught, after all, with a terrible legacy of the past. They are, after all, faced not just with fresh and open choices, but also with tragic choices, where each alternative is tinged with evils and fraught with peril. They face the more common human condition than absolutely fresh starts. They must begin in the middle of a situation that is already wrong, but cannot be completely undone.

But the dark legacy of the past and conflict of values and the inability to know the full consequences of their actions were not the only elements of that scene: they brought to that complex real situation the moral agency, and the limitations of human beings. It was not just that the decisions were tough; it was also that the human agents were weak, and, in some cases, worse then weak.

We may grant that here most clearly is the tragic dimension of the founders' situation. But surely we may not then use that fact to absolve them of the responsibility for the actions they took, and did not take, in the range of freedom that still remained. They were the founders of a nation more insistent than any other that human beings have the freedom to make and remake the world, and then to take the responsibility for what they have made.

Many Hands

One

WAS MADISON THE FATHER OF THE CONSTITUTION? That is the wrong metaphor, for Madison or for anyone else. The singleness of the metaphor of fatherhood is inappropriate to the collaborative complexity of this successful republican state-making. A later president, John F. Kennedy, quoting a "Chinese proverb" that no one has been able to find, would remark that "victory has a hundred fathers. Defeat is an orphan."

Was Madison the most important of the several parents of the Constitution? Madison failed to carry not only the two big points, very important to him—the federal "negative" of state legislation, and state equality in the second house—but also a variety of other positions. One could make—and historian Forrest McDonald has in fact made—a list of the items that Madison at one time or another favored that did not emerge in the final product. After extracting from the debates at the convention and from the fifteen points of the Virginia Plan a long list of specifics that Madison spoke for, voted for, or can be inferred to have supported, McDonald concluded: "Overall, of seventy-one specific proposals that Madison moved, seconded, or spoke unequivocally in regard to, he was on the losing side forty times." McDonald wrote, therefore, that a "Madisonian" constitution "bears limited resemblance to the document that was drafted by the convention." McDonald had begun this passage in his book—three full pages of Madisonian defeats—by remarking that "the myth that Madison was the father of the constitution dies hard"; he does his best, one might say, to kill it. But without complete success, so far as this reader is concerned. The writing of a new constitution, by "many hands," in a circumstance of actual and potential disagreement—of "deliberation and consent," with the awareness that the people of thirteen widely differing colonies will be asked to ratify it, in the shifting circumstances of almost four months of debate and argument, of course entails making (and seconding and voting for) particular proposals that do not prevail. That is the nature of such a deliberation. One shifts positions with the ebb and flow of argument and decision, partly because one thinks again, partly because the reality check of others' views limits and corrects one's sense of possibilities, partly because when one thing is decided the terms for the next are changed. All high politics is aiming at a moving target—a target which one's shot itself affects. One must say of many proposals: if the people would accept and act on it this way, fine, but if that other way, not. In other words the shaping of law and policy is not a matter of static and abstract designing but of a set of relationships in a particular time and place—dynamic. James Madison in Philadelphia, unlike James Harrington in his country home in England, or David Hume at his desk in Edinburgh, was responding to a changing configuration of forces and possibilities in a real world in which, of course, he did not have anything approaching complete control. A new-modeling state-maker at his desk does have such control: he can start from scratch, he can decide what to assume away, he can make his puppets behave. But not so with Madison or Wilson or Hamilton in Philadelphia.

Madison had prepared for the convention more thoroughly than anyone else, and that preparation, both in his memos and in the Virginia planning, was important. He had played a key role in issuing the call from Annapolis that made the convention happen. He had helped to persuade George Washington to lend his indispensable support. He endangered his health by keeping the notes from which (primarily) we learn what happened in the convention. And then, after the convention was over and the Constitution written he was a central figure in getting it ratified.

At the convention itself, he attended every session and spoke regularly and often—161 times, more than any other delegate. He came to be very highly regarded by his fellow delegates.

All of that is before we reach the substance of the convention itself. He had led in developing the Virginia Plan that had not only formed the basis of the first weeks' discussion, but also, despite the summer's changes, was still the skeleton of the Constitution as it emerged at the end. Madison had written to Jefferson, Randolph, and Washington before the convention, and put in his memos, his convictions on these large matters: that there ought to be a "new system," and not a patchwork on the Articles; that in the new system the central government should be strong, with powers beyond those of the Congress under the Articles; that while the consolidation of the states into "one simple republic" would be neither possible nor desirable, the continuing independence of the states would make union impossible, so that he sought a "middle ground," retaining the states but with a supreme central government—in other words in the very broad outline what we have in fact in the American federal union. He held that the central government should act directly upon individuals and not upon states only—in other words, that there would be the two governments both acting upon the individual citizens, surely a key to the success of our actual federal union; that the federal judiciary be supreme over the states, and independent of the other branches; that the whole structure should rest, through however many and complicated steps, on the whole and undivided people; that the constitution be ratified by the people in conventions called for that purpose. In other words, in his thinking and his arguing there were present, before the convention began, or during the convention after the compromise in July, most of the key ideas that made the Constitution an advance not only over the Articles but also over those previous republics and confederacies that young Madison had studied in his memos.

Two

Nevertheless, Madison was not the single great Constitution-maker of the new United States. Neither was James Wilson. Neither was Gouverneur Morris, who played a large role as draftsman and in other ways. Neither was John Adams, who was in England at the time of the framing but whose role in the previous decade, making the argument that the states should form new governments and giving them advice about what that government should be, and serving as the chief writer of the Massachusetts constitution of 1780, was a large one indeed. None of these nor any of the other candidates was the single great lawgiver.

When many years later—in 1825—an admirer stuck on Madison the label "Father of the Constitution," Madison of course declined it; the Constitution, he said, was the work of many hands and many minds. He was one of a group of advertent and inadvertent collaborators who through their deliberations constructed the new government which was not exactly what any one of them would have designed or wanted, and not what most of them wanted exactly after it was done, either. The United States, as he was to write in *Federalist* 38, unlike all previous governments founded "with deliberation and consent," was framed not by "some individual citizen of preeminent wisdom and approved integrity" (Draco, Solon, Lycurgus) but by "a select body of citizens, from whose common deliberations more wisdom, as well as more safety," might be expected.

One can imagine that Madison really meant that. It is not impossible that he really did think it was better that a government should be shaped not by one lawgiver, not even himself, but by the deliberations of a body of citizens—by the checking and correcting and resisting and improving and stimulating of each other, which guards against the ego and interests and idiosyncrasy of any one, and gathers the wisdom of many, and adjusts the governmental form to the habits and characteristics and interests of a particular people. The United States was to a much greater extent than other nations the product of collaborative human contrivance, of reason and conscience, of deliberation. It might even be said to have been brought into being as a result of moral reasoning; its own beginning might itself be an example of that governance by mutual persuasion which is its own main point.

Of course we Americans, with that pride and self-congratulation of which all peoples are guilty, exaggerate the newness and the wonderfulness and the element of sheer human concoction in what was done—but, still, it was in some ways new, and it was also in some ways wonderful. And we are not altogether wrong to believe that it was, to an unusual degree, *done*. It was done by human hands, or rather by human minds, and not by mysterious superhuman powers from another world or inexorable subhuman forces in this one. It was done not by the long unconscious accumulation of dozens of generations but by quite specific human beings thinking it through at specific times and places in a relatively short period. The United States was brought into being not by an oracle in Delphi but by a committee in Philadelphia.

The framers were like the lawgivers of old, except that there was no single figure but many, and they composed the law in Williamsburg and Boston and now supremely in Philadelphia, rather than bringing it down from Sinai. There was no Solon or Romulus or Moses. There was no single figure who gathered up into his symbolic real or legendary self, by his foundational lawgiving or glorious deeds, by his connection with divine powers or charismatic leadership, the whole originating and defining action of the people. No doubt the monarchical impulse in human beings, to deposit all collective feeling in one king or queen or leader, applies double strength to the legends of a people's beginnings and moments of decisive self-definition. But the Americans, born in an age of post-Puritan Enlightenment and the intellectual clarity of the printing press, did not do it that way. In this regard, too, the American founding may be itself an example of the principle the founded nation was ideally to exemplify. One might say that the Americans resisted monofounderism (not a word I except ever to use again) as they did monarchy, on republican principle—the republican principle that was the moral content of their Revolution and of their founding of the nation.

Three

Some among the many hands that shaped the American government were not present in Philadelphia. John Adams's advice on the state constitutions in 1776, and especially his work on the Massachusetts constitution in 1780, set in motion ideas that would appear in Philadelphia in 1787; the first volume of his book defending the American constitutions, which he wrote in haste in London while he was the American minister, landed on the desks of the delegates just before the convention began.

James Madison, who did not think much of the ideas in that book, was no doubt much more influenced by his correspondence with his great collaborator in Paris. One may sense something of Madison's awareness of Jefferson from his letters. On October 24 he wrote from New York the long letter, already mentioned, to Thomas Jefferson in Paris telling him about the convention that had concluded the month earlier. That is an interesting moment: these two correspondents, the younger man now with this work in Philadelphia under his belt, Jefferson in Paris much interested, corresponding busily of course, the two of them intellectual and political companions already for eight years. After the preliminaries about which letter came when and what happened to a parcel of rice, and the like, Madison's long letter was, as one might expect, a long report on the convention and a set of explanations of the Constitution it had written: the executive, on which subject there were "tedious and reiterative discussion"; the Senate, the "great anchor of the government"; the due partition of power between the general and the local governments. But abruptly in the middle of this straight reporting there came a long and surprising editorial digression, in which Madison defended, and defended at great length, his support for that idea of his, that the new federal legislature should have had a veto—a "negative"—over the laws of the states. One wonders what Jefferson, over in Paris reading this letter, made of this extended digression on a point that was, as the lawyers say, moot. Madison had fought for that "negative," and fought hard, and been very disappointed to have lost out on it, but at the convention he had gathered himself together and kept on working to make the Constitution as good as it could be without that pet proposal of his; Madison was not one to gather up his marbles and go home when he did not get what he wanted as, some might say, Alexander Hamilton had done after his speech of June 26 at the convention, and as perhaps one might say of other delegates who left Philadelphia. Madison in that gathering of supreme importance in his life and in the new nation's life was, as always, thoroughly conscientious. He stayed, of course, right through the convention, participating, arguing, taking his notes and filling them in, in the evenings and weekends, endangering his health by how hard he worked on it, and finally, on September 17, with everybody else who was present except for three, signing the result. But here he was a month later in New York, writing his long and more or less objective account of the convention to his friend Jefferson, when suddenly he goes off for page after page of argument in behalf of that defeated negative. One might conclude that that defeat had really stung him, and that he had not got over it. Or, if that is too personal and emotional a way to put it, that he was still intellectually convinced that that proposal had been (almost) a necessity, and that even though defeated he wanted to get his position down on paper. He says in this letter that the union under this Constitution, without that federal veto, will be just a "federal system of republics," which is better than the "Confederacy of independent States" that it was under the Articles—"I admit the differences to be material"—but far short of what it might be and should have been, in Madison's view. Apparently, he really did have a strong disapproval of what the states had done and would do. He *really* had wanted the federal legislature to be able to veto the acts of states. And he had a theoretical position, worked out in those memos, that required greater strength at the center than he thought this Constitution provided. He *almost* said—this "Father of the Constitution" (put that very much now in quotes)—that the Constitution without it wouldn't work.

There may be another aspect, in this long digression in his letter to Jefferson, that is personal between them, these great collaborators. Madison had of course, in the run-up to the convention, written to Jefferson his idea about the negative. Jefferson had responded dismissively: the proposed congressional power to veto any state law "fails in an essential character, that the hole and the patch should be commensurate. But this proposes to mend a small hole by covering the whole garment." Madison did not think the hole was so small.

Near the end of the convention, on September 6, he had written Jefferson that the Constitution they were about to sign (that is, without that negative) would "neither effectually answer its national object nor"—and here perhaps is his more clear-cut and stronger objection—"prevent the local mischiefs which everywhere excite disgusts against the State governments." Madison himself certainly had his disgusts excited by those local mischiefs.

So now when he is writing to Jefferson to give a full summary of the convention he suddenly branches out into this extended defense of his defeated proposal—a defense, one might say, in part against Jefferson himself. It is so long and such an interruption that at the end of it he wrote: "Begging pardon for this immoderate digression."

And of what, now, does this immoderate digression, this extended defense of his defeated negative—defense against Jefferson, defense against the majority at the convention, defense perhaps against the judgment of history—consist? It consists of almost everything in *both* of his memorandums (in his vices memo, from item eleven) and in the key parts of this preconvention letters, now expanded somewhat; it consists of an anticipation of the argument that will shortly appear in his greatest *Federalist* papers, the ones that are number 10 and 51. It is the core result of his research project, and of the reason Madison has achieved historical distinction. And it is here all slugged into this letter to Jefferson, in defense of the defeated negative. One can say that that must have been of enormous importance to him. Or one can say that, once he got going, he just reached for the material he had worked out and put it in.

In this section of Madison's postconvention letter to Jefferson there are all the elements of his analysis in the vices memo, including that point with which its important item eleven begins, that people differ—that all civilized societies exhibit a range of interests and parties and factions—and that under the stimulus of this letter-writing he adds phrases that are illuminating:

> Those who contend for a simple Democracy, or a pure republic, actuated by the sense of the majority, and operating within narrow limits, assume or suppose a case which is altogether fictitious. They found their reasoning on the idea, that the people composing the Society, enjoy not only an equality of political rights; but that they have all precisely the same interests, and the same feelings in every respect. Were this in reality the case, their reasoning would be conclusive. The interest of the majority would be that of the minority also; the decisions could only turn on mere opinion concerning the good of the whole, of which the major voice would be the safest criterion; and within a small sphere, this voice could be most easily collected, and the public affairs most accurately managed.

But that is "altogether fictitious." It never is that way, in any elaborated society. People do *not* have precisely the same interests, or the same feelings in every respect. "We know however that no Society ever did or can consist of so homogeneous a mass of citizens."

That last is an important sentence. Madison is rejecting what seems to be implied in some notions of a republic founded on virtue, or in an ideal like Sam Adams's of a "Christian Sparta," and in many of the localist attitudes of the Antifederalists: that in order for a republic to work there must be a tight unity of attitude and interest, such as we may imagine at least sometimes to be found in small bands of human beings with some thick layer of common training, a commune or religious order. Or "approached," Madison himself says, in "savage societies." But a modern civilized state is not going to be like that. Human beings are going to differ.

Madison, in this letter to Jefferson, once more spells out the bases of these differences, a little more elaborately now than in his memo on the vices, and in particular beginning with and featuring differences based on property and varying economic function.

> A distinction of property results from that very protection which a free Government gives to unequal faculties of acquiring it. There will be rich and poor; creditors and debtors; a landed interest, a monied interest; a mercantile interest, a manufacturing interest. These classes may again be subdivided according to the different productions of different situations & soils, & according to different branches of commerce, and of manufactures. In addition to these natural distinctions, artificial ones will be founded, on accidental differences in political, religious or other opinions, or an attachment to the persons of leading individuals.

Madison then, for the only time in his several repetitions of this point, writing now to his fellow intellectual Jefferson, indulges in a comment, just among us philosophers, about the ground of some of these factions: "However erroneous or ridiculous these grounds of dissention and faction, may appear to the enlightened Statesman, or the benevolent philosopher, the bulk of mankind who are neither Statesmen nor Philosophers, will continue to view them in a different light."

Madison will not repeat that particular observation in his public presentations, when the bulk of mankind—nonstatesmen, nonphilosophers—was listening, but he will repeat the general point, most notably in *Federalist* 10: those differences of faction among human beings are a given.

Jefferson was an epistolatory participant in the great seminar surrounding the Constitution, if only in that in Madison's head was a voice that he had to answer, a mind to which he had to make explanations.

Four

In the work of the many hands who made the United States Constitution, in Philadelphia itself and elsewhere, may it not be said that there was an element of disinterestedness, of objectivity, of service to a lasting public good?

Of course there were small-state and large-state factions, and nationalists and localists, and protection of particular interests, notably slavery, and men of lesser as well as greater stature. Of course those persisting differences of interest and attachment that Madison had been analyzing since he wrote his memos, and analyzed again in his letter to Jefferson, were represented in the very convention itself. Of course there were deals. There were unedifying moments. Nevertheless, one cannot read about the proceedings without being impressed by the serious intention to serve the long-term good and the common good that moved above and through these disputes—indeed, the long-term and the common good not only of this republic, but of republicanism in human history.

Our idealism never comes pure, and it only sometimes appears as the chief ingredient of our position. Always there are mixtures. The naive idealist expects a purity that will never be. (And then is disillusioned when he doesn't find it.) The naive cynic sees a rigorous self-interest that rarely is so simple. If you are an American, gentle reader, filled with the American Creed, and you went to some universal conclave on political life, and you there defended, say, the great civil liberties, and their mixture with majority rule—might not someone from a vastly different political culture say you are just reflecting the self-interest of America? But that would not be right. If you said—we have to have those bases in the Philippines, *that* would be the self-interest of America (although that can be set in a larger frame of others' interests, too). But your defense of the principles of government that carry some universal moral ideal, although it would be limited and maybe even warped by the particularities of your own national experience, and by other things perhaps too ingrained for you even to identify, and although of course you and I have much to learn from others, as they from us—still, there is in your defense of those principles (freedom of conscience, say) something that transcends tribalism and touches what is universally worthy. In the best of the framers, and in the spirit of their meeting, there was an unusually high proportion of this fragile and worthy ingredient.

The framers and the other founders, judging by their speeches, certainly did feel the responsibility of the task that fell to them—the historic responsibility and the opportunity. They saw it as no merely provincial or temporary matter, but an extraordinary moment in the history of the world. Sometimes that appeared in a fear of failure. Thus Rufus King said on June 30 "that his feelings were more harrowed & his fears more agitated for his Country than he could express, that he conceived this to be the last opportunity of providing for its liberty & happiness."

Madison himself was a major source of statements about the large significance of their collective undertaking. He said in the Federal Convention on June 26: "It was more than probable we were now digesting a plan which in its operating wd decide for ever the fate of Republican Govt." Three days later he said that this was "a Constitution which we wished to last forever."

One of the most sweeping statements was that of Gouveneur Morris. He said on July 5 that "the whole human race will be affected by the proceedings of this Convention. He wished gentlemen to extend their views beyond the present moment of time; beyond the narrow limits of place from which they derive their political origin."

These statements by framers echoed that of John Adams more than a decade earlier, about the unique "fair opportunity" offered to the statemakers of the newly independent British colonies in America; now, however, with eleven years of sobering experience the United States have the further and grander opportunity to reconstruct their continental union. These statements also echo Thomas Paine's sweeping claims in '76, but now with a specific proposed government to give them substance.

They would continue through the contest over ratification. James Wilson would make one of the most striking statements in his defense of the Constitution in Philadelphia in November after the Constitutional Convention's end: "Numerous states yet unformed, myriads of the human race, who will inhabit regions hitherto uncultivated, were to be affected by the result of their proceedings."

Madison may in general have lacked eloquence but he could be counted on to soar when the topic was the significance of the American founding. In the peroration of *Federalist* 14, with the proposed Constitution now before the people, he celebrated the accomplishments so far and appealed to the people's better side: "Happily for America, happily we trust for the whole human race, [the American citizens] pursued a new and more noble course [than that of a "blind veneration for antiquity, for custom, or for names"]. They accomplished a revolution which has no parallel in the annals of human society. They reared the fabrics of governments which have no model on the face of the globe. They formed the design of a great confederacy, which it is incumbent on their successors to improve and perpetuate."

Then in late June of 1788, at the Virginia ratifying convention, he said at the beginning of his last major speech:

Mr. Chairman—Nothing has excited more admiration in the world than the manner in which free governments have been established in America. For it was the first instance from the creation of the world to the American revolution, that the free inhabitants have been seen deliberating on a form of government, and selecting such of their citizens as possessed their confidence, to determine upon, and give effect to it. But why has this excited so much wonder and applause? Because it is of so much magnitude, and because it is liable to be frustrated by so many accidents.

The "so much magnitude" of the American project was memorably noted then, after the Constitution was ratified and the new government begun, by the first president, in his inaugural address, drafted by Madison. George Washington would say that "the sacred fire of liberty, and the destiny of the Republican mode of Government, are justly considered as deeply, perhaps as finally staked, on the experiment entrusted to the hands of the American people."

Many quotations on this kind from American pens and voices could be gathered, of course, continuing down to the present. One supreme later echo, coming when the union was threatened with dissolution, will occur to everyone; it included the assertion that that contest was "testing whether this nation, or any nation so conceived and so dedicated, should long endure."

The Americans made some large claims. They said that their moment was a quite unusual opportunity in the history of the human race. They said that the form of government they were setting up, given that opportunity, was unique, new, without parallel in the annals of human society.

This unparalleled realization of an unparalleled opportunity to build a social order unparalleled in worthiness was a project carried out by an unparalleled work of conscious thought, of mutual deliberation; by "reflection and choice," as Hamilton put it in *Federalist* 1. It was done not for the benefit of residents of formerly British America alone, but for most, or all, of the peoples of the world, and not for the people now alive only but for "numerous states yet unformed, myriads of the human race."

Citizens of other countries, old and new, who believe that their nation is the bearer of important and universal ideals may bridle at what they may see to be the inflated claims of these Americans—that the entire history of liberty turns on their experiment. But the moral quality of this picture of the work of the American founders depends, to be sure, very heavily on its timing and context. At least in the context of the making and defending of the Constitution—if not in later moments—this high concept of America's world role appears primarily to have been not bragging or self-congratulation or pretense but a sobering effort to rise to the largest vision and highest purpose and to take the work, as yet undone and problematic, with the utmost gravity.

The Cloudy Medium of Words

AFTER HE SIGNED THE NEW CONSTITUTION on September 17, 1787, James Madison stayed for a few days in Philadelphia to write letters and complete his notes, and then departed, a good summer's work done, on September 21, for New York. The Congress—the decrepit old Congress under the Articles, which this Constitution proposed to supplant—was still meeting, and Madison was still a Virginia member. He passed through Princeton on his way to New York and doubtless learned that he was about to be given an honorary degree in recognition of his high public service; John Witherspoon, "the old Doctor," transmitted the diploma to his former student with words of praise and deep satisfaction. But despite what we may think today, Madison himself was not at the point of completed accomplishment at which one can sit back and calmly gather up honorary degrees and paragraphs of congratulation from one's old teachers; Madison was in the midst of, or perhaps one should say at the beginning of, an intense and enormously important political battle, the outcome of which was very much in doubt.

Looking back more than two centuries Americans may feel that the Constitution, once written and signed in that hot room in Philadelphia, slipped neatly into its place in the ongoing life of the new nation. But that is not what happened. It is very hard to recapture the doubt and uncertainty and difficulty that were very real on the other side of a great continental divide in history, after which all the waters that might have flowed in one direction flow instead in another. But there was no guarantee that a working Constitution would be written in Philadelphia, and perhaps even less that it would be ratified by enough states to set it in motion. That enough states did in the end is perhaps another miracle.

Madison was hurrying to New York to be a part of that battle. If the Philadelphia Constitution failed in ratification it would have been only a confusing footnote in history—but in whose history? Of what nation or collection of nations? Occasionally in the debates in Philadelphia the fear and uncertainty of the delegates would show through. If they failed to construct a union, a successful Constitution, then the colonies might fall into several warring confederacies, each making its deals with foreign powers. And now that they had written a Constitution there was still that same danger as the document they proposed was sent to Congress for transmittal to the ratifying conventions of the states. It might all have fallen to the ground; it was in the end a very close thing; and in the fall of 1787 Madison and Hamilton and the others could not know the outcome.

In the Congress in New York—step one—Madison and other delegates newly arrived from Philadelphia overcame the opposition (from Richard Henry Lee among others) by arranging that the Congress should simply submit the proposed Constitution to the states for their decision, without any recommendation one way or the other. For such a resolution the vote could be unanimous (a unanimity of states, of course).

The unanimity was another political stroke, about which the opponents grumbled; the use of the word suggested that the Congress unanimously recommended ratification, whereas in fact there was unanimity only on the point of submitting the Constitution to the states to consider ratification.

Madison was a leader in the group in New York that began politicking to get the Constitution ratified, writing strategic letters defending it, even though he had many reservations about it. In November, Alexander Hamilton, meanwhile, despite his much more severe reservations about it, had agreed to write a series of papers for New York newspapers making the case for the Constitution, and had begun to recruit some help. Therein lies a big story indeed.

From *Federalist* 1: "It has been frequently remarked that it seems to have been reserved to the people of this country, by their conduct and example, to decide the important question, whether societies of men are really capable of establishing good government from reflection and choice, or whether they are forever destined to depend for their political Constitutions on accident and force."

Alexander Hamilton, who wrote those sentences in the first of the *Federalist* papers, was perhaps the most "brilliant" (was he not?) of the major American founders. Hamilton came from nowhere to the top of

American leadership in an astonishingly short time. He had no family connections to give him his start, and no family plantation to provide his support. He had no Montpelier, Monticello, or Mount Vernon. He was not related to the Boylstons (John Adams's mother) or the Quincys or the Randolphs (Thomas Jefferson's mother). He was, in the contemptuous phrase of John Adams's that always is repeated (and I repeat it now) the "bastard brat of a Scotch pedlar" (Adams and Hamilton did not like each other) and he came from a remote West Indian island. Although he would marry into the upper levels of the New York state wealth and political leadership, he was not himself encumbered with any historic attachment to any of the states. He could think continentally, and did. He did not have college mentors like John Witherspoon or William Small or George Wythe or Adams's Harvard teacher John Winthrop; at King's College in New York, Hamilton was one of those students—from the point of view of professors an awkward presence—who are smarter not only than their fellow students but also than their professors. He turned out distinguished pamphlets in the scribblers' argument about the Revolution when he was nineteen years old. He rose rapidly in the Continental army and became one of the seven aides-de-camp to General Washington, certainly the ablest and closest to Washington; he wrote many of the general's papers. Ironically—and also perhaps revealingly—he was one of the very few Americans in the late eighteenth century who did not particularly respect George Washington—Hamilton was smarter than Washington was, too, and Hamilton certainly knew it—and Hamilton eventually got himself disengaged from the general. Washington was, however, loyal to Hamilton, and impressed with Hamilton's talents, whatever the story might be in the other direction, and remained his sponsor until his death. Washington as president gave to Hamilton the most important—as it was then—of the handful of cabinet posts, and Hamilton as Washington's secretary of the Treasury made those contributions to the nation's life that are the primary reason, or one of the two primary reasons, for his importance as an American founder. The other reason, of course, is his activity surrounding the Constitution—and especially the papers that now, in November of 1787, he began to write for New York newspapers.

When Hamilton and Madison, on their separate schedules, left Philadelphia for New York in September 1787, the first signs suggested that the prospects for the new Constitution were good. But by the end of October the opposition had begun to show its strength, especially in New York, where Governor Clinton was the leading opponent. In late September and early October the New York newspapers carried many articles attacking the Constitution. Alexander Hamilton's decision to produce (with others) the series of articles explicating and defending the Constitution arose in the context of the journalistic and political debate about it in New York state. Hamilton went to Albany in early October to a session of the New York supreme court and, apparently, made the decision while he was in Albany to organize and partly to write a series of essays defending the Constitution.

According to the legend repeated in all these retellings, he wrote the first number in the cabin of his sloop while he was returning from Albany to New York on the Hudson River. On October 27 the first number, signed as they were all to be with the pseudonym Publius, appeared in New York newspaper called the *Independent Journal;* Hamilton sent a copy of it to George Washington. It outlined the proposed series, appealed to the reader for moderation and reasoned judgment, and included the lines quoted above. The United States, he said, is to a greater extent than other nations the product of collaborative human contrivance, of reason and conscience, of thinking, of deliberation. And the outcome matters not only to Americans, but also to the world. Hamilton wrote that for "all good and considerate men" the "inducements of philanthropy" were added to those of patriotism, considering this great choice, because a mistake now by the Americans would be "the general misfortune of mankind."

From *Federalist* 2:

> Providence has been pleased to give this one connected country to one united people—a people descended from the same ancestors, speaking the same language, professing the same religion, attached to the same principles of government, very similar in their manners and customs, and who, by their joint counsels, arms, and efforts, fighting side by side throughout a long and bloody war, have nobly established their general liberty and independence.
>
> This country and this people seem to have been made for each other, and it appears as if it was the design of Providence that an inheritance so proper and convenient for a band of brethren, united to each other by the strongest ties, should never be split into a number of unsocial, jealous, and alien sovereignties.

"So proper and convenient for a band of brethren"! The Americans then often asserted that Providence had designed the match between their land, their ideals, and their nationhood—their union. But readers today may find a little startling Publius's claim that this people professes the same religion, and is descended from the same ancestors—that they are in blood and faith "a band of brethren." There may even have since come questions as to whether they speak the same language and have similar manners and customs. The better understanding of this new nation was already foreshadowed elsewhere in the *Federalist*. In spite of the fact that Americans do *not* have any of those traditional bases of national unity—

of blood, of religion, of manners or customs—nevertheless they are in another and better way unified: in attachment to a social creed. At its best the cement of this great nation was not to be tribal or territorial but ideal: a shared attachment to social principles of universal application. One hundred and fifty-six years after John Jay, writing as Publius in the second *Federalist,* wrote the paragraphs quoted above, the Swedish social scientist Gunnar Myrdal wrote, in perhaps the most important of twentieth-century studies of the United States, *An American Dilemma,* that

> Americans of all national origins, classes, regions, creeds, and colors, have something in common: a social ethos, a political creed. It is difficult to avoid the judgment that this "American Creed" is the cement in the structure of this great and disparate nation. . . . America, compared to every other country in Western civilization, large or small, has the most explicitly expressed system of general ideals in reference to human interrelations. This body of ideas is more widely understood and appreciated than similar ideas are anywhere else.

Hamilton never intended to write the whole series alone, and perhaps intended to have more collaborators than in the end he was to have. He asked a fellow New York political leader William Duer for contributions, but what Duer wrote was not up to the standard that was soon set for the series, and his essays were not included in the book publication. Hamilton "warmly pressed" Gouverneur Morris, the stylist and high nationalist from the convention, for his help, but Morris turned him down. John Jay, on the other hand, who had not been at the convention, accepted and was part of the plan from the start.

Jay was ten years older than Hamilton, six years older than Madison, an established New York lawyer and political leader who was at that time more distinguished than either of them. Jay had written the New York state constitution of 1777, one of that first crop of state constitutions following upon the May 10–15 resolution promoted by John Adams. That constitution in its turn, like Adams's constitution for Massachusetts and some others, had been a source for the Federal Constitution-writers in Philadelphia. Jay had also been one of the fledgling nation's leading diplomats; he had joined with Adams and Franklin to negotiate the Treaty of 1783 that ended the Revolution, and he had served as the secretary for foreign affairs—the equivalent of the later secretary of state—for the new nation under the Articles. He was later to negotiate the treaty that is named for him, and to serve as chief justice of the Supreme Court. He was to write, and did write, numbers of the *Federalist* having to do with foreign affairs. He wrote numbers 2 through 5, which celebrate the strength of union, and decry the weakness of disunion, in a hostile world. But after writing those numbers Jay had had a severe attack of rheumatism, and could not write anything more through the hard going of the winter; he was to produce only one later essay, number 64, defending the Senate's role in treaty-making.

Hamilton himself wrote the three numbers following Jay's set, numbers 6 through 9 pounding away on the weakness and danger of government under the Articles, or any loose confederation; he gave many historical examples, and conjured a frightening prospect of conflict among the American states, and entanglement in the intrigue and warfare of Europe, unless the American states were unified. For these and others of the early essays Hamilton drew upon the five-hour speech he had given back on June 18 in Philadelphia, while he was still attending the Federal Convention as a delegate from New York. That speech had been Hamilton's major, and nearly his only, contribution to the deliberations of the framers, and it was not a contribution that led much of anywhere. It had come while the convention was still sitting as a Committee of the Whole, with both the Virginia and the New Jersey plans before it; Hamilton had said—of course he would—that "he was obliged to declare himself unfriendly to both plans." His unfriendliness—stronger against the New Jersey than the Virginia plan—arose from the insufficient vigor, energy, union, strength at the center. He himself at the end of his extended and learned and energetic (but in context rhetorically ineffectual) speech had offered the nubbin of a plan of his own, which was that the American states approach as closely to the British system, with something like a king and something like a House of Lords, as they could, and that they stay as distant from democracy, from dependence upon the will of the people, as could be. That was not a program that was going to sell well to these newly independent and very "republican" Americans!

Hamilton had to assure the delegates the next day after his speech that he had not quite intended "a total extinguishment of state governments" (as Yates's notes put it) but he came close enough to require his unconvincing explanation. And his proposals of an elective kingship, which king would *appoint* the governors of the states and have the power of veto over *all* legislation, and of a Senate elected for life representing the wealthy few, and his endorsement of the patronage system of England ("corruption" to the whigs) were all sufficiently far outside anything the delegates could or would endorse that this long speech of Hamilton's, "brilliant" though it may have been, seems to have fallen to the floor of the Pennsylvania State House with a thud.

But Hamilton—who left Philadelphia soon after that speech—still had the extensive notes he had made in preparation for it, and could now draw upon them, in double anonymity, for the *Federalist* essays. Nobody knew he was writing the essays, because they were signed with the pseudonym Publius, and nobody knew he had given that speech, because the proceedings were secret. It would only be after the passage of many years that the public would come to know both. Hamilton could draw upon his outline for materials for *Federalist* 6 through 9, and again for 11, 12, 13, and again for 15 through 17 and 21 and 22. He could in those numbers attack the weakness and lack of energy of government under the Articles, or in any loose confederation or disunion, without his readers knowing that the writer's own solution to these weaknesses was a "high toned" anti-democratic government that they would be very disinclined to support.

But meanwhile Hamilton had attained another collaborator whose ideas about government were different from his, whose knowledge of the Constitutional Convention was much deeper than his, whose facility at high-level composition was almost as great as his, and whose capacity as a speculative political philosopher was greater than his. With this new collaborator, he would then join in producing what would become (though they surely did not think of them in this way at the time, turning them out at the rate of one thousand words a day, three or four essays a week) in spite of its time-bound polemical object, the greatest among American political classics.

When, in the middle of November, Hamilton asked James Madison to join in the project he turned for the first time outside the circle of New Yorkers (Jay, Deur, Morris) who were collaborating in an undertaking that had arisen in the context of New York state's battle over ratification. The joining of Hamilton and Madison in this great enterprise may appear to be yet another example of that strangeness of bedfellows that politics is said regularly to make. So it may appear from the perspective of the years, after what was to happen between them in the 1790s, and between their admirers and followers throughout subsequent American history. They would later be leaders of opposing parties on the Jay Treaty, the national bank, the alien and sedition laws, the commercial-eastern versus the agrarian-western interpretations of America's direction, and the loose versus the strict construction of the Constitution they had joined in making and defending. And it is true that Hamilton and Madison were rather different sorts of persons, and it is true that their political values were different and in some degree antagonistic—not only later, but also at this very time, and in these very essays, in which the inclinations that would one day make them opponents may already be discernible.

But politics not only makes but also keeps changing the strange bedfellows, by changing, and changing again, lines of division. On the very large topics by which the new nation was divided in the 1780s—whether government under the Articles was adequate, or whether there should be greater strength at the center of the union, and then whether the Constitution written in Philadelphia should be ratified, Hamilton and Madison were in agreement.

On the first of those questions they had been in agreement for some time. Madison and Hamilton had met in the Congress, then meeting in Philadelphia, in 1782—the Congress descended from that first gathering to which John Adams had gone in the fall of 1774, now acquiring a legitimacy under the Articles of Confederation (proposed in 1777, but not ratified until 1781) but also losing altitude fast in power and prestige and efficiency. The two young delegates—Madison had been thirty-one in 1782 and Hamilton four years younger—agreed with each other in deploring the weakness of Congress and the weakness of the union. They were part of a group in Congress—younger, for the most part—working to overcome its defects and to strengthen the national center. James Wilson of Pennsylvania was a part of this group. Madison has most often been thought of as a collaborator with Thomas Jefferson, as so he was, for all of his life. *The Great Collaboration,* by Adrienne Koch, describes their working together for almost half a century through the nation's beginnings. But in the 1780s, the most important stage of Madison's public life, he had other co-workers. Jefferson was in Paris. In the Constitutional Convention itself, as we have seen, there was a wide area of common purpose with the other most substantive delegate, James Wilson. And throughout the whole period leading up to that supplanting of the Articles by the Constitution, a ten-year period, there was a sharing of purpose, if not an overt collaboration, with Alexander Hamilton.

At the Annapolis convention in September 1786 they were prime movers, planning the call to the states for delegates to the convention the following May. They had time for long conversations—one might say, while waiting for other states to arrive (only five states sent delegations)—about their shared nationalist purposes. Then they played their contrasting roles in Philadelphia in the summer of 1787. And now, in the middle of the following November, Hamilton had asked James Madison for his help in this series—another important moment in the making of the United States—and Madison had agreed.

Madison was in New York ostensibly to serve as a Virginia delegate to Congress—the old Congress, now breathing its last breaths—but actually to politick for the ratification of the Constitution. While serving in that Congress he was working for a new government that would take that Congress's place. He was in touch with the "federalists," as they called themselves, the pro-ratification forces, in the states, and they with him. They urged him to publish a full and reasoned defense of the Constitution for their use in the ratification struggles in their states. And so when Hamilton asked him to join the Publius project, he set to work.

Though they were very different and although they wrote their essays independently of each other (there wasn't time to do otherwise) it was to be, all the same, another great *intellectual* collaboration—as was the founding as a whole.

From *Federalist* 10: "The latent causes of faction are thus sown in the nature of man; and we see them every where brought into different degrees of activity. . . . So strong is this propensity of mankind to fall into mutual animosities, that where no substantial occasion presents itself, the most frivolous and fanciful distinctions have been sufficient to kindle their unfriendly passions, and excite their most violent conflict."

On November 24 Madison's first entry was published—the number that would become, in the twentieth century, the most famous of all the *Federalist* papers and one of a handful of the most important documents in American history, the tenth *Federalist*.

In this essay he gathered up material from his memo on the vices, and from his speech on June 6 in the convention, and from his long letter to Jefferson of October 24. Madison in that now-famous number made the argument against those who insisted that republics had to be small. Montesquieu had written that it was so, and others had, too, and it was the conventional view. Hamilton had already attacked that idea in *Federalist* 9, quoting, as one does in such debates, Montesquieu from another spot. But Madison, drawing upon the clue he had from David Hume, carried the argument in favor of a *large* republic much further, to the point that it is usually said that he turned the argument of the opponents on its head: A republic *had* to be large—extended, compounded—in order to be lasting and successful.

If you are going to have a free country you are going to have contending groups: the assumption that there will be harmony is dangerous and wrong. Liberty leads to "faction." The causes of those factions are sown "in the nature of man." Madison went through a compressed list of the different kinds of division and contention that he had made on those previous occasions, and made more of the divisions of an economic kind that Hume had done: "But the most common and durable source of factions, has been the various and unequal distribution of property. Those who hold, and those who are without property, have ever formed distinct interests in society."

Madison then stated the effect that these factionalized interests have upon the mind and judgment of human beings, especially in groups, more effectively than he had done before:

No man is allowed to be a judge in his own cause; because his interest would certainly bias his judgment, and, not improbably, corrupt his integrity. With equal, nay with greater reason, a body of men are unfit to be both judges and parties, at the same time; yet what are many of the most important acts of legislation but so many judicial determinations, not indeed concerning the rights of single persons, but concerning the rights of large bodies of citizens; and what are the different classes of legislators, but advocates and parties to the causes which they determine?

Don't depend on enlightened statesmen to solve all of this: Madison wrote in one of the oft-quoted sentences: "Enlightened statesmen will not always be at the helm." Don't depend on religion or morality to restrain a passionate, self-interested majority faction either: "If the impulse and the opportunity be suffered to coincide, we well know that neither moral nor religious motives can be relied on as an adequate control." And there then comes a remnant of the notion of the increased immorality of groups that we found in his memo on the vices: "They [religions and moral motives] are not found to be such [an adequate control] on the injustice and violence of individuals, and lose their efficacy in proportion to the number combined together, that is, in proportion as their efficacy become needful." The more, the worse.

So what is the solution? Not an authoritarian state, repressing these contending self-interested groups: this is to be a *republican* government, a government in which liberty is preserved. And Madison was a good deal more aware than was Alexander Hamilton that the doctrine of human self-love, and the warp of our reasoning by self-love, affects authorities or rulers, and the "rich and well-born," at least as much as everyone else.

So what is the *republican* solution? It is twofold. The one most noted by twentieth-century readers of Madison's essay is to extend the sphere of the society to be governed, so that you take in "a greater variety of parties and interests," and thus make it less probable that a majority will have a common motive to invade the rights of others, and more difficult for them to do it if they do: there is a kind of safety in size and multiplicity. This was the point at which Madison, with that hint from Hume, directly contradicted the conventional view to which the opponents of the Constitution were appealing: that republics had to be small, that a republic could not work for so large a territory and population as the American states. Madison replied, yes it can—and it will be more likely to *stay* a republic, and to *last,* than would a pure little town hall democracy, which, he said, presents "spectacles of turbulence and contention," "as short in their lives as they have been violent in their deaths."

The collaborators under the pseudonym Publius were not, however, producing a treatise in political philosophy; they were arguing a concrete case for a specific political choice—for a specific document—in a close contest. The essays 15 through 22, including the three (18 through 20) that Madison got in part out of his old memo on confederacies, flailed away at the defects of government under the Articles; that section of Hamilton's plan for the series was completed with the publication of *Federalist* 22 on December 15, 1787. They were turning these pieces out at a remarkable speed, even if they did have some papers and notes in a drawer that they could draw upon. At the height of their production the essays were published, in a complicated scheme in the several New York newspapers, at a rate of four a week.

The two essayists now divided the task into big blocks of essays under large rubrics: Hamilton took the next set, on "the necessity of a Constitution at least equally energetic with the one proposed." The "at least" is interesting, given the deep reservations we know that Hamilton had about the Constitution he was defending. But this was congenial material to Hamilton: energy, energy, energy; vigor, vigor; union, union. You will at times have to use force, and from the national center, not just the state militias. There has to be armed strength. And there must be the power to tax, without depending upon the states to yield up "quotas." These essays by Hamilton ran from 23 through 36, the last one published on January 8, 1788. Presumably Madison in the meantime, there at a lodging house at 19 Maiden Lane in New York City through Christmas, was busily writing, storing up the essays he would be responsible for in the next block. He was now to defend—according to the original plan back in *Federalist* 1—"the conformity of the proposed Constitution to the true principles of republican government," and then to examine the Constitution part by part.

When Madison took over the wheel his first essay in this long sequence—twenty-two consecutive essays from his hand—was number 37, which was once better known than *Federalist* 10. In it Madison engaged in some very interesting introductory reflections on the problems faced in the work of the convention, and indeed in any such undertaking: "A faultless plan was not to be expected." As Aristotle had said, so now he is saying, do not expect more exactitude in politics than the nature of the subject allows.

From *Federalist* 37: "When we pass from the works of nature, in which all the delineations are perfectly accurate, and appear to be otherwise only from the imperfection of the eye which surveys them, to the institutions of man, in which the obscurity arises as well from the object itself, as from the organ by which it is contemplated, we must perceive the necessity of moderating still farther our expectations and hopes from the efforts of human sagacity."

Political thinking is difficult. The convention, says Madison, faced the further difficulty of a complex task, "combining the requisite stability and energy in government with the inviolable attention due to liberty and to the republican form."

Madison's discussion of the difficulty of conveying political ideas and decisions in *words* is one of the most interesting passages in all that he wrote, and has a distinctly modern ring:

> Besides the obscurity arising from the complexity of objects, and the imperfection of the human faculties, the medium through which the conceptions of men are conveyed to each other, adds a fresh embarrassment. The use of words is to express ideas. But no language is so copious as to supply words and phrases for every complex idea, or so correct as not to include many equivocally denoting different ideas. When the Almighty himself condescends to address mankind in their own language, his meaning, luminous as it must be, is rendered dim and doubtful, by the cloudy medium through which it is communicated.

The cloudy medium. Madison, though not as felicitous a writer as Jefferson nor as ready and fiery a writer as Hamilton, did his best with that cloudy medium, words. Consider the intricate complexity, a hall of mirrors, in James Madison's discussion, in *Federalist* 37, of the difficulties of the work of the convention—and of our relationship to it, now. He is writing, as though from outside, and in anonymity, about a convention of which he himself had in fact been an active member. We know now, as the readers then did not, that he wrote this essay. And we also know, as the public would not really know for decades (until after the death of the last surviving member of the convention—James Madison himself—in 1836) the exact shape and detail of the battles with that convention, and who said what, and who was on what side. And we now know those details including the role of the participant James Madison—primarily from the notes kept by the reporter James Madison.

And here now is a paragraph published in 1788 under the pseudonym Publius, written we now know by Madison, interpreting that most intense of all the battles in the convention, over the equal representation of states—most intense, especially to delegate James Madison. All the shifting lights of that prism of relationships shine through this calm interpretive paragraph:

> To the difficulties already mentioned, may be added the interfering pretensions of the larger and small states. We cannot err in supposing that the former

would contend for a participation in the government, fully proportioned to their superior wealth and importance; and that the latter would not be less tenacious of the equality at present enjoyed by them. We may well suppose that neither side would entirely yield to the other, and consequently that the struggle could be terminated only by compromise.

"We may well suppose" indeed! Madison is supposing what he knows, and what he much regretted at the time. And then he states what "it is extremely probable" happened: "It is extremely probable also, that after the ratio of representation had been adjusted, this very compromise must have produced a fresh struggle between the same parties, to give such a turn to the organization of the government, and to the distribution of its powers, as would increase the importance of the branches, in forming which they had respectively obtained the greatest share of influence."

There is evidence in the resulting document, writes this pretended outsider Publius, that something like that happened: "The convention must have been compelled to sacrifice theoretical propriety to the force of extraneous circumstances." It "must have" indeed.

Given all the difficulties, writes Madison, the "real wonder" is that they were surmounted. Madison does not often write in a pious tone, about a "finger of the Almighty hand," but here he does. "It is impossible for any man of candor to reflect on this circumstance, without partaking of the astonishment. It is impossible for the man of pious reflection not to perceive in it a finger of that Almighty Hand which has been so frequently and signally extended to our relief in the critical stages of the revolution."

Madison must have been working very hard and writing very fast through the last half of January and the month of February. In number 39 he defined what *republicanism* is, one might say, in a way that allows both the state governments and this Federal Constitution to fit it (he had given the defining of republicanism another whack back in *Federalist* 14), and then he descanted on the combined national-federal character of the proposed government in a way that Patrick Henry was to mock in the Virginia ratifying convention. One might also say that he made this argument in *Federalist* 40: (1) that the Convention did not exceed its powers; (2) it is good that it did.

In the next essays he examined the specific powers granted by the Constitution, and kept reassuring his readers about the powers the states will retain, a political necessity in his rhetorical situation. His readers knew, and cared about, their states; they did not know, and did not know whether to care about, this new *national* thing. Starting with *Federalist* 47 Madison explained the separation of powers. That doctrine emerged with particular clarity in the Convention, and in Madison's own mind, in the last half of the summer: the three branches are separated and independent, but also linked in certain ways to provide both a check on each other and a functioning government. He quoted from his friend Thomas Jefferson's *Notes on the State of Virginia* both in *Federalist* 48 and 49, in the second case, more to disagree than to agree with him. In the now-famous *Federalist* 51 he gave his view that the right kind of separation of powers provides a solution to the problem of government. He called up again the ideas about humankind and about pluralism from his memo on the vices and his other readings and thinkings; *Federalist* 51 now seems like a parallel to or continuation of *Federalist* 10. Whereas number 10 showed that the checking and balancing provided by multiple groups in an extended republic would help to preserve republican government in the social order at large, 51 shows how the checking and balancing provided by multiple separated powers help to preserve republican government within the federal structure: set ambition to check ambition. Several passages from 51 have become familiar, especially "If men were angels, no government would be necessary."

In this familiar passage Madison links government to human nature in a quotable way. He was dealing only with a subpart: how to contrive the "interior structure" of the federal government so that "its several constituent parts" may "by their mutual relations, be the means of keeping each other in their proper places." But in discussing this point—important to be sure but subordinate in the largest scheme of the argument—he was led to write passages and sentences that summarize the larger frame. Though in the last part of the twentieth century this passage has become a cliché—different parts of *The Federalist* are featured at different times in American history—perhaps nevertheless we should quote it here. In the immense pluralist democracy that James Madison helped to create, a cliché in one neck of the woods is fresh material in another.

From *Federalist* 51: "Ambition must be made to counteract ambition. The interest of the man must be connected with the constitutional rights of the place."

So far Madison is thinking about the Senate, the House, the president, the courts checking each other. But then comes his speculative flight: "It may be a reflection on human nature, that such devices should be necessary to control the abuses of government. But what is government itself but the greatest of all reflections on human nature? If men were angels, no government would be necessary. If angels were to govern men, neither external nor internal controls on government would be necessary."

One may disagree with him slightly: even angels would need government. Government is necessary even for angels because the essence of government includes not only coercion but also consent, not only restraining order but also clarifying order. When the angels play serious volleyball someone will need to say when to start and where the lines are and what the score is and whether the ball is in or out, even though there will not be any argument (each side yielding always to the other would be as confusing as each side always claiming its own). Order is a social good, a need of all creatures, dangerous though it be; we *want* and *need* it, and so would angels. The anarchists think not; some hold that voluntary cooperation solves all. But at least on any large scale for any serious purpose one needs something that looks very much like government; even angels could not build a transcontinental railroad—assuming angels would want to do that—by a Quaker meeting. The point of all this is to resist definitions of government that make it exclusively coercion, necessitated only by the Fall (by human sin—self-seeking, self-interested). Government is instead an interweave of coercion and consent, arising from an original social nature, and not our selfishness alone.

With the angels out of the way, Madison, in *Federalist* 51, went on to one of his important little summaries of American government: "In framing a government which is to be administered by men over men, the great difficulty lies in this: You must first enable the government to control the governed; and in the next place, oblige it to control itself."

The phrase "checks and balances" does not fully capture the complexity that Madison is here and elsewhere describing. The point is not simply to check and restrain the governors; it is also, first, before that, to be able to govern. Madison, like Hamilton and Wilson and others, had gone to Philadelphia to create a strong central government, in contrast to their frustrating experience under the Articles. They were not anarchists; they were not least-government people; they were not exclusively, or even primarily, intent upon erecting protection against government. They did not have the later American presumption against or hostility to government; their opponents, the antifederalists, had something on that order. The writers and supporters of the Constitution, on the contrary, were primarily and centrally intent upon producing a government that governed—an effective national government. But then—it must itself by governed, checked, balanced, held accountable, held within a republican frame.

> A dependence on the people is no doubt the primary control on the government; but experience has taught mankind the necessity of auxiliary precautions.
>
> This policy of supplying by opposite and rival interests, the defect of better motives, might be traced through the whole system of human affairs, private as well as public.

Madison himself has traced this policy through three *Federalist* papers. In number 46 Madison meanwhile had discussed that further dimension of checking and balancing, dropped into American laps by the accident of history and appropriated by the framers: that the states and the new federal government would be mutually restraining powers. *Federalist* 10, 46, 51: checks and balances among social interests; between states and the federal government; among the separated powers within government.

In numbers 52 through 58 Madison discussed the House of Representatives—in 54 the federal ratio in the composition of the House, of which more in another chapter; in 55, as we have noticed, with respect to the number of representatives. Madison at this point had produced twenty-two consecutive essays in a six-week period, and no doubt needed to shake his wrist and rest his fingers. Hamilton, home from court in Albany, took over with 59 through 61 on problems about the elections to Congress. Then a rested Madison took over for two long papers on the Senate, numbers 62 and 63, which were the last he was to write. He faced a delicate problem on one point in *Federalist* 62: how should he write about state equality in the Senate? In fact, as we know he himself had opposed and fought against it on principle almost to the point of pulling the convention apart. What would he now write? He did not write a defense of a position he did not hold, but simply noted the compromise as a fact to be accepted in amity, as such things must be, in a free society.

After the one late essay by Jay, Hamilton then carried the whole burden to the end, defending in eleven essays on the presidency the congenial doctrine of "energy in the executive," in six essays on the judiciary defending its independence and, as we have seen in 78, the practice of judicial review; in 84 attempting to justify the absence of a bill of rights, and then concluding. The last essay to be published in the series in the New York newspapers was number 79, on April 12, 1788. Meanwhile the first volume of the collection into book form had already been published, and was being rushed to the appropriate people: federalists who would use its arguments in New York and other states. Hamilton's last eight essays, making eighty-five in all, were added to the second collected volume.

Madison and Hamilton and Jay had not written their essays in a vacuum, or merely for what Abigail Adams called "futurity," or for the admiration of pedants; they had written those essays as part of an intense current political argument, with enormous consequences. They had opponents. There was another side.

Many of the points that they made which we today, studying *The Federalist* as a political classic, examine in isolation, were in fact written in response to a point made by their opponents. The passage from John Jay's *Federalist* 2 about the Americans as one united people, as we said, was an implicit response to the antifederalists' charge that the colonies were too heterogeneous to form a united republican government. Madison's idea, in *Federalist* 10 and elsewhere, about enlarging the sphere to make an extended, compound republic, was a trump card played upon the antifederalists' ace: their claim, backed by the authority of "the illustrious Montesquieu" and many others, and by the common sense of the time, and, as one antifederalist pamphlet said, by "the whole experience of mankind," that a republic had to be small. Although the paragraphs of Hamilton's on the role of the judiciary, in *Federalist* 78 and following, have been quoted again and again in subsequent American history as authoritative interpretation of the courts in the constitutional system, they did not come down out of the heaven of pure and abstract reasoning. They arose from the current debate; Hamilton was quite directly responding to a New York antifederalist essayist who signed himself Brutus, in the scamble of particular argument in a particular context. Hamilton's rather contradictory argument in *Federalist* 84 about the Constitution's lack of a bill of rights—that it does not need one, and already has one—is a response to what would be in the end the antifederalists' strongest point.

Why did Madison have to spend two essays—Federalist 52 and 53—defending the two-year term for Representatives? Because the antifederalists had made a point of it. They argued that two years was too long for a representative to be in office without coming home and mingling with the people and facing the votes: "Where annual elections end, there tyranny begins." Well, said Madison of this old radical whig slogan, although generally such proverbial sayings are founded in reason, once they harden into bumper stickers they may be "applied to cases to which the reason of them does not extend."

Why did Madison spend parts at least of no fewer than four essays (number 55, 56, 57, and 58) defending the small size of the House of Representatives? Today we would not think that, among all the questions that might be raised about the Constitution, that one was the most pressing. But the antifederalists kept raising that issue, so Madison answered.

The argument between these two groups was our first nationwide American political contest, carried on in thirteen different venues but with ideas, arguments, pamphlets, correspondence, and some organization crossing state lines. While Madison was producing his essays he was also energetically writing letters arguing strategy and substance in the ratification battles in the states. The smaller states, as Madison had predicted, ratified easily. For various reasons they *needed* the union. The important battles would be in the four big states. Pennsylvania had ratified, by means that do not bear close examination, before he and Hamilton began writing their essays. Massachusetts, in a close and important contest, ratified while they were writing. But the Constitution would never work without New York and, above all, Virginia. Conventions in both of those states would meet in June, and it was there, in the home states of the two chief writers of *The Federalist,* that the fate of the Constitution would be decided.

On March 4, 1788, cutting it pretty close, Madison had put down his pen and left New York for Virginia. Already in early February friends in Virginia had been insisting that they needed Madison's help, and that he must return home in order to be elected to that ratifying convention. He barely made it.

The Peculiar *Federalist* Paper

BEFORE WE FOLLOW MADISON to the fight in Virginia in the spring we may pause to lift into view one of the *Federalist* papers that Madison wrote in the winter. This one, if you read between the lines, has a poignancy that sets it apart from the others. It is number 54, published on February 12, 1788, part of the sequence of papers defending the Constitution's provisions for the House of Representatives.

Perhaps on a first reading a reader will not find it any different from the papers that go before and after—just another dose of closely argued political science. But when one scrapes off layers to lay bare its subject, and when one notes who is writing it (at the time the reader did not know who wrote it, but we do) then one realizes that underneath the dry lines of political argument there is that tragic dimension, mentioned before, that Americans sometimes think that they have escaped.

The division of labor with Hamilton meant that Madison had to defend, along with other constitutional provisions about the House, the federal ratio—the three-fifths ratio—by which each state would be assigned its number of representatives. In the decades to come that provision was destined to be notorious—a major item in the grievances of the free states toward the "slave power." It would be widely denounced in the North; abolitionist journals, in the 1830s and after, would regularly cite the accretion of extra and, in their view, altogether unjust representation that would accrue to the slave states as a result of this provision: as many as 25 representatives in a House of not many more than 200 throughout the second quarter of the nineteenth century. Maybe more. In the reappointments following the 1820 Census, two free states would have 64 representatives, and 8 slave states, with only a tad larger population, would have 100 members. The outcome of many important votes would be altered by margins like that. In 1843, the legislature of Massachusetts passed a resolution drafted by Charles Francis Adams, which his father John Quincy Adams then introduced to the House: "to amend the Constitution by doing away with the right of slaveholding states to count every five slaves as equal to three white men in establishing representation." The effort failed in the House (a House skewed by the provision the resolution was directed against) by an overwhelming vote: 156 to 13. The next year the House refused three times a resolution to the same effect. The ratio continued to affect the foundation of power in Congress until it was altered not by resolutions or votes but by the force of arms— practically, until the "gentlemen of the South" withdrew in 1861, and constitutionally until the thirteenth amendment rendered it obsolete in 1865, after the Civil War.

Did Madison, faced with the job of defending the provision back before it was adopted, "believe in" this curious expedient from the Philadelphia summer? He wanted the Constitution to be adopted, so he had to defend it.

The issue was this: Do slaves count in a state's population for the purpose of assigning a state its number of members of the House—the body in the new government that is based on population? It will be remembered that the Federal Convention had borrowed that federal ratio from the arrangement made under the Articles of Confederation for a quite different purpose: that of assessing a state's capacity to pay when assigning *taxes* among the states. In that case the amount of *property* in the state was an appropriate criterion. But now this curious formula was to be used in counting a state's population to see how many House members the state should have. It was to be used, in other words, to shape the foundation of power in the new republic: states with large numbers of slaves would have those *extra* representatives, beyond those they would have on the basis of free persons. The formula was also to be used, in what was to give the appearance of compromise, for assigning proportions of direct taxes to the states, but direct federal taxes never became an significant source of revenue for the new government.

And in order to give this weird provision some kind of a logic there had to be a carefully controlled admission that the slave was a human being (otherwise why count slave property and not horse property?) but—not too much of a human being (or else why not count him the same as other persons?). In order for the provision to make such sense as it could make, it had to be argued that the slave was a fractional combination of property and person, with the latter, as compared to whites, somewhat diminished. The peculiarities of the power-political situation meant that in this context those ordinarily least likely to insist on the humanity of the slave—the slaveholders and their state spokesmen— were *most* insistent upon it, because the more the slave was a person, the greater the justification for his being "represented," and therefore the greater the slaveowners' power—therefore the more representatives their states had in the House. And conversely, those otherwise most likely to resist the categorization of the slave as sheer property—those from free states, or states with few slaves—in this context were most insistent that the slaves were simply property, like the property they owned, in the North, which did not count in assigning numbers of representatives.

The flavor of a southern defense of the provision may be discovered in the speech made back home by a man who had been a delegate to the Constitutional Convention—one of the framers—named William R. Davie, from North Carolina. In July of 1788 at that state's convention considering the ratification of the Constitution it fell to him to defend this provision. "The Eastern [i.e. northern] States had great jealousies on this subject. They insisted that their cows and horses were equally entitled to representation; that the one was property as well as the other."

But over against that position the slaveholding states had a power-political interest that Davie stated straightforwardly: "It became our duty, on the other hand, to acquire as much weight as possible in the legislation of the Union; and, as the Northern States were more populous in whites, this only could be done by insisting that a certain proportion of our slaves should make a part of the computed population."

This was what was at stake throughout: "In order [for the slaveholding states] to acquire as much weight as possible in the legislation of the Union," Davie said, they had to insist on counting slaves, and in order to justify counting slaves they had to insist that these slaves were (somewhat) human.

The northern states arguing *against* this extra representation, maintained, among other points, as Davie reported to his Carolina colleagues "that, in a time of war, slaves rendered a country more vulnerable, while its defence devolved upon its free inhabitants." But he told his Carolina colleagues how he and his fellow slave-state delegates responded: "On the other hand, we insisted that, in time of peace, they [the slaves] contributed, by their labor, to the general wealth, as well as other members of the community—that, as rational beings, they had a right of representation, and, in some instances, might be highly useful in war. On these principles the Eastern States gave the matter up, and consented to the regulation as it has been read."

The point most to be noted slips by quickly in Davie's argument: the slaves as "rational beings" had a "right to representation." This did not, of course, mean that the slaves had the "right" to be represented by representatives whom they, as rational beings, helped to choose; far from it. For slaves to have had a vote, or civil liberty of any kind, was out of the question to the white population of the slave states, and to most of that of the free states as well. Their "right" to representation would be exercised altogether by their masters; the net result of noting their rationality would be an increase in their masters' power. The slaveholders and defenders of slavery asserted, for the moment, in this context only, up to a point, the rationality and humanity of the slave—because it served their own political interest to assert it.

It was this twisted moral-political provision that Madison, scribbling away in New York, had to defend, back in February of 1788, a few months before Davie would make his presentation in the North Carolina ratifying convention.

Madison faced a quite different rhetorical situation from that of Davie. He was writing under a pseudonym, shared with Hamilton and Jay, so that the reader did not know from what region the writer came, or whether the writer was a slaveholder or how he stood on slavery. Madison was not in a position to appeal to the interests or values just of one state or region; although *The Federalist* was in the first instance directed toward the voters in New York state, it quickly became a handbook for supporters of the Constitution in other states as well, North and South. So Madison as Publius had to defend this provision, as it were, to all comers.

And how did Madison defend it? First, characteristically, he stated the challenge clearly. Madison was scrupulous in stating clearly his opponents' points: "Slaves are considered as property, not as persons. They ought therefore to be comprehended in estimates of taxation which are founded on property, and to be excluded from representation which is regulated by a census of persons." So his opponent would say.

How then does he answer the objection he has himself so accurately put? The most striking feature of his answer is the rhetorical device that in this delicate situation he chose to use—for the only time in *The Federalist*. This device, in addition to its strategic value, may also suggest the fundamentally bad conscience, the moral faultline, underneath his discussion.

The device was this. Madison, already hidden behind the anonymity of the collective pseudonym Publius, now invented another layer of distancing. Having briefly stated the challenge of this provision "in its full force," he announced that he would be "equally candid" in stating "the reasoning that may be offered on the opposite side," which he then did for four pages. But he did not do so in his own right. He invented an anonymous one of "our Southern brethren," and gave the defense of the federal ratio as from the mouth of this fictitious spokesman, put in quotation marks for almost four pages.

"We subscribe to the doctrine, might one of our Southern brethren observe," he wrote, and continued, in the voice of this southern brother, "that representation relates more immediately to persons, and taxation more immediately to property, and we join in the application of this distinction to the case of our slaves. But we must deny the fact that slaves are considered merely as property, and in no respect whatever as persons. The true state of the case is, that they partake of both these qualities: being considered by our laws, in some respects, as persons, and in other respects as property."

Madison's fictional-rhetorical southerner coolly identifies those regards in which a slave is property: "In being compelled to labor not for himself, but for a master; in being vendible by one master to another master; and in being subject at all times to be restrained in his liberty, and chastised in his body, by the capricious will of another, the slave may appear to be degraded from the human rank, and classed with those irrational animals, which fall under the legal denomination of property."

Does one detect in the way Madison (as Publius as southern brother) puts this point a suggestion of moral disapproval, in language—e.g., "capricious will"—that might not be used by a true believer?

He then put as a parallel those regards in which a slave is nevertheless a person: "In being protected on the other hand in his life and in his limbs, against the violence of all others, even the master of his labour and his liberty; and in being punishable himself for all violence committed against others; the slave is no less evidently regarded by the law as a member of society; not as a part of the irrational creation; as a moral person, not as a mere article of property."

And so this fictional character concludes: "The federal constitution therefore, decides with great propriety in the case of our slaves, when it views them in the mixt character of persons and property. This is in fact their true character." It had been James Madison, of course, who in Philadelphia had explicitly condemned admitting in the Constitution's text that there could be "property in man." But in this polemical context, behind his two masks, he must justify its recognition.

Madison's fictitious southerner then makes an argument that one may guess not many real slaveholders would have made:

It [the mixed character of persons and property] is the character bestowed on them by the laws under which they live; and it will not be denied that these are the proper criterion; because it is only under the pretext that the laws have transformed the negroes into subjects of property, that a place is disputed them in the computation of numbers; and it is admitted that if the laws were to restore the rights which have been taken away, the negroes could no longer be refused an equal share of representation with the other inhabitants.

This paragraph implicitly admits the moral illegitimacy of slavery, if you take the word *rights* seriously, as Madison and the founding generation certainly did. "The laws under which they live" have "taken away" a slave's rights (would a real and average white slaveowner acknowledge that?). If the law should "restore" those underlying, suppressed rights— then of course these human beings would be entitled to full representation.

Madison's southern spokesman answers other points, taking seriously the "compromise" that joins apportioning taxes, which favors one side, with apportioning representation, which favors the other.

Slaves are not counted for apportioning representation in the governments of southern states themselves? But—his spokesman answers—by the convention's rule there should be "no regard for the policy of particular states toward their own inhabitants." So, in theory, slaves should be counted *fully*, (just as inhabitants disqualified from citizenship elsewhere in the states) since it is none of the union's business what states do in that regard. But we—the slaveholding states—those who would be gainers— waive that consideration, says Madison's character grandly. "All that [we] ask is, that equal moderation be shewn on the other side. Let the case of the slaves be considered, as it is in truth a peculiar one. Let the compromising expedient of the constitution be mutually adopted, which regards them as inhabitants, but as debased by servitude below the equal level of free inhabitants, which regards the *slave* as divested of two fifths of the *man*."

All of this is in the voice of the southern spokesman. When Madison had finished his argument from that voice he said in his own right [Publius's own right]: "Such is the reasoning which an advocate for the southern interests might employ on this subject: And although it may appear to be a little strained in some points, yet on the whole, I must confess, that it fully reconciles me to the scale of representation, which the convention have established."

"May appear to be a little strained in some points"! Thus Madison brackets the argument he has made in the mouth of an invented spokesman, and sets it at a distance from his own view, and then, with this touch of a reservation "strained in some points"—he accepts it—but only "on the whole." The most revealing aspect of this paper is this distancing rhetorical device—unique in *The Federalist*.

If in addresses to general American audiences in the bicentennial time one included references to James Madison, then almost invariably the question period would generate the query—more potent today than anything about factions or federalism—what was Madison's relationship to slavery? Repeatedly the question would be asked, coolly at best, by black persons—distancing themselves in their turn from this lifelong slaveowner whom many of their white countrymen were seeming uncritically to celebrate, along with the other founding fathers.

But—to try to respond to that challenge—all of us should be judged in the context of our own time, identity, and circumstance—eighteenth century or twentieth, black or white. Very few human beings move out of the line, toward a larger justice, from what is accepted, habitual, and institutionalized in their own time, group, and place. And still fewer do so wisely, and effectively. James Madison, with the help of a unique revolutionary moment, is one of the few who did so—not only on republicanism but also—to a lesser degree—on the subject of slavery, which he knew to be a contradiction to that primary faith of his.

The real James Madison, who in this essay was hidden under two layers of disguise, condemned slavery all his life. His most recent biographer, the biographer of his old age, as it were, Drew McCoy, wrote that "on the level of principle . . . Madison's antislavery credentials can be fairly described as impeccable. Throughout a long public career (and an even longer life) he never waivered for a moment in utterly condemning the institution."

He opposed that institution not only in principle but to an extent—more one may presume to say than most of us would have done—in action as well. Personally, he did so, or tried to do so, in his youth—exactly in the decade of the great research project described in these pages—by attempting to disentangle his own financial support from the institution of slavery. As the oldest son of James Madison, Sr., he was the heir to the plantation, Montpelier, with 118 slaves—the largest slaveowner in Orange County. That was the foundation of his economic well-being. How many twentieth-century Americans, black or white, would in a comparable conflict of moral conviction with personal economic well-being strive to the degree that Madison did to disentangle themselves from a morally repulsive inheritance? Young Madison, the child of the republican revolution, did try to arrange his life so that he would not be dependent economically on slavery—by uncongenial law studies, and by uncongenial speculations in land and by other projects. He was not successful. He was caught up in public duties, that took his time and energy across five decades. At the end of his life—long after the years considered here—after he had served in the great office he helped to design, president of the United States, he returned with Dolley to Montpelier, but even in that period, in which he settled into the life of a slaveowner on a plantation, he continued to oppose slavery not only in his statements about it but, by his lights, in his actions as well. A knowledgeable modern reader of pages on Madison could even write in the margins "Madison spent the last thirty years of life opposing slavery!"

As to his treatment of slavery in his public thought and action, there were as we have seen abrupt flashes of lightning on the subject of slavery suddenly breaking through his memos—a moment only. These were sparse and rare but very important interventions in the deliberations of the Philadelphia convention—his insistence that the Constitution not recognize "property in men," and his exclamation of woe at the eight-year extension of the period during which the slave trade could not be interfered with.

We have noted in an earlier chapter the hitherto little noticed writings of Madison, made in 1791, in which he stated more explicitly than elsewhere the opposition between republicanism and slavery not only in principle but also in the kind of society that slavery creates. These writings are some notes Madison made in preparation for essays he would write in the new Jeffersonian-Madisonian journal, edited by a Princeton classmate of Madison's, the *National Gazette*. These notes or jottings constitute almost, one might say, yet another memo to himself in the sequence of his studies. And they do include, again, references to various ancient and modern confederacies and republics. One section treats the "Influence of domestic slavery on Government," and spells out succinctly and unequivocally the contradictions hinted at in the lightning flashes in his earlier memos. He began plainly enough: "In proportion as slavery prevails in a State, the Government, however democratic in name, must be aristocratic in fact. The power lies in a part instead of the whole; in the hands of property, not of numbers. All the ancient popular governments, were for this reason aristocracies. The majority were slaves." But the question then arises: On the same principle, what about the slave states of the United States? Madison answered forthrightly: "The Southern States of America, are on the same principle aristocracies."

He continued, nailing down another point, with his respect to his home state: "In Virginia the aristocratic character is increased by the rule of suffrage, which requiring a freehold in land excluded nearly half the free inhabitants, and must exclude a greater proportion, as the population increases. At present the slaves and non-freeholders amount to nearly ¾ of the State. The power is therefore in about ¼."

Does that make a difference in policy? Of course it does. Madison wrote: "Were the slaves freed and the right of suffrage extended to all, the operation of the Government might be very different." And he was willing to concede that that made the South less "republican": "The slavery of the Southern States, throws the power much more in the hands of property, than in the Northern States."

It was a candid and intellectually honest page.

But if one would defend Madison, as a representative of a rare public virtue, against the easy condemnations of persons from a different time and circumstance, one would in the end also have to acknowledge that he is vulnerable to judgment exactly by the high standards he himself set. Those 1791 jottings spelling out the contradiction between a slave society and republicanism, to which Drew McCoy calls our attention, were never made public. They did not appear in speeches, essays or public argument, in the way the material from his memos had done—these are private reflections only. They never found a publisher. Madison's later career, with respect to slavery, as McCoy describes it, is marked by a dimension of tragedy; to a degree, so is his earlier career, even in the high point of the 1780s.

What do we mean when we speak of the tragic dimension of politics? Something more, presumably, than that human beings in politics make choices in a situation they did not choose, among restricted alternatives, involving the sacrifice of many goods—although that is part of what we mean. A political person—which is to say any of us—is born in some Orange County, with some heritage of the accumulated decisions and nondecisions of others, like African slavery, already an entrenched institution: we did not choose it. (One mark of Thomas Jefferson's writings when they touch on slavery is the sharp insistence with which he blames it all on somebody else—in the failed paragraph of the Declaration of Independence, on the British king—and of course that assigning responsibility to somebody else is 95 percent correct. But not 100 percent correct.) And in a profound political situation every choice we have entails some sacrifice of good, some acceptance of evils. If one is engaged in a great moral project—the primary commitment, to construct after the world's first successful colonial revolt the world's first large-scale lasting republican government—then one must accept the terms that history presents and subordinate other commitments.

But all of human life is marked by such limitations; high politics has a deeper level of the tragic because it is the realm of *power*—of the larger impact of the will of some on the life of vast numbers of others. What thirty-nine men in Philadelphia do, and do not do, on a few summer afternoons—to write into the Constitution of the New Order of the Ages, the three-fifths ratio, and the provision for the recovery of fugitive slaves, and the period of toleration of the slave trade—will reach into the lives of the 4 million persons—including particularly 700,00 black persons— across fifteen hundred miles of Atlantic coastline in the late eighteenth century, and beyond that into the lives of the growing numbers of their children for seven decades to come, down to the "terrible scourge of war," and long beyond that, too, and outside those boundaries, too: it will reach into African villages where eight extra years of the United States market for slaves will bring 40,000 new slaves into the New Order for the Ages. Part of what we mean by the tragic in politics—by no means an exact term—is the *disproportion* of causes to effects, as in Shakespeare, when a character's not-too-unusual obtuseness or indecision or ambition in the early acts has by the last act littered the stage with falling bodies and pitiful and terrible destruction.

But magnified effects and hard choices do not alone constitute tragedy: one must add the effect of the humanness of the agents who make those choices and produce the effects. The aspect of the tragic that hovers over high politics springs not only from what is *outside* the political actor, but *inside* him (or now her), too. Although James Madison would oppose slavery as a moral evil all his life, both in his personal life and in his public positions, both in thought and in action, he did so in the context of other beliefs and commitments that subordinated that conviction. Where we stand on a great matter is not the only question to be asked; another is, Where do we place that great matter in the hierarchy of decision—down with the lesser numbers, among those matters deferred or set aside, or at the top? The historian Don Fehrenbacher, summarizing for the purpose of recounting later episodes in the history of this matter, wrote that at the Constitutional Convention and for the first half century of the nation's life, slavery was an *interest* ("concentrated, persistent, practical, and testily defensive") whereas antislavery was only a *sentiment* ("diffuse, sporadic, moralistic, and tentative"). The failures of the founders, and particularly the framers, to do more of what we now believe they could have done to restrict slavery, even within the limits of practical reality, comes from the contrast those two terms imply—the blunt strength of the pro-slavery side, the weakness on the other side.

Suppose that Madison had put as high a priority on restricting slavery—"putting it in the road to ultimate extinction," to borrow a term from later politics—as he did with these two other matters: religious liberty and making state power in the new Congress proportional. On the second matter he and James Wilson and some other big-state people were willing to oppose the small-state delegates, on the issue of state equality, fiercely and consistently, to the point of bringing the Federal Convention to the brink of dissolution on July 16–17. But as we have already said, they did not engage in any test of wills with South Carolina and Georgia over slavery remotely comparable to their test of wills with Delaware and New Jersey over state equality.

On religious liberty, Madison and Jefferson in Virginia after the revolution were leaders of opinion, well out in front of most others, aggressively shaping opinion and calculating political forces; Jefferson in the previous decade had gone out of his way to promote the radical change in the law code of Virginia represented by his bill establishing religious freedom, and in the 1780s Madison not only produced the greatest defense of its principles—the anonymous Memorial and Remonstrance against Religious Assessments—but took bold political initiatives as its floor leader in the Virginia General Assembly to get it passed. Together these two young Virginia statesmen took a position that was by no means the dominant one in the state, one that had fierce opposition—Jefferson said at the end of his life that the fight over religious liberty in Virginia was the severest contest he was ever engaged in—and put together the alliances, and the arguments, and the legislative strategy, against the odds, to get it passed. On issues touching slavery Madison took no comparable initiatives or risks, and exercised no comparable political leadership.

Although it is clear that Madison was distressed by aspects of the compromises with slavery in the Constitution, in the end he acquiesced, and in *The Federalist* defended the three-fifths ratio. Here were writings with a pin on the rind of a young oak of another kind than Paine intended—minute writings—that would reveal themselves in large character on the full-grown tree in a burgeoning empire of slavery and a conflict that would rend the union.

In the last years of his life, settled into Montpelier as a slaveowning Virginian, Madison endorsed two dubious schemes with respect to slavery. One of these was the idea of "diffusion" that was put forward by some slave-state people at the time of the Missouri question in 1820— Thomas Jefferson also endorsed it, more avidly than Madison. The nation faced its first big contest over the territory into which slavery would be allowed to move, and southerners putting forward this idea held that the institution should, for everyone's good, be "diffused" throughout the entire nation, thus by spreading it to share its burdens—including its moral burdens—more fairly among the states and regions. What that would have meant in fact was the creating of a slave nation. It was the opposite of the "containment" policy that Lincoln and the Republicans would hold to in the 1850s—confine the institution absolutely to its present boundaries.

The other idea the elderly Madison not only endorsed but took a leading role in sponsoring was colonization. The program of the American Colonization Society was: the gradual emancipation of slaves— solely at the discretion of the slaveowners, voluntarily manumitting their slaves—and the emigration of the freed slaves to another place, a colony (hence the name) in the West Indies, in South America, or, as it developed, in Africa, and specifically to the newly established nation of Liberia with its capital of Monrovia (named for President Monroe). That program was loaded with convenient ambiguities and was therefore ideal for politicians and public leaders caught in a hard spot either with their constituencies or with their consciences. Was the emigration of blacks to be voluntary or were they to be—deported?

Colonization attracted the support of many of the nation's worthiest citizens. The talented straddler Henry Clay was one of the founders of the society; his young admirer out in Illinois Abraham Lincoln supported the idea almost all of his life, right up into the President's House; Thomas Jefferson in his old age supported it and many of the nation's "most eminent divines," as they used to call them, and statesmen and public benefactors supported it. James Madison, the last of the "fathers," was in his old age and eminence the head of the colonization society.

The colonization idea could be presented, because of its useful ambiguity, in radically different ways. It could represent a genuine effort, however misguided, to bring an end to slavery; Abraham Lincoln, addressing the local colonization society in 1853 and 1855, would trace the history of abolition, of the ending of the slave trade, of the action of heroes like Wilberforce, would enter into his notes for the talk the phrase "All the while—individual conscience at work" and then would bring the history of this work of conscience against slavery to a climax with the society to which he was speaking, the American Colonization Society.

No doubt a major motive of many in that society—young Lincoln and old Madison included—was a genuine opposition to slavery. Many abolitionists started as colonization people. Colonization was sufficiently antislavery to draw the ire of the most excitable defenders of slavery; proposals that Congress appropriate funds to support colonization were one item in the list of frightening developments that provoked the frenzied atmosphere in South Carolina after 1830.

But colonization could at the same time be presented as a way to rid the nation of free negroes (an anomaly, embarrassment, and danger, from the point of view of a race-based slavery) and also to deflect antislavery agitation.

The colonization movement included under its great tent of ambiguity a wide range of opinion on slavery and race; it also corresponded to that mixture that a great many Americans, then and now, have within themselves, in the emotion-fraught issues of race and slavery: to want to end slavery—but not too soon. To want to see evils overcome—but not with any disruption. To want a better world for everybody—but gradually. Not too fast. What would happen if slavery were ended tomorrow? Can you imagine it? The well-disposed portion of the broad American public had in it a very great tendency to evade this difficult complex of issues: not to face it. To avoid it. To keep it ambiguous. When the abolitionists would come on the scene in the 1830s they would direct their scornful fire most of all at the colonizers: by their method American slavery never would be ended.

In Drew McCoy's *The Last of the Fathers* there is suggested another dimension of the older Madison's connection to slavery: he drew back, and compromised, and remained silent, and endorsed the meretricious proposal of the colonization society, not in spite of but exactly because of his intense commitment to the republican legacy his whole life had served. It is one of the poignant features of the tragic that the destruction comes not from malice or simply from weakness but from misguided strength.

But the shadow of tragedy over Madison's connection to slavery is not the end of the story, nor are the compromises of the Constitution the only legacy of the framers and the founders. When we identify the claim that stood counter to the *interest* of slavery we should not stop with the founders' *sentiment* of antislavery, with its comparative weakness and lack of persistence. In an earlier chapter, listing the accomplishments of the founders with respect to slavery, we listed, along with items specifically touching that institution, the institutions of liberty in the constitutional system they devised—especially the freedoms of thought and speech and petition and "free argument and debate." And we should add the premises implicit in those institutions, and explicit in the great Declarations and Bills of Rights that defined the nation's moral core. Out of these there would be generated, beginning at about the time Madison in his eighties was dying at Montpelier, an antislavery movement, and a social conviction, which was now no mere sentiment—which was now organized and persistent and given by some persons the highest priority. There would come the "terrible scourge of war"—"and the war came," and 600,000 dead and lasting scars. Nevertheless, although the stage of this tragedy was, at the curtain, littered with fallen bodies and terrible destruction, it was not a result that offered pity, terror, and catharsis only, with no meaning or accomplishment. Far from that. During and after the terrible war America came to grant three essential nation-making points which had not been unambiguous in the founding, and without which the

United States could have come to play no positive role in the moral history of mankind. These three points—continuous despite his own limitations with the republican commitments of the young James Madison of the 1780s—were that the union was prior and superior to the states; that human slavery was a contradiction to the nation's meaning; and that black Americans had rights equal to those of all other Americans. There really was then to be, despite all the faults and perplexities that remained, a new birth of freedom.

But in 1787 all of that was still far in the future.

13

Traveling toward the Constitution or
Never Turn the Hands Backward

1787
James Madison in New York to Thomas Jefferson in Paris,
December 20

SINCE THE DATE OF MY OTHER LETTER [October 24, reporting on the Federal Convention], The Convention of Delaware have unanimously adopted the new Constitution. That of Pennsylvania has adopted it by a Majority of 46 agst. 23. That of New Jersey is sitting and will adopt pretty unanimously. These are all the Conventions that have met. I hear from North Carolina that the Assembly there is well disposed. Mr. Henry, Mr. Mason, R. H. Lee, and the Governour [Edmond Randolph], continue by their influence to strengthen the opposition in Virginia.

1788
Rufus King in Boston to James Madison in New York, February 3

I inclose a newspaper of yesterday containing the propositions communicated by Mr. Hancock to the [Massachusetts] Convention, on Thursday last. Mr. [Samuel] Adams who contrary to his own Sentiments has been hitherto silent in convention, has given his public & explicit approbation of Mr. Hancock's propositions.

We flatter ourselves that the weight of these two characters will insure our success, but the Event is not absolutely certain.

Alexander Hamilton in New York to James Madison in Orange, April 3

I send you the Foederalist from the beginning to the conclusion of the commentary on the Executive branch. If our suspicions of the author be right, he must be too much engaged to make a rapid progress in what remains. The Court of Chancery & a Circuit Court are now sitting.

We are told that your election has succeeded; with which we all felicitate ourselves.

James Madison in Orange County to George Washington at Mount Vernon, April 10

Col: Nicholas, who is among the best judges, thinks on the whole, that a majority in the Convention will be on the list of fœderalists; but very properly takes into view the turn that may be given to the event by the weight of Kentucky if thrown into the wrong scale, and by the proceedings of Maryland and South Carolina, if they should terminate in either a rejection or postponement of the question. The impression on Kentucky, like that on the rest of the State was at first answerable to our wishes: but, as elsewhere, the torch of discord has been thrown in and has found the materials but too inflammable. I have written several letters since my arrival, to correspondents in that district, with a view to counteract antifederal machinations.

Edmund Randolph in Richmond to James Madison in Orange County, April 17

Two objections have always struck me, as deserving consideration on the subject of previous amendments; one, that under their cover, a higher game might be played, the other, that the hope of obtaining them might be frustrated by the assent of too many states. The former I fear more and more, daily; not knowing how far the schemes of those who *externally* patronize them, may internally *extend,* believing that personal irritation has roused some to enlarge their original views of opposition, and having myself no disposition to enjoy the credit of establishing my own opinion at the expence of public safety. I mention these things in confidence; especially as my final determination will not be taken, until I hear something from Maryland at least.

George Washington at Mount Vernon to James Madison in Orange County, May 2

The body [Maryland ratifying convention] . . . by a large and decided Majority (of Sixty odd to twelve) have ratified the New Constitution . . . Mr. [Luther] martin did something—I know not what—but presume with vehemence—yet no converts were made—no, not one. So the business, after a very short Session, ended; and will if I mistake not, render yours less tiresome.

Thomas Jefferson in Paris to James Madison in Orange County, May 3

By mr. Warville I send your pedometer. To the loop at bottom of it you must sew a tape, and, at the other end of the tape, a small hook (such as we use under the name of hooks & eyes). Cut a little hold in the bottom of your left watchpocket. Pass the hook & tape through it, & down between the breeches & drawers, & fix the hook on the edge of your kneeband, an inch from the kneebuckle. Then hook the instrument itself by it's swivel-hook on the upper edge of the watchpocket. Your tape being well adjusted in length, your double steps will be exactly counted by the instrument, the shortest hand pointing out the thousands, the flat hand the hundreds, & the long hand the tens & units. Never turn the hands backward. Indeed it is best not to set them at any given place, but to note the number they stand at when you begin to walk. The adjusting the tape to it's exact length is a critical business, & will cost you many trials. But, once done, it is done for ever.

Alexander Hamilton in New York to James Madison in Orange County, May 11

These [elections] are now over in this state, but the result is not known. All depends upon Albany where both sides claim the victory. Our doubts will not be removed till the latter end of the month. I hope your expectations of Virginia have not diminished.

Respecting the first volume of Publius I have executed your commands. The books have been sent addressed to the care of Governor Randall. The second we are informed will be out in the course of a week, & an equal number shall be forwarded.

Alexander Hamilton in New York to James Madison in Orange County, May 19

As [Governor George] Clinton is truly the leader of his party, and is inflexibly obstinate I count little on overcoming opposition by reason. Our only chances will be the previous ratification by Nine states, which may shake the firmness of his followers; and a change in the sentiments of the people which have been for some time travelling towards the constitution, though the first impressions made by every species of influence and artifice were too strong to be eradicated in time to give a decisive turn to the elections. We shall leave nothing undone to cultivate a favourable disposition in the citizens at large.

. . . . .

We think here that the situation of your state is critical. Let me know what you know think of it. I believe you [the Virginia ratifying convention] meet nearly at the time we [the New York ratifying convention] do. It will be of vast importance that an exact communication should be kept up between us at that period; and the moment *any decisive* question is taken, if favourable, I request you to dispatch an express to me with pointed orders to make all possible diligence, by changing horses &c. All expences shall be thankfully and liberally paid.

James Madison in Richmond to George Washington at Mount Vernon, June 4

I found, contrary to my expectation that not only a very full house [at the Virginia ratifying convention] had been made on the first day, but that it had proceeded to the appointment of the President & other officers. Mr. Pendleton was put into the chair without opposition. Yesterday little more was done than settling some forms and Resolving that no question general or particular should be propounded till the whole plan should be considered & debated clause by clause. This was moved by Col. Mason, and contrary to his expectations, concurred in by the other side. To day the discussions commenced in Committee of the whole. The Governor [Edmund Randolph] has declared the day of previous amendments past, and thrown himself fully into the federal scale. Henry & Mason made a lame figure & appeared to take different and awkward ground. The federalists are a good deal elated by the existing prospect. I dare not however speak with certainty as to the decision. Kentucke has been extremely tainted, is supposed to be generally adverse, and every piece of address is going on privately to work on the local interests & prejudices of that & other quarters. In haste.

George Washington at Mount Vernon to James Madison in Orange County, June 8

... though it is yet too soon to rejoice. . . . What I have mostly apprehended is that the insiduous arts of its opposers to alarm the fears and to inflame the passions of the Multitude may have produced instructions to the Delegates that would shut the door against argument and be a bar to the exercise of the judgment. If this is not the case I have no doubt but that the good sense of this Country will prevail against the local views of designing characters and the arragent opinions of chagreened and disappointed Men. The decision of Maryland & South Carolina by such large Majorities and the moral certainty of the adoption by New-Hampshire will make *all* except desperate Men look before they leap into the dark consequences of rejection.

The Ratification by eight States without a negative—By three of them unanimously—By Six against one in another—by three to one in another—By two for one in two more—and By *all* the weight of *abilities* & *property* in the other is enough one would think to produce a cessation of opposition. I do not mean that Number alone is sufficient to produce conviction in the Mind, but I think it is enough to produce some change in the conduct of any man who entertains a doubt of his infalibility.

Alexander Hamilton in New York to James Madison in Orange County, June 8

The elections had turned out, beyond expectation, favorable to the Antifoederal party. They have a majority of two thirds in the Convention and according to the best estimate I can form of about four sevenths in the community. The views of the leaders in this City are pretty well ascertained to be turned towards a *long* adjournment say till next spring or Summer. Their incautious ones observe that this will give an opportunity to the state to *see how the government works and to act according to circumstances.*

My reasonings on the fact are to this effect. The leaders of the party hostile to the constitution are equally hostile to the Union. They are however afraid to reject the constitution at once because that step would bring matters to a crisis between this state and the states which had adopted the Constitution and between the parties in the state . . . . They therefore resolve upon a long adjournment as the safest and most artful course to effect their final purpose. They suppose that when the Government gets into operation it will be obliged to take some steps in respect to revenue &c. which will furnish topics of declamation to its enemies in the several states and will strengthen the minorities. If any considerable discontent should show itself they will stand ready to head the opposition. If on the contrary the thing should go on smoothly and the sentiments of our own people should change they can then elect to come into the Union. They at all events take the chances of time and the chapter of accidents. . . .

. . . . .

. . . the more I can penetrate the views of the Anti-foederal party in this state, the more I dread the consequences of the Non adoption of the Constitution by any of the other states, the more I fear an eventual disunion and civil war. God grant that Virginia may accede. The example will have a vast influence on our politics. New Hampshire, all accounts give us to expect, will be an assenting state.

The number of the volumes of the Foederalist which you desired have been forwarded as well the sec[c]ond as first; to the care of Governor Randolph. . . .

In a former letter I requested you to communicate to me by express the event of any decisive question in favour of the constitution authorising changes of horses &c. with an assurance to the person sent that he will be liberally paid for his diligence.

James Madison in Richmond to George Washington at Mount Vernon, June 13

Appearances at present are less favorable than at the date of my last. Our progress is slow and every advantage is taken of the delay, to work on the local prejudices of particular setts of members. British debts, the Indiana claim, and the Missippi. are the principal topics of private discussion & intrigue, as well as of public declamation. The members who have served in Congress have been dragged into communications on the first which would not be justifiable on any other occasion of on the present. There is reason to believe that the event may depend on the Kentucky members; who seem to lean more agst. than in favor of the Constitution. The business is in the most ticklish state that can be imagined. The majority will certainly be very small on whatever side it may finally lie; and I dare not encourage much expectation that it will be on the favorable side.

James Madison in Richmond to Alexander Hamilton in New York, June 16

The contents of your letter confirm the idea that a negociation for delay is [on] foot between the opposition here & with you. We have conjectured for some days that the policy is to spin out the Session in order to receive overtures from your Convention; or if that cannot be to weary the members into an adjournment without taking any decision. It [is] presumed at the same time that they do not despair of carrying the point of previous amendments which is preferable game. The parties continue to be nicely balanced. If we have a majority at all it does not exceed three or four. If we lose it Kentucke will be the cause, they are generally if not unanimously against us. . . . the business is wearisome beyond expression.

Alexander Hamilton in Poughkeepsie to James Madison in Richmond, June 19

Yesterday, My Dear Sir, The Convention made a house. That day and this have been spent in preliminary arrangements. Tomorrow we go into a Committee of the whole on the Constitution. There is every appearance that a full discussion will take place, which will keep us together at least a fortnight. . . . Our adversaries greatly outnumber us. . . . So far the thing is not to be despaired of. A happy issue with you must have considerable influence upon us.

James Madison in Richmond to Alexander Hamilton in Poughkeepsie, June 20

Our debates have advanced as far as the Judiciary Department against which a great effort is making. . . . A few days more will probably produce a decision. . . . At present It is calculated that we still retain a majority of 3 or 4; and if we can weather the storm agst. the part under consideration I shall hold the danger to be pretty well over. There is nevertheless a very disagreeable uncertainty in the case.

Alexander Hamilton to James Madison in Richmond, June 21

Our debate here began on the clause respecting the proportion of representation &c. which has taken up two days. Tomorrow I imagine we shall talk about the power over elections. The only good information I can give you is that we shall be sometime together and take the chance of events.

The object of the party at present is undoubtedly conditional amendments. What effect events may have cannot precisely be foreseen.

I believe the adoption by New Hampshire is certain.

James Madison in Richmond to Alexander Hamilton in Poughkeepsie, June 22

The Judiciary Department has been on the anvil for several days; and I presume will still be a further subject of disquisition. The attacks on it have apparently made less impression than was feared. But they may be secretly felt by particular interests that would not make the acknowledgement, and wd. chuse to ground their vote agst. the Constitution on other motives. In the course of this week we hope for a close of the business in some form or other. The opponents will probably bring forward a bill of rights with sundry other amendments as conditions of ratification. Should these fail or be despaired of, an adjournment will I think be attempted. And in case of disappointment here also, some predict a secession. I do not myself concur in the last apprehension; though I have thought it prudent to withold, by a studied fairness in ever step on the side of the Constitution, every pretext for rash experiments. The plan meditated by the friends [of] the Constitution is to preface the ratification with some plain & general truths that can not affect the validity of the Act: & to subjoin a recommendation which may hold up amendments as objects to be pursued in the constitutional mode. These expedients are rendered prudent by the nice balance of numbers and the scruples entertained by some who are in general well affected. Whether they will secure us a majority, I dare not positively to declare.

James Madison to Richmond to George Washington at Mount Vernon, June 23

We got through the constitution by paragraphs today. Tomorrow some proposition for closing the business will be made. On our side a ratification involving a few declaratory truths not affecting its validity will be tendered. The opposition will urge previous amendments. Their conversation to day seemed to betray despair. Col. Mason in particular talked in a style which no other sentiment could have produced. He held out the idea of civil convulsions as the effects of obtruding the Government on the people. He was answered by several and concluded with declaring his determination for himself to acquiesce in the event whatever it might be. Mr. H—y endeavoured to gloss what had fallen from his friend, declared his aversion to the Constitution to be such that he could not take the oath; but that he would remain in peaceable submission to the result. We calculate on a majority, but a bare one. It is possible nevertheless that some adverse circumstance may happen.

George Washington at Mount Vernon to James Madison in Richmond, June 23

I will yet hope that the good sense of this Country . . . will ultimately decide right on the important question now depending before the Convention.

I hear with real concern of your indisposition. . . . Relaxation must have become indispensably necessary for your health, and for that reason I presume to advise you to take a little respite from business and to express a wish that part of the time might be spent under this Roof on your Journey thither. Moderate exercise, and books occasionally, with the mind unbent, will be your best restoratives. With much truth I can assure you that no one will be happier in your company than your sincere &

Affecte. Servt Go: Washington

14

Rocking Cradles
in Virginia

MADISON HAD FINISHED THE LAST *FEDERALIST* PAPER he was to write,
number 63, at the beginning of March 1788 and had then left New York
on March 4 to make his way to Montpelier in order to stand for election
to the Virginia ratifying convention. He spent a week in Philadelphia, and
he stopped at Mount Vernon for dinner and a long talk with Washington,
who took the day off from his chores; it was the first time they had seen
each other since the Philadelphia convention. Then on the way on to
Orange he had a meeting with the noted Baptist preacher John Leland.
Leland and many Baptists had objected to the Constitution's failure to
include a protection for religious liberty, but Madison, as an old
comrade-in-arms from the great Virginia struggle on that issue, was able
to persuade him that the failure to ratify the Constitution would not serve
religious liberty or any other good purpose. Ratify first; amend later.
Madison's meeting with Leland was one of the several settings in which
the federalists made an agreement with their critics or foes: if you will
support ratification without attempting *prior* amendment (which attempt
would unstick the whole bargain) then we will support the addition of a
bill of rights by amendment *after* the government is in place. This consultation between Leland and Madison figures large in Baptist legend, and
comes complete with an oak tree at which they are supposed to have met.

Madison arrived in Montpelier on March 23, cutting it close; the
next day was the traditional court day election at which the delegate to
the ratifying convention would be chosen. Madison made a speech defending the Constitution, and was an easy winner over his antifederalist

neighbor and also over the man who had beaten him eleven years before—his only defeat ever—for a seat in the House of Delegates by providing free booze, as the young Madison had declined to do.

The Virginia ratifying convention that gathered in Richmond on June 2, 1788, was to be one of the most remarkable gatherings in American history because of the eminence and talent of the leaders of both sides, the seriousness and high level of the debate, the issue at stake, and the closeness of the contest and the outcome. In the Virginia convention the antifederalists had in Patrick Henry and George Mason their most eminent spokesmen in the whole of the union.

And the federalists had their most informed spokesman in James Madison, together with other luminaries from the nation's largest state. The Virginian who was not long after this event to be described by another participant in this convention—Light-Horse Harry Lee—as "first in war, first in peace, first in the hearts of his countrymen," although not present in Richmond for the convention, was known to favor ratifying the Constitution; Madison in their meeting at Mount Vernon had encouraged Washington to make his support widely known.

I will draw heavily in what follows not on more recent studies but on an ornate and colorful mid-nineteenth-century history of this extraordinary Virginia ratifying convention of 1788. It was written by a president of the Virginia Historical Society and a chancellor of the College of William and Mary, an old Virginian in other words, named Hugh Blair Grigsby. Although he gives full value to all his Virginia characters, Grigsby, writing in the atmosphere of the Civil War, is more sympathetic to Patrick Henry and George Mason, and to their resistance to ratifying the Constitution, than would be the dominant historians and biographers of a later time or a different geography. The effort, in particular, of Patrick Henry, to defend the sovereignty and rights of *states* receives full sympathy. Henry's first long speech (two and a half hours) was to feature among much else an attack on the phrase "We the people." (In Henry's view it should have been "We the states.") Grigsby, in his account of that speech, wrote that "the influence of character"—we might use the word reputation—was essential to the final outcome. He attached to the sentence about the influence of character a footnote that I am going to quote in full, not only because it conveys Grigsby's style and a certain amount of information but also because it includes at the end a wonderful and unusual theory about the motives of statesmen.

> As an illustration of "the influence of character," it may be said that no four men excited more influence in favor of the Constitution in Virginia, than George Washington, Edmund Pendleton, George Wythe, and James Madison, and four purer names were probably never recorded in profane history; yet to

those who look into the secret motives that unconsciously impel the most candid minds on great occasions, which involve the destinies of posterity, it may be said that they were all men of wealth, or held office by a life tenure, and that, though married, neither of them ever had a child. In the same spirit it may be mentioned that Mason and Henry were men of large families, and that hundreds now living look back to "Gunston Hall" and "Red Hill." In the case of Henry, the cradle began to rock in his house in his eighteenth year, and was rocking at his death in his sixty-third.

Gunston Hall was George Mason's family home; Red Hill was Henry's. If James Madison and George Washington had had some rocking cradles in Montpelier and Mount Vernon, would they then have been moved to oppose the Constitution?

Both sides had a lineup of luminaries: this ratifying convention had the most eminent cadres of combatants on the two sides of any of the state ratifying conventions.

The names and lives of the participants are woven into the early history of America, back to the earliest harbinger of independence in the Stamp Act crisis and forward into the nineteenth-century beginnings of the new nation's most serious crisis, in the Civil War. There was the earliest great voice of American liberty, who had introduced the Virginia Resolves to a remnant of the House of Burgesses in 1765, protesting taxation without representation, and including some line in response to the charge of "treason" out of which an American legend was woven, Patrick Henry. Now, twenty-three years later, he was to give his last great performance on the stage of American history—a metaphor quite appropriate to Henry. There was also, on the other side, now as throughout most of their careers, a very different figure, also in the last stages of his public life, who came in on crutches and had to be helped to his seat. This was the much respected and distinguished conservative Edmund Pendleton, who had opposed Henry on the Virginia Resolves and on many other issues through the years. Grigsby, identifying as he tends to do with Henry, says "in all the great conjectures of our history, in which he [Henry] had borne a conspicuous part, he had been opposed by Pendleton": "In the House of Burgesses, in the debate on his own resolutions against the Stamp Act; . . . on the resolutions of the March Convention of 1775, putting the Colony into a posture of defence; and on nearly all the dividing questions in the Convention and in the House of Delegates, that old man . . . had opposed him [Henry] with untiring zeal."

Pendleton, one of the Grigsby quartet of the childless supporting the Constitution, though a generation older and of a different political persuasion, was a friend of Thomas Jefferson. Pendleton had served with Jefferson on the committee to revise Virginia's law code in 1777–79, although they were often on different sides. In the great fight over the "general assessment" to support religion, Patrick Henry and Edmund Pendleton were on the same side—it was Henry's bill in fact—with Jefferson and Madison on the other. Pendleton was now a judge, and had been so often chosen to be chairman of so many Virginia gatherings as to be almost the automatic choice in this one.

Also on the side opposite Henry there was George Wythe, the first professor of law in America, the "Socrates of Virginia," who had first come to the House of Burgesses in 1758, had been the friend of the royal governors Fauquier and Botetourt, who was the only possible rival to Pendleton for the chair, and himself foreclosed any contest by nominating Pendleton. He was himself then chosen as chairman of the Committee of the Whole, in which parliamentary form the convention was to spend much of its time. Wythe had been an active participant in the events leading up to the Revolution, a signer of the Declaration of Independence, the Virginia delegate for whom John Adams first composed his *Thoughts on Government,* and a Virginia delegate to the Federal Convention, although he had had to leave very early because of the illness of his wife. He was the teacher of many other active participants, including Thomas Jefferson, and, in this convention, among many others, the great orators for the federalist side George Nicholas and James Innes. On the same side with Henry there was the chief author of the Virginia Declaration of Rights of 1776, the antecedent of bills of rights worldwide, another "husband and father" in Grigsby's terms, George Mason. These men, in their fifties and sixties, had been through many battles with and against each other through the whole story of the coming of American independence, and were now in Richmond in what was to be for many of them their last major appearance in public life.

But there were also among the antifederalists the young James Monroe, who would one day be president under the Constitution he was here opposing, and James Tyler and Benjamin Harrison, whose families would furnish additional presidents under the Constitution they here opposed. On the other hand, among the younger delegates the *supporters* of the Constitution included the dashing young general from the Revolutionary War, yet another of the many students of Witherspoon whose names are woven into the early history of the republic, a man who had entered Princeton just as Madison was leaving it, Henry Lee—Light-Horse Harry Lee. His son, Robert E. Lee, would seventy-three years later be the greatest hero of the forces seeking to break asunder the union that the father was here helping to construct. There was also, among the federalists, the young John Marshall, who would one day, as chief justice of the United States under the Constitution he was here in Richmond supporting, write the most important of all court opinions about the reach of that Constitution and the role of the Supreme Court. Both Marshall and Monroe, leaders of tomorrow, who made their maiden speeches on opposing sides one after the other in the middle of the convention, had been George Wythe's students, who in this Virginia convention though not in the whole nation's councils would outnumber those of Witherspoon: Marshall, Monroe, Madison.

Each side had its leaders great in their time whose names are less well known now. George Nicholas was another student of Wythe's, and another member of a notable Virginia family; Virginia politics had a powerful dynastic element. He was the son of that Robert Carter Nicholas, the longtime treasurer of the Colony of Virginia. This George Nicholas was a fat man, who was caricatured in a famous cartoon, in the days before there were cartoons, as a plum pudding on sticks. He was another fearless orator and the one on the other side whom Henry is said to have feared most. Nicholas had moved to the part of Virginia over the mountains that would one day be Kentucky, the votes of which area were of great importance in this convention. The federalists saved until almost the end a man named James Innes, who was said to be still greater as an orator; it was a time and place of great orators. On the antifederalist side there was William Grayson, an early reader and follower of Adam Smith's *Wealth of Nations,* who through Henry's influence would be one of the first United States senators from Virginia under the Constitution he tried to defeat. The debate was carried on by people I have named and only a few more; most of the 170 delegates never spoke.

The federalists had the presiding officers—Pendleton and Wythe—and the better organization and plan. They had chosen the candidates for delegate with care (as part of which planning they had written James Madison in New York insisting that he come back to Virginia in time to stand for election); and they selected which speakers should speak when on what. The antifederalists had no such coordination.

Henry and Mason were the leaders of the opposition. Each in his own way was something of a loner, a free-wheeling individual, and their opposition was not coordinated. Patrick Henry attacked the Federal Convention itself for going beyond its mandate, but George Mason, having participated actively throughout that convention without opposing it on that ground, could not properly now turn around and do so.

And this difference between the two antifederalist leaders led to what some would conclude was their initial, and decisive, strategic mistake: immediately at the commencing of business Mason moved that the Constitution be debated *clause by clause.* That was just what Madison and the federalist wanted. In such a controlled procedure, taking the Constitution item by item, Madison with his unmatched detailed knowledge, and his analytical powers, would be at his best, and the federalist cause, in the contained situation dealing with specifics, could make their best case. But Mason also wanted to deal with specifics, because his objections to the Constitution were not general but quite particular and detailed. They may be said to have represented the objections of one old constitution-writer to the work of others; they were refinements of those he had written down on September 16, 1787, or perhaps a few days before that, when still in Philadelphia and attending the Federal Convention, but grumpy and dispirited and refusing to sign the Constitution, he wrote them on the blank pages of his copy of the report of the Committee of Style, his Objections to the Constitution. They had then been widely circulated, beginning in the fight for ratification in Pennsylvania. The noted author of the Virginia Declaration of Rights protested that there is no declaration of rights; "there is no declaration of any kind, for preserving the liberty of the press, or the trial by jury in civil cases." Mason objected to the size of the House of Representatives; saying it was too small to be truly representative; to the Senate's role in treaties, appointments, and impeachments, and to its having any role in money bills; to the federal judiciary, which he said would destroy the judiciaries of the several states; to the absence of a constitutional council to advise and restrain the president; to the unrestrained presidential power of granting pardon for treason; to the making of navigation laws by a mere majority (southern exporting states wanted the protection of a two-third's majority; northern antifederalists would not have shared in that one); to the "sweeping" clause, as they called it then—later the "elastic" clause—at the end of the enumerated powers of Congress, which would allow all sorts of mischief. And he objected to the "unnecessary" office of vice president—on which matter a modern reader may think he had a point, except that he centered his objection on the vice president's presiding in the Senate, which he said dangerously blended executive and legislative power.

Henry's objections had no such particularity. They were broad, and they were fervent, and they seemed to include anything and everything that came to hand. The rule of the house to the contrary notwithstanding, Henry promptly at the beginning proceeded to take up the issue of the new Constitution as a whole, and not part by part.

This ratifying convention in some ways was built to Henry's taste. It differed from some others of the great meetings of the American founding—including the Constitutional Convention whose work it was considering—in that it was bigger and that it was open. It was not held in secret. There were 170 members, 2 from each of Virginia's eighty-four counties, and 1 member each from Williamsburg and Norfolk. This was a large assembly, not a small conference like the Federal Convention, with its 55 delegates and its regular attendance of 30 or 40. In Richmond the informal separation between the dozen or so leaders who spoke and the other delegates who listened was more marked, and oratory much more important. In particular there was the row of delegates from the western counties that would be Kentucky, whose votes would be decisive, standing at the back of the hall. Although there was scarcely room for the delegates in the new Academy building on Shockoe Hill in Richmond, there was a gallery of the public, so that in contrast to the secret Philadelphia Convention the Richmond convention felt the daily flow of opinion and reaction from what they used to call in those days "out-of-doors." For the first time in Virginia history, the delegates, though chosen by counties, would vote *individually*. That was a big departure from the tricky politics of voting by units (states or counties), as had been the case in Virginia's past and in the Federal Convention and in Congress under the Articles. So the Richmond meeting partook in all those ways more of the popular assembly in which the momentary flash of oratorical fire can fan the flames and play a larger role—in other words, an assembly in which the gifts and talents of Patrick Henry might have the advantage over the gifts and talents of James Madison.

As it was to Grigsby the last great encounter between Henry and Pendleton, so we may see it even more to have been the last great encounter between Henry and Madison. There is some justification to make it personal in that way. Many in the listening audience had heard and followed Henry through the years of the Revolution and of independence, some going all the way back to his first famous speech against the Stamp Act in 1763. Old-timers in years to come would say that as they remembered the great days of the coming of independence they would hear again the sound of Patrick Henry's voice. He was a very different sort of person from James Madison or Thomas Jefferson. He did not use the learned allusions, or close reasoning, that marked the speeches of his more educated colleagues; he used instead the repetitions and pauses, the gestures, histrionics, and emotional appeals that he learned in his youth from revivalist preachers—Samuel Davies and others—of the Great Awakening.

But when agitation changed to governing, to planning, thinking, making distinctions, Henry's talents faded. At least Madison and Jefferson's opinion of Henry faded—in private they came to speak of him with some disdain. Jefferson commented as early as 1774 on Henry's laziness about reading anything. Grigsby unconsciously reveals something about Henry's defects when he says that Henry's "best school of preparation on any great question was listening to the speeches of those engaged in the debate." Grigsby, quoting a brother of Chief Justice Marshall, adds that "when [his opponents] were done speaking Mr. Henry knew as much of the subject in hand as they did." Then—said Marshall—Henry's superiority would show itself in his perfect mastery over the subject and if he spoke three times on the same subject the last would be "the clearest and most striking that could be conceived."

One does get a sense of Patrick Henry through these reports as a kind of person not unknown in other times and settings. Thomas Jefferson, in a moment of admiration, had said that "he spoke as Homer wrote," or as we might say today, with the baseball analogy, he was a natural. A natural at what? At the public performance of political debate and oratory. He was an actor, a beneficiary of the skills learned from the traveling evangelists of the Great Awakening, a combination of some of the old oratory taught to the few in the colleges with the new popular speech-making that appealed to the many. And above all he was a participant throughout his life in the assemblies and conventions of "revolutionary" politics—a revolution fought with guns and bullets and violence in part, but before and after and during that fighting fought even more with words and phrases and gestures and two-hour speeches (most of all as we have said—but not by Henry—with pamphlets and broadsides and declarations in print).

What are the talents of a Henry? To sense the mood and attitude of a public. To know what will "work" as an appeal. To be able instinctively to formulate that appeal in the most forceful way, refining it and refining it as the quotation from John Marshall's brother implies, getting it right—rhetorically right. For such a person the substance can almost be said to be subordinate to the performance and the effect. The admiration for Henry's great speeches echoes through the literature of the American Revolution, from people on both, or all, sides. It is almost as though he could have done the same for either side, like a hired gun of rhetoric, like a modern lawyer, like a debater. And yet that is not right. Henry did have certain persistent themes—fear of governmental power, soaring defense of liberty (whatever he might mean by that in each instance). They were themes most readily available in the surface feelings of the largest audience, and did not involve any second thoughts, or complications, or unpleasant limiting considerations.

That is not to say he resembled in all regards the "great communicators" of later times and different means. He spoke at great length—two and a half hours at a sitting, and one of his contemporaries noted "the perfection of his periods"—praise that is unlikely to be forthcoming for his successors in the ages of the telegraph, mass publication, radio, and television. He had, apparently, great talents as an actor, accomplishing much by means that cannot be discerned in the written record of the proceedings. Grigsby reports, in another of his footnotes: "Mr. Madison, in his latter days, told Governor Coles that when he had made a most conclusive argument in favor of the Constitution, Henry would rise to reply to him, and by . . . a shake of the head or a striking gesture . . . undo all that Madison had been trying to do for an hour before."

Grigsby as historian is dependent upon the official note-taker at Richmond—a man named Robertson, who, as he will often remark, could not do justice even to the words, let alone the full effect, of Patrick Henry's presentations. I am going to reproduce here one of Grigsby's footnotes on the point of Henry's prowess which is profoundly revealing, in a different way from Grigsby's intention. It reveals the underlying attitude not only of the most popular leader in this Virginia slaveholding society in 1788, and by inference those who heard him—those of whom he could expect a favorable response—but also of the Virginia historian of 1857–66, who tells the tale not to Henry's discredit but rather with a sort of relish and admiration. Here is Grigsby's footnote:

> On one of the occasions which the reporter passes over with some such remarks as, "Here Mr. Henry declaimed with great pathos on the loss of our liberties," I was told by a person on the floor of the Convention at the time, that when Henry had painted in the most vivid colors the dangers likely to result to the black population from the unlimited power of the general government, wielded by men who had little or no interest in that species of property, and had filled his audience with fear, he suddenly broke out with the homely exclamation: "*They'll free your niggers!*" The audience passed instantly from fear to wayward laughter; and my informant said that it was most ludicrous to see men who a moment before were half frightened to death, with a broad grin on their faced.

Henry returned to this appeal to white Virginia's racial fears, and economic interest in slavery, near the end of the convention, when he appeared to be losing. "It has been repeatedly said here [he then claimed] that the great object of a national government is national defence. . . . In this State there are two hundred and thirty-six thousand blacks, but there are few or none in the Northern States. . . . if the Northern States shall be of opinion that our numbers are numberless, they may call forth every national resource. May Congress not say that every black man must fight?"

That was one fear—that the war power in the union would lead to emancipation. Joined to it, said Henry, was northern opinion.

> Another thing will contribute to bring this thing about. Slavery is detested; we feel its fatal effects; we deplore it with all the pity of humanity. Let all these considerations, at some future period, press with full force upon the minds of

Congress. They will search that paper and see if they have the power of man-
umission. And have they not, sir? said Henry. Have they not the power to
provide for the general defence and welfare? May they not think that these call
for the abolition of slavery? May they not pronounce all slaves free, and will
they not be warranted by that power? . . . The majority of Congress is to the
North, and the slaves are to the South. In this situation I see great jeopardy to
the property of the people of Virginia, and their peace and tranquility gone
away.

One might say that, in his perverse way, Henry was prescient: what
he feared is not far from what, after three quarters of a century, actually
did happen. Fortunately.

Virginians of that time, unlike South Carolinians, characteristically
would feature a double reverse in their arguments about slavery that may
be confusing to a modern reader. On the one hand they would denounce
the inhumanity, the immorality, of the slave *trade* (as Mason had done,
and Madison had done, in Philadelphia), and acknowledge the evil also
of slavery itself (as Henry apparently does here). But then the point about
the *immorality* of slavery is that it will press upon the mind of the North,
and lead the union government to threaten the *property* of Virginians.
Therefore Henry opposes joining in a constitutional union with those
northern states.

Henry worked his magic—whatever we may think of his devices—
again and again in this convention. Henry spoke on all but five of the
twenty-two days of the convention, as many as eight times in one meeting, almost a quarter of the total speaking time at the convention. Typically, he swayed even those who were in calm moments clearly on the
other side; typically, he had no coherent program for the convention.

The federalists had a coordinated attack. After the early presentations by Mason and Henry attacking the Constitution, the federalists
brought forward a powerful multigun response. With the hall still echo-
ing with the moving cadences and exclamations of Patrick Henry, they
did not just yet send up the inaudible analytic James Madison, but rather
another key figure in the story, Edmund Randolph.

Randolph was still the governor of the state, the delegate to Philadelphia who had introduced the Virginia Plan—and one of the three delegates to Philadelphia who in the end had declined to sign! Virginia, in
fact, had not done well in the Constitution-signing department, as the
state's opponents of the Constitution pointed out. Of the group of seven
delegates originally chosen by the Virginia General Assembly to go to
Philadelphia, only three, in the end, signed the Constitution. If you were
a Virginia antifederalist you could almost make it sound as though from
all the outstanding Virginia delegation only James Madison had really

supported the Constitution. Patrick Henry, although chosen as a delegate, had "smelt a rat" and declined to go (Henry was still smelling rats the following June). George Mason and Edmund Randolph—who had been there through the entire convention and played important roles—had in the end refused to sign. Virginia provided, in Mason and Randolph, two of the three nonsigners in Philadelphia (the third was Elbridge Gerry of Massachusetts). So where then did Virginia stand?

What Mason and Henry and the antifederalist forces did not know as the Richmond convention began was that Edmund Randolph had by this time changed his mind yet again. James Madison and George Washington—Washington encouraged by Madison—had helped him to change his position. While Madison was in New York in the winter of 1787–88 writing the *Federalist* essays he had kept up his correspondence with Randolph, treating him almost as at one with the federalists, and carefully answering his arguments. In a letter of January 10, 1788, for example, Madison carefully explained to Randolph why a second convention was a bad idea. Randolph was two years younger than Madison, both of them still in their thirties despite all the history they had lived through in commanding positions. They were both, as Randolph would put in a speech in this convention, children of the Revolution. Randolph and Madison had known each other since 1776, had worked together, and had become close friends. Randolph came from one of the great families of the state; he was big, handsome, and eloquent, in contrast to Madison, whom he may have seemed superficially to have outshone. He had already been attorney general of the state, as a Randolph had been throughout much of Virginia's history; he held that office before he was a delegate to Williamsburg and then to Philadelphia and then—now—governor. In the notes on the Philadelphia Convention Randolph appears to be volatile, and more than a little unpredictable. Although he had localistic anticentralist impulses that sometimes coincided with the fears of the small states, he was also a heavy Virginia patriot, and therefore a big-state partisan. He was the one on July 16 who apparently proposed to adjourn the convention and threatened that the big states might go their own way, to which William Paterson of New Jersey had made a retort in kind, and after which the convention had come close to falling apart. And yet when the Constitution had been hammered together in September, Randolph objected that it had insufficient protection against centralizing power, insufficient protection for the states and in particular his state (some of Randolph's vagaries may be explained as attempts to respond, as a local politician, to the perceived currents of opinion and state's interests in Virginia). Randolph had proposed, in September in Philadelphia, that there be a *second* convention. He wanted the Constitution submitted to the states in order to gather their proposed amendments, after which this second convention would patch up a new one. James Madison, and apparently everyone else, thought that quite a bad idea. So Randolph declined to sign the Constitution. And—more than that—he had given his objections to the Constitution and stated his reasons for not signing in a public letter to the Speaker of the Virginia House of Delegates. So the opponents of the Constitution were certainly justified in expecting him to be on their side. And yet, in the event, in his first speech in the first week, immediately after Henry's first great blast, he argued *for* ratification.

His speech did have certain defensive aspects, as perhaps was to be expected. He said that the only question for him had always been whether there should be amendments before ratification, or afterwards, and that now that eight states had ratified the answer should be afterwards. He had always stood, he said, for the Constitution as against anarchy.

Randolph is not an easy man to interpret. Patrick Henry, understandably, asked him to explain his switch. In fact Henry went to town with him. "Did he not tell us that he withheld his signature? . . . He was not led by the illumined, the illustrious few. . . . what alterations have a few months brought about? The internal [eternal?] difference between right and wrong does not fluctuate. . . . It is immutable."

The reference to "the illumined, the illustrious few," is a touch of sarcasm about the eggheads and big shots on the other side from Henry, whose influence he thought was a key reason the Constitution had so much support. But Randolph had been independent of that. What happened? Henry presented himself, mock-modestly, as having been much influenced by Randolph's earlier position: "I had the highest respect for the honorable gentleman's abilities. I considered his opinion as a great authority. . . . When I found my honorable friend in the number of those who doubted, I began to doubt also."

This taunting and goading by Henry came in the second week of the convention. Randolph and Henry had already had some exchanges in the first week, including Henry's pouncing on Randolph's use of the word *herd*. But Henry used this slip the way debaters do, then and now: "The honorable gentleman has anticipated what we are to be reduced to by degradingly assimilating us to a *herd*."

I have quoted more than once Randolph's remark about being "a child of the Revolution." He used this phrase in his first long speech on June 6, which he began by saying "I am a child of the Revolution." Henry in his reply argued that "requisitions" (on the states, for money) had been effective during the war—Henry even caressed the word *requisitions* and said what a wonderful word it was—and appealed to Randolph as a *child* of the Revolution to recollect how effective requisitions had been, giving the word *child*, Grigsby tell us in a footnote, a significance Randolph had not intended.

These simmering exchanges between Henry and Randolph came to a boil in the second week, after the long speech of Henry's to which I have referred, calling upon Randolph to explain his switch. Randolph responded "with evident emotion" that he had been "attacked in a most illiberal manner" by Henry and insisted that he had always been attached to the union. As evidence he threw down upon the clerk's table a letter he had written to his constituents ("a paper which I hold in my hand"—an anticipation of later political melodrama) and declared that it might lie there "for the inspection of the curious and the malicious," the last word of course an implied dig at Henry. In oldtime Virginia this was too much, and Henry's second that evening "waited upon" Randolph. But to everyone's relief a reconciliation was effected and the matter settled "without resort to the field."

However difficult an ally he was—to whichever side he was allied— Randolph was of great importance strategically to the federalists in Richmond.

But others were more important for the steady substance of the federalists' argument. There were many remarkable speeches, and many remarkable days, but perhaps no day more notable for the federalists than the first full day of their argument, in which they answered Patrick Henry and set forth their case, Friday, June 6. Evidently they had planned the order in which they would speak, and the responsibilities of each speaker. For the first response to Henry they sent up not their ultimate intellectual champion, James Madison, but this convert to their cause, the governor Edmund Randolph, with his greater physical stature, more oratorical style, and louder voice; this was the speech that Randolph began with his self-identification as a child of the Revolution. Then with the air somewhat cleared of the echoes of Henry's voice James Madison did arise, and in a manner and voice and content vastly different from Henry's gave his comprehensive defense of the Constitution he and the others had written in the previous summer. When he sat down the federalists' nearest answer, perhaps, to Henry as an orator, George Nicholas, arose to complete the day. Nicholas, according to Grigsby's ornate nineteenth-century Virginia judgment, was "as potent in the war of wit as he was irresistible by the force of logic." When Nicholas sat down, at the end of this session on June 6, wrote Grigsby, "even their opponents could not deny that three such speeches as had been delivered at that sitting had never before been heard in a single day in a deliberative assembly in Virginia." And some might add—if not in eighteenth-century Virginia, then where? Grigsby goes on to quote Bushrod Washington's letter to his Uncle George as having said that there may even have been some votes changed by the careful speech, sandwiched between the two orators, given by James Madison.

June 6, 1788, was a year to the day after Madison's first major speech in the Federal Convention in Philadelphia, and the two June 6 efforts have similarities and common themes, going back to his notes and memorandums and letters.

If, as would certainly be defensible, we regard James Madison as Henry's chief opponent, then we may say that there could scarcely be a sharper contrast between the opposing intellectual warriors. Although Madison spoke somewhat more than did any other federalist, he did not speak nearly as often or as much as Henry. He did not carry the federalist case by himself, but coordinated his quiet work of clarification, logic, and careful correction of historical and constitutional points, with the fireworks of his federalist colleagues Edmund Randolph, George Nicholas, and Henry Lee, and the important speech defending the article on the judiciary by young John Marshall. Madison engaged in none, and was drawn into none, of the personal exchanges, sarcastic sallies, and oratorical displays that marked the speeches of many of the other principal speakers on both sides—certainly of Patrick Henry. Where Henry's voice would fill the Academy for hours, Madison could often scarcely be heard; at more than one point David Robertson, the recording secretary, wrote about Madison something like this: "He spoke so low that his exordium could not be heard distinctly." Where Henry, despite the formal decision of the convention to take up the Constitution in sequence clause by clause, nevertheless, ignoring that decision, engaged in sweeping attacks on the Constitution as a whole, Madison kept to the schedule and urged others to do the same. On June 11, after the convention had been meeting for eight days of attacks by Henry and was still technically stuck on Article I, sections 1 and 2, Madison said: "I presume that vague discourses and mere sports of fancy, not relative to the subject at all, are very improper on this interesting occasion. I hope these will be no longer attempted, but that we shall come to the point. I trust that we shall not go out of order, but confine ourselves to the clause under consideration. I beg gentlemen would observe this rule. I shall endeavor not to depart from it myself." There cannot be much doubt who it was primarily, in Madison's view, who was indulging in "vague discourses" and "sports of fancy" not relative to the subject, or that his plea would be unsuccessful in that quarter. On June 12, responding to another of Henry's sweeping attacks on the Constitution, Madison began: "Mr. Chairman, pardon me for making a few remarks on what fell from the honorable gentleman last up. I am sorry to follow the example of gentlemen of deviating from the rule of the house: but as they have taken the utmost latitude in their objections, it is necessary that those who favor the government should answer them. But I wish as soon as possible to take up the subject regularly." On the next day, June 13, after Henry raised (again) the specter that the new government under the Constitution would give away the right to navigate the Mississippi River—a continuing thread of Henry's attack, and from Madison's point of view a total distraction and scare tactic—the convention went into a Committee of the Whole to ask the members of the convention who had also been members of Congress when a treaty with Spain on that question had been debated to tell what they knew about it. It was not something that Madison thought this convention should be doing, but he could not stop it. He was himself one of the delegates who had been a member of Congress when the treaty had been considered. There were four such delegates, as it happened two on each side of the present question, Grayson and Monroe, who opposed the Constitution, and Henry Lee and Madison, who supported it. Madison probably arranged that Lee would speak first, so that he could then have a later speech. When Madison did speak he began thus: "Mr. Chairman—It is extremely disagreeable to me to enter into this discussion." Nevertheless, perforce, he did enter into it, and told what he remembered, and argued that the rights of navigation, like other rights, would be *more* secure, not less, under the Constitution.

The question of the navigation of the Mississippi was a particularly potent topic for the opponents of the Constitution. All Virginians felt strongly about it, but those in the West, across the mountains in the counties that would one day be Kentucky, felt especially strongly. The two sides knew by now that the vote would be *very* close, and also that the delegates from those Kentucky counties were swing votes that in all likelihood would determine the outcome. Commerce on the Mississippi was essential to the economy, and the pride, of these western counties, as to a lesser degree of Virginia as a whole, and the South as a whole. So raising the issue served Henry's purposes.

In negotiations that had been carried on by the American secretary of foreign affairs under the Articles (John Jay) several "eastern" (northern) states had voted for instructions that would have allowed him to strike a deal that would have given over to Spain navigation rights on the great river for twenty-five years. The deal did not come about, and these talks took place under the severe pressure of American needs in wartime, in conditions of a quite different period. Henry linked the emotions tied to the river to the issue of the Constitution. His point was that in those negotiations the northern states had shown themselves willing to give away the navigation rights on the Mississippi, and that that kind of thing could be expected under this consolidated national government. After Madison made his answer in the Committee of the Whole, William Grayson (also a congressman) gave an antifederalist rebuttal, and then Patrick Henry rose again. About this speech Grigsby gets carried away: "The occasion, the theme, the immeasurable issues which might be swayed by the deliberations of a single day, threw such an inspiration over his genius that he seemed to be wrapt into a higher sphere, and his lips appeared to glow as if touched with the coals from the altar."

Henry, with those glowing lips, described, it seems, two contrasting conditions of the Mississippi and the Mississippi Valley:

> One described the great valley of the Mississippi as stretching from the Alleghenies to the nameless mountains of the distant West, as teeming with a mighty population, cultivated farms, thriving villages, towns, cities, colleges, and churches, filling the vision in every direction—the Mississippi covered with ships laden with foreign and domestic wealth—the West the strength, the pride, and the flower of the Confederacy. Such would be the valley of the West with a free navigation of the Mississippi. . . . The other picture was a reverse of the scene, and presented a prospect of unalloyed calamity. The Mississippi was no longer alive with ships—its unburdened waters flowing idly to the sea—no villages, no towns, no cities, no schools, no churches, no cultivated plains; the original solitude of the forest unbroken, save here and there by the rude hut of an outlaw; capital flying from a land where it would turn to dross. Such would be the West with the loss of the Mississippi, and under a consolidated government to be controlled by those who had no interest in its welfare.

How to answer this kind of thing? After a pause the answer for the federalists was given by their number-one orator, George Nicholas, who was already himself planning to move to Kentucky. It would not be effective any longer just to argue (as Madison certainly and probably Nicholas believed) that all of this had nothing whatever to do with the question at hand. What Nicholas did, fighting Henry's fire with his own fire, was to paint his own glowing picture of future Mississippi commerce and prosperity, and to make his own fierce condemnation of the shocking possibility that all that might have been sacrificed—and then, after a dramatic pause, to turn suddenly toward Henry and to ask: by whom had this fearful act been contemplated? By the gentleman's own *favorite* confederation!

Eventually the convention did creep forward a little through Article I on the powers of Congress, item by item; but on June 16 Patrick Henry attacked them all, more or less, dwelling particularly on the power to raise armies and to call forth the militia. Madison began his response by saying "Mr. Chairman—I will endeavor to follow the rule of the house, but must pay due attention to the observations that fell from the gentleman." He went on to say that without this power, there is no government: "I should think, that if there were any object, which the general government ought to command, it would be the direction of the national forces." That some of the antifederalists—Henry certainly—reached for any objection they could find was shown later on the same day when Henry expatiated on the dangers of the exclusive power of Congress to legislate for the federal district. Madison responded: "I am astonished that the honorable member should launch out into such strong descriptions without any occasion. Was there ever a legislature in existence that held their sessions at a place where they had not jurisdiction?"

We have listed George Mason's criticisms of the Constitution; Patrick Henry's are harder to list, because they were not specific. It seems that he used every argument and appeal that came to hand. Behind the many appeals he made there was a fearful attachment to the way things were in Virginia. Henry was one of those—John Tyler was another—who when he said "my country" meant Virginia. To be sure, he said he was strong for "union," too—but a union, as the sympathetic Grigsby, writing in the era of the Civil War, makes very clear, of *sovereign* states—a union in which Virginia's power was undiminished. He gathered up all the fears and worries about change, all the attachment to the way things were, and gave them a powerful voice. In particular he gave voice to the latent hostility to government, to the *principle* of government, that may be discernible anywhere and certainly could be found in English colonials of the radical whig and radical Dissenting tradition, and in their American successors. This government, said Henry again and again and in many ways, was a threat to our rights and liberties.

For Madison and the federalists, this government was necessary to *protect* our rights and liberties. James Madison argued from first to last that the alternative to this union was chaos. This union with this genuine government was necessary to the survival of the republic. The individual states, or a collection of three or so confederations of states, could not deal with foreign nations, could not provide for the common defense. James Madison kept steadily to his central theme, that the issue was "whether the Union shall or shall not be continued." And of course in his speeches he went back yet another time to the notes and memorandums had had written to himself, and to the *Federalist* papers he had drawn from them. In his first major speech, on June 6, Madison gave his analysis of factions and of the compound republic, as they were presented in *Federalist* 10. On the next day, June 7, again speaking after Governor Randolph and in response to Henry's challenges, he surveyed the weakness of confederations yet again, as he had first done, in his notes on ancient and modern confederacies—in the spring of 1786, and as he had written them out in numbers 18 through 20 of *The Federalist*. In his speech on June 11, on the central issue of the power to levy direct taxes, he drew upon two *Federalist* papers, numbers 56 and 45. He drew upon *The Federalist* again on June 14, in defending the power of Congress to regulate the militia against one of Henry's attacks against uniting "the power of the purse and the power of the sword." In his speech of that day he made a good Madisonian formulation about power: "Where power can be safely lodged, if it be necessary, reason commands it cession. In such cases it is imprudent and unsafe to withhold it. It is universally admitted that it must be lodged in some hands or other." One could hold a full semester seminar on those few sentences. Madison certainly had a sufficient awareness of the dangers of power, but he was also aware of the dangers of the lack of power. Power does corrupt, as stated in that excessively well known aphorism of Lord Acton, but lack of power corrupts also, in a different but equally important way.

In that speech on June 14 Madison, provoked perhaps by the outpouring from Henry, made that unusually personal testimony that we have quoted before: "I profess myself to have had a uniform zeal for republican government. If the honorable member, or any other person, conceives that my attachment to this system arises from a different source, he is greatly mistaken. From the first moment that my mind was capable of contemplating political subjects, I never, till this moment, ceased wishing success to well regulated republican government. The establishment of such in America was my most ardent desire."

Fairly early in the twenty-two-day session (June 3–27) the leaders of the two sides, both of which had politicians, perceived that the outcome would be incredibly close, as indeed it was to be. There were eighty votes, plus or minus, in favor of the Constitution and about eighty votes against it, too. The convention moved more rapidly toward the end, because the Virginia House of Delegates was to assemble on June 23 and several members of the ratifying convention were delegates, and also because the opponents to ratification perceived that they had not changed any votes in the last great exchange, on the judiciary (John Marshall and James Madison giving able explanations of how the new federal judiciary would work) and resorted to their last tactic, the introduction of a long list of proposed amendments.

Throughout the convention, one might almost say, the latent issue had been whether to ratify the Constitution without prior amendment or whether to insist on prior amendments as a condition of ratification—that at least is the way George Mason would see it. For James Madison that was the same as the question, whether to ratify, yes or no. Henry, who had been answering no in every way he could find, now on the border of a close defeat, prepared a list of *forty* (as Madison said, no less than forty!) amendments, twenty in a bill of rights, and twenty "other alternatives" of which Madison said, some were "improper and inadmissable." But the federalists knew that they had to do something about amendments, and particularly about a bill of rights; the absence of a bill of rights in the Constitution was by far the strongest argument that the opponents had. So on the day—June 24—when it was known that Henry would present and defend his enormous list, George Wythe arose immediately when the convention assembled and got the floor—and introduced *his* list, of almost forty amendments, *also* including a bill of rights. But Wythe presented these amendments as *recommendations* only. He moved a form of ratification which surrounded the act of ratification with language of this recommendation. But that surrounding did not disturb his fellow federalists, or satisfy the antifederalists. The core issue was ratify or not; the core issue was enclosed in a covering of *previous* or *subsequent* amendments. To vote for subsequent amendments was to vote to ratify; to vote for previous amendments was to vote not to ratify.

Henry, thus somewhat forestalled, arose and among many other arguments attacked Wythe's list for some of its omissions, and himself said that in such lists what is not named is implicitly given away—which was exactly the federalist argument against any bill of rights, in *Federalist* 84, and in a speech after Henry's in this convention by Madison.

Henry, after Wythe beat him to the punch with amendments, made the appeal to racial fears that we have already described, and then went on, responding to Wythe on the subject of "subsequent amendments," in Grigsby's account:

> He said he was distressed when he heard the expression from the lips of Wythe. "It is a new thought altogether. It is opposed to every idea of fortitude and manliness in the States or in anybody else. Evils admitted in order to be removed subsequently, and tyranny submitted to, in order to be excluded by a subsequent alteration, are things totally new to me. . . . I ask, does experience warrant such a thing from the beginning of the world to the present day? Do you enter into a compact of government first, and afterwards settle the terms of the government? . . . I believe it to be a fact that the great body of the yeomanry are in decided opposition to that paper on your table. . . . These men will never part with their political opinions. Subsequent amendments will not do for men of this cast. You may amuse them by proposing amendments, but they will never like your government."

The vote technically was on an amendment proposed by Henry to the ratification motion by Wythe. Henry's amendment reversed the Wythe motion's point, and would have had the convention resolve that a declaration of rights and amendments to "other exceptionable parts" of

the Constitution should be referred to "other states in the American confederacy" for their consideration *previous* to any ratification of the Constitution.

Madison in his last major speech began this way:

Nothing has excited more admiration in the world, than the manner in which
free governments have been established in America. For it was the first instance from the creation of the world to the American revolution, that the free
inhabitants have been seen deliberating on a form of government, and selecting such of their citizens as possessed their confidence, to determine upon, and
give effect to it. But what has this excited so much wonder and applause?
Because it is of so much magnitude, and because it is liable to be frustrated by
so many accidents.

He appealed to the delegates, in something of the manner of *Federalist* 37, not to expect perfection, to make great allowances: "We must calculate the impossibility that every state should be gratified in its wishes,
much less that every individual should receive this gratification." Even at
the Federal Convention, where men's minds could be "calm and dispas-
sionate," "mutual deference and concession were absolutely necessary.
Had they been inflexibly tenacious of their individual opinions, they
would never have concurred."

A considerable feature of the argument in Richmond was the progress of ratification in other states, and Virginia's place in the sequence.
The fact that eight states had already ratified when the Virginians con-
vened had been said by Edmund Randolph to have been the decisive point
in his switching sides, and the federalists leaned on the already accomplished fact of the other ratifications to urge Virginia to join. But the antifederalists thought they had found a counter to that. Early in the
proceedings, on June 9 and again on June 12, Henry introduced a letter
from Thomas Jefferson, written in February, which, deploring the absence of a bill of rights, had suggested that after nine states had ratified,
perhaps the next four—with the Constitution thus secure—should refuse
to ratify until a bill of rights was added. Henry had argued that since New
Hampshire was on the point of ratifying, and would become the ninth
state, then as Jefferson had suggested, Virginia should *withhold* its ratification pending such a bill. Madison's reply, on June 12, is particularly
interesting, given his close friendship and lifelong collaboration with Jefferson. In the first place he said that such an outside name should not be
introduced: "The honorable member in order to influence our decision,
has mentioned the opinion of a citizen who is an ornament to this state. I
was much surprised. Is it come to this then, that we are not to follow our
own reason? Is it proper to introduce the opinions of respectable men not
within the walls?"

Then he said that if it came to that, could we not adduce a character equally great on our side? He was referring indirectly, as everyone knew, to George Washington.

Having thus countered the great name of Jefferson with the hint of a still greater name, Madison then delicately alluded to his own personal knowledge of Jefferson's position: "I am in some measure acquainted with his sentiments on this subject. It is not right for me to unfold what he has informed me." But Madison did unfold enough to say that he believed that if Jefferson were there he would favor ratification of this Constitution, and that in addition he approved the particular clause under discussion (the power to levy taxes) because it enabled government to function. In a letter to Jefferson later Madison explained what he had done.

In his last speech Madison urged that Virginia join with these other states that had ratified. "Virginia has always heretofore spoken the language of respect to other states, and she has always been attended to. Will it be that language, to call on a great majority of the states to acknowledge that they had done wrong?" He also reminded the house several times of the solemn historic decision they were about to make. Madison did not have Henry's colorful extravagance, but it may be that his words, being fewer and more carefully considered, in the end weighed for more.

Henry made of course a last speech, a last appeal—one might almost say, like Sarah Bernhardt's farewell tours, several times. One of the last acquired legendary features from the accompaniment by "striking manifestations of the elements." Henry's speech must have been rather striking, too.

> The gentleman [Madison] has told you of the numerous blessings which he imagines will result to us and the world in general from the adoption of this system. I see the awful immensity of the dangers with which it is pregnant. I see it—I feel it. I see beings of a higher order anxious concerning our decision. When I look beyond the horizon that binds human eyes, and see the final consummation of all human things, and see those intelligent beings which inhabit the ethereal mansions, reviewing the political decisions and revolutions which in the progress of time will happen in America, and the consequent happiness or misery of mankind, I am led to believe that much of the account of one side or the other will depend on what we now decide. Our happiness alone is not affected by the event. All nations are interested in the determination. We have it in our power to secure the happiness of one-half of the human race. Its adoption may involve the misery of the other hemispheres.

Grigsby then quotes the description of the scene "with great animation," by one who was present:

A storm suddenly rose. It grew dark. The doors came to with a rebound like a peal of musketry. The windows rattled; the huge wooden structure rocked; the rain fell from the eaves in torrents, which were dashed against the glass; the thunder roared; and the lightning, casting its fitful glare across the anxious faces of the members, recalled to the mind those terrific pictures which the imaginations of Dante and Milton have drawn of those angelic spirits that, shorn of their celestial brightness, had met in council to war with the hosts of Heaven. In the height of the confusion Henry stood unappalled, and, in the language of a member present, "rising on the wings of the tempest, he seized upon the artillery of Heaven, and directed its fiercest thunders against the head of his adversaries."

In the final votes James Madison's federalists, and the Constitution of the United States, survived this combined assault of Patrick Henry and the artillery of heaven. The key vote, as so often happens in parliamentary bodies, came not exactly on the fundamental question, to ratify or not—reflected in Wythe's original motion—but on the amendment to that motion offered by John Tyler, that Henry's long list of amendments and alterations be acted upon *prior* to ratification. The vote moved through the counties of Virginia in alphabetical order. When it reached Northumberland County the vote was tied, at sixty. After Randolph County (now part of West Virginia) it was tied at sixty-nine. A few counties later the old pros of the Virginia political scene—Edmund Pendleton and others—knew what had been suspected by both sides in the closing days, that although it was very close the federalists had a slight lead. The final vote was eighty-eight to eighty. (eighty-eight nay, against Tyler's amendment, and eighty yay.) A switch of five votes would have defeated the Constitution in the largest state, and altered American history and— as is not too much to say and as both Henry and Madison had said in their closing speeches—the history of humankind. Although the majority of the delegates from the Kentucky counties voted in favor of the Tyler motion (therefore in effect against ratification) four of the fourteen did not, and the defection, if that is what you call it, of those four, despite Henry's performance on the issue of the Mississippi River, was one important element of the winning combination. But of course when a vote is as close as that the analysts, especially on the defeated side, can find a dozen places to say if this, if that, if another little change.

After the decisive vote there came, on June 25, the formal vote on Wythe's motion to ratify, on which one delegate switched, to make the vote 89–79. Madison promptly dispatched his promised letter to Alexander Hamilton giving him the good news about Virginia, which had its effect in the New York convention. New Hampshire, which had declined to ratify in February, had in fact ratified on its second try on June 21, although the Virginia delegates did not know that, so Virginia was not the decisive ninth state, but the tenth. At the New York convention in Poughkeepsie the federalist delegates led by Alexander Hamilton used the clinching ratification by New Hampshire, which made the union certain, and the ratification by the biggest state Virginia, to help to persuade the reluctant delegates finally, a month after Virginia, to ratify. With these eleven states the union was secure. North Carolina did not ratify until November 1789, and rapscallion Rhode Island not until May of 1790; they came into a union that had already chosen its first president, George Washington, and its first Congress, and was under way.

To return briefly to the meeting in Richmond: the victorious federalists, Grigsby tells us, did not crow and strut but had a due solemnity. The convention spent a day on the list of proposed amendments. It even defeated an attempt to remove the worst of them (from the federalist point of view), an amendment that would have effectively removed the new government's direct taxing power. It stayed in the list—but after all only as a proposal.

Opponents congratulated each other. Apparently there was a feeling, about their convention, that transcended the two sides and the outcome. As Pete Rose at bat said to the opposing catcher Carleton Fisk in the extra-inning game in the 1975 World Series, Isn't this a wonderful game? Great just to be in it.

Pendleton made a last speech. Let us close with Grigsby's prose. Pendleton is speaking.

> Old men, who had heard his parting benediction twelve years before to the Convention which declared independence, and called to mind his manly presence and the clear silver tones of a voice now tremulous and faint from infirmity and age, bowed their heads between their hands and wept freely. But in the midst of weeping the deep blue eye of Pendleton was undimmed. When he concluded his speech he descended from the chair, and, taking his seat on one of the nearest benches, he bade adieu to the members individually, who crowded around him to press a parting salutation. The warmest opponents were seen to exchange parting regards with each other. For it was a peculiar and noble characteristic of our fathers, when the contest was decided, to forgive and forget personal collisions, and to unite heart and hand in the common cause. On the breaking up of the House many members ordered their horses, and were before sunset some miles on their way homeward; and before the close of another day all had disappeared; and there was no object to remind the citizen of Richmond, as at nightfall through deserted streets he sought his home, that the members of one of the most illustrious assemblies that ever met on the American continent had finished their deliberations, had discharged the high trust confided to them by their country, and had again mingled with the mass of the people.

15

Was the United States
Founded on Selfishness?

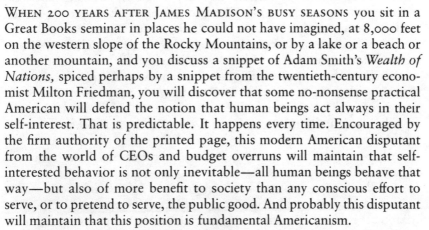

WHEN 200 YEARS AFTER JAMES MADISON'S BUSY SEASONS you sit in a
Great Books seminar in places he could not have imagined, at 8,000 feet
on the western slope of the Rocky Mountains, or by a lake or a beach or
another mountain, and you discuss a snippet of Adam Smith's *Wealth of
Nations,* spiced perhaps by a snippet from the twentieth-century econo-
mist Milton Friedman, you will discover that some no-nonsense practical
American will defend the notion that human beings act always in their
self-interest. That is predictable. It happens every time. Encouraged by
the firm authority of the printed page, this modern American disputant
from the world of CEOs and budget overruns will maintain that self-
interested behavior is not only inevitable—all human beings behave that
way—but also of more benefit to society than any conscious effort to
serve, or to pretend to serve, the public good. And probably this disputant
will maintain that this position is fundamental Americanism.

Although the New World had become, by the late twentieth century,
a jumble of philosophies, the seminar's hard-line proponent of a ubiquitous and beneficent self-love would be by no means alone; his outlook
would be one of the most influential of popular American perspectives
from the late nineteenth century onward. One could hear his theme in
other American places, usually less pleasant than the mountain retreat
and the lake. The trucking executive, with his own firm in Anderson,
Indiana, discussing philosophies by accident in the club car, belligerently
asserts that human beings act only from self-interested motives, and besides, "that's what buys the bourbon and the beef," examples of each of

which on the table are available for his gesture. One young business executive will maintain, when asked why poets become poets, that such persons can't "make it" in the world of market competition—as she has done in the Bell South Company—so their self-interest takes them elsewhere, safely out of the battle. A public relations executive, of advancing years, a founder of a firm, seated at the Pinnacle Club at the top of a New York skyscraper, looking back over his life and giving voice to his philosophy, with the stock market ticker ticking in the background, remarks that it had to begin with human selfishness.

The snippet from *The Wealth of Nations* in the mountain top readings will probably include some of Smith's memorable description of the great advantages of the division of labor, featuring his famous pin factory—by dividing the labor the number of pins produced is increased many fold—and his finding that this division of labor arises from the human propensity to trade: to truck, barter, and exchange one thing for another. Out of this trucking, bartering, and exchanging, the reading explains, the superior bow-maker learns to stick to making bows and to let somebody else make the arrows, and everything else: he trades his excess of bows for these other goods. And conversely with the arrow-maker. And—a sentence the practical twentieth-century American will seize upon—each does this "from regard to his own interest." The society as a whole has a bigger supply of bows and arrows than it would otherwise have—the public good in that quite tangible sense is served—even though neither the bow-maker nor the arrow-maker, or any other in the vast division of labor, intends directly to serve the public good. "It is not from benevolence of the butcher, the brewer, or the baker that we expect our dinner," wrote Smith, unaware that he would be quoted triumphantly by an American oil executive two centuries later," but from their regard to their own interest."

Smith wrote the most famous paragraph in *The Wealth of Nations* in Scotland while his friend Hume was publishing his essays, and across the Atlantic the young Virginia statesman James Madison was pursuing his education. Smith's paragraph made the rejection of any motive of public good, on the part of merchants and producers, explicit: "[The individual], indeed, neither intends to promote the public interest, nor knows how much he is promoting it . . . he intends only his own security; and by directing . . . industry in such a manner as its produce may be of the greatest value, he intends only his own gain and he is in this, as in many other cases, led by an invisible hand to promote an end which was no part of his intention."

Smith then went on to put public service in its lowly place: "Nor is it always the worse for society that it [service to the public good] was no part of it [the individual's motive]. By pursuing his own interest he frequently promotes that of the society more effectually than when he really intends to promote it. I have never known much good done by those who affect to trade for the public good."

If in the late twentieth-century executive-seminar readings there is a contribution from Milton Friedman it will be his widely circulated article rejecting any "social responsibility" of business, in which Friedman remarks, "I share Adam Smith's skepticism about the benefits that can be expected from 'those who affect to trade for the public good.' "

The sentence from Adam Smith, following those quoted above, suggested that his derogation of conscious service to the public good applied, and was intended to apply, only to merchants, and only to merchants (or businessmen) in their capacity as merchants: "It [the affecting to trade for the public good] is an affection, indeed, not very common among merchants, and very few words need be employed in dissuading them from it."

But the attack on "affecting to trade for the public good" certainly has not been confined to merchants as merchants as the decades have rolled on in the New World. The "public good" came to be regarded by some as properly, for everybody, "no part of his intention"; as a pretense; as a menace; as served better by the unconscious working of market forces, and large social forces, than by the deliberate and purposeful action of human beings. Sometimes it seems even stronger than that: that the "public good" is never served by those who try to serve it. Or even: there is no such thing as the "public good."

And so in the seminar in the pines the defender of the iron law of selfishness, fortified by the prestige of Smith and Friedman, may proceed—like a sophomore in an introductory ethics class—to apply his doctrine far beyond the narrow range of bakers, brewers, and bowmakers, and the realm of economic behavior. He may even, under pressure, apply it to saints and martyrs, to the mothers who devote their lives to their children, to the soldiers who perform above and beyond the call of duty, to the persons who have so great a love as to lay down their lives for their brothers—not to mention political leaders who affect to care about the commonweal and judges who seek to serve justice and citizens who care about the larger goods of humankind. All of these—the hardline party will say—are simply following their (rather extraordinary versions of) "self-interest." To which an opponent will just shake her head, not only at such failure of moral perception but also at such terminological confusion. She may even make a remark that resembles David Hume's: "He has forgotten the movements of his heart. . . . he calls not things by their proper names."

But there in the readings, a few pages over from Adam Smith, the hard-line proponent of egotism will be pleased to find James Madison—*Federalist* 10 or 51. And he will seize on some paragraphs in these to serve his purpose: See! The Father of the American Constitution held to the same view! Self-love, self-interest, balanced and checking each other! It is the American way.

And, as a reader of these pages will know, there is on the surface a plausible foundation for this claim—not only in *Federalist* 10 and 51 but in the core of Madison's thinking about politics going back at least to his memorandums. Madison did indeed ground his defense of the "extended" or "compound" republic partly in his view of human self-love, which leads inevitably to contending interested factions. He did repeatedly affirm, in many different formulations, that men are not angels; moreover, he came to a pluralist conception of republican politics that saw in the multiplicity of factions, reflecting various interests, checking each other, a protection from majority tyranny and a way that republicanism could work and last in a large nation. He and the main proponents of the Constitution of 1787 had come to see, in some contrast to the euphoric revolutionary idealism, or the provincial Puritanism, of 1776, that this union was not going to be a "Christian Sparta," grounded in a self-denying and virtuous people sacrificing interest to the good of the republic. The experience in the newly independent states, including the experience in and among the state governments that Madison's memos had recorded, showed that plainly. So this republic had to have some other foundation than pure and simple and universal "public virtue."

But, *recognizing* that it would not be simple or pure does not mean there is no such things as a worthy public motive; and *perceiving* the ubiquity of human self-love is very different from *endorsing* it. The United States was not founded on the self-justifying vision of universal selfishness posited by popular economic philosophies of the late nineteenth and the twentieth centuries. That is another thought-world from the founders. Neither, to be sure, was it founded on the "optimism" about humankind—the trustworthy "goodness" and infinite malleability of "the people"—also popular in later centuries, and sometimes said to be the necessary foundation of democracy and the creed of Madison's friend Jefferson. The climate of thought about human nature in which James Madison moved was more complex, and perhaps more profound, than either of these simple later alternatives. And the practical moral and institutional conclusions drawn from the view of humankind were very different from either—in particular, different from that view attributed, wrongly it may be, to Adam Smith

In the first place, just with respect to Madison himself: Madison's view of human nature was by no means peculiar to him but was ubiquitous in his time and place; and second, his view, compared to the most important opponents, the antifederalists who opposed the constitution, placed *more* confidence in the possibilities of human virtue.

Set over against the simple optimism, even the insistent optimism, about human nature that is one very powerful strand in the popular culture of America's mass democracy in the late twentieth century, and the views on this point attributed whether correctly or not to Madison's life-long friend Thomas Jefferson, and the views also of a considerable segment of the American intelligentsia in the middle and later part of the twentieth century, James Madison's views, of persistent and ineradicable human self-serving, do indeed seem distinctive. But they were not, in comparison with others in his own time and circumstance. Such a view of human nature was, on the contrary, very widespread, in a culture still to an extent permeated by the teachings of Reformed Christianity, including English Puritanism, and of the radical whig tradition in England.

One could go to the record of the Federal Convention—Madison's notes and the other records—and find references again and again and again to the premise of human selfishness, "depravity" and "vice." And so it had been throughout the Revolutionary period. Bernard Bailyn, the Harvard scholar who collected and commented on the many American revolutionary pamphlets, wrote this in his summary of the ideas of those pamphlets: "What turned power into a malignant force was not its own nature so much as the nature of man—his susceptibility to corruption and his lust for self-aggrandizement." (H. Richard Niebuhr once said, about Acton's famous dictum, that it is not so much that power corrupts as that we corrupt power). Bailyn goes on to say—about this theme in the pre-Revolutionary pamphlets—"On this there was absolute agreement. . . . it was not simply a question of what the weak and ignorant will do. . . . it concerned mankind in general." Bailyn gives many quotations. Then in a footnote Bailyn wrote: "This basic concept of human nature, which would attain its greatest fame in *The Federalist,* appears full blown in the colonies well before the revolutionary years, and may be traced back, intact, to the early eighteenth-century transmitters of English opposition thought." And surely, one may surmise, one aspect or version or source of it still further back, in one major tributary feeding into that English opposition thought, to a thousand preachers and teachers of Puritan Protestanitism in England, and of Reformed Christianity in Scotland and Switzerland and Holland and elsewhere, and in some part again all the way back to St. Augustine and St. Paul.

James Madison in *Federalist* 10 and 51 and elsewhere was therefore by no means alone or original or out-of-step with his fellows in noting the inclination of self-aggrandizing humankind to corrupt power or be corrupted by power. Quite the contrary: what he said on that point was the common currency.

To say that, of course, does not answer the claim of the CEOs in the modern seminars, that Madison's perception of human self-love resembles theirs; perhaps it may appear indeed to strengthen that claim, by extending a "realistic" view of humankind out beyond a few sentences in the *Federalist* papers to the whole thought-world of the founding generation.

But it is necessary then to note something further about Madison within that world: Madison and the federalist proponents of the Constitution both softened and complicated, and made a different application of, this widely shared perception. To make that point we may refer again to the outlook Madison and his party were arguing against, their opponents, the antifederalists.

These opponents of the Constitution were even more convinced of humankind's "political depravity" than the federalists, and they regarded the proposed Constitution as an example of it. There was a strand of grumpiness and cynicism running through many varieties of antifederalism. The antifederalists across the states were united only in what they were opposed to, not in their reasons for opposing it. They did not have to propose anything; they just said no to what was proposed by others. One argument of the antifederalists in Massachusetts and Pennsylvania was that the Constitution tied them to slave states; one argument of antifederalists in Virginia and in South Carolina, was that this Constitution linked them to those "eastern" states opposed to slavery. In the North Carolina ratifying convention there was opposition to the Constitution's prohibition against religious tests: that prohibition, it was said, would open the door to pagans, deists, Mahometens, Jews and heathens; someday in the future the pope of Rome might be elected president. More commonly in other states the antifederalist argument, one of those most often repeated, went in the opposite direction: the Constitution was criticized because it did not explicitly protect, in a bill of rights, liberty of conscience and freedom of religion.

The antifederalists generally represented a particularly strong attachment to a particular state. The antifederalists in Pennsylvania tended to be radical democrats who were attached to the state constitution of 1776; those in New York, supporters of Governor Clinton and his faction; those in Massachusetts, old leaders of '76 and those less shocked than their opponents by Shays's Rebellion; those in Virginia, followers of the state's most powerful politician Patrick Henry, who, as we have seen, would appeal to fears of the "eastern" states on the issues of the Mississippi River and of slaves. Each of the states had its individual circumstances and particular story.

There was among the antifederalists rather more of the suspicion and hostility toward other states—those others, those foreigners, those folk from another region with its wrong ideas—than might be found, generally speaking, among the more nationally minded federalists. Antifederalism would feed on the state xenophobias and narrow interests in each state. If you had tried to have a convention of antifederalists you would be bringing together the extremes; you would have had some of the sharpest antagonisms in the union.

The antifederalists, then, with this collection of localisms and grumpiness, accused the proponents of the new Constitution like Madison of trusting too much, of having too *optimistic* a view, too *favorable* a view, of human nature, and therefore of building a giant new intercolonial engine of power that was too little restrained. One of the earliest and best known postwar scholars studying the antifederalists, Cecilia Kenyon, called them "men of little faith." These opponents of the Constitution regarded their opponents—like Madison—as men of, in a sense, too much faith.

It is necessary then to make some further distinctions:

(1) Madison's view of human nature was mixed and realistic, not relentlessly negative or cynical. When he turned to argue with those antifederalists he had a quite different emphasis from twentieth-century readings of *Federalist* 10. Alongside self-love there was a virtue that it was the task of state-makers to encourage.

(2) There was no assumption that self-love would automatically serve—"as by an invisible hand"—the public good; rather, there was the opposite—the assumption that although, particularly in large groups, pervasive and ineradicable—it was a menace to be checked. It was to be checked and restrained not by central authority but by the free play of pluralism, in order that other motives might have their chance to serve the public good. The upshot was a calculating effort both to check and make use of it.

(3) Madison and company, in contrast to much of the past thought, made a progressive rather than a conservative application of realism about mankind.

(1) That Madison's view of humankind was not systematically bleak, but rather mixed, appears at many spots in the *Federalist* essays, not only in the implication of the many references to justice and virtue and the public good but directly. One such clear statement directly on the point of human nature comes in *Federalist* 55.

Madison's clear statement calls to mind the formulation of Reinhold Niebuhr, the twentieth-century American theologian and political thinker—a formulation that is quoted so often in the circles in which he is known as to have become a cliché. It goes like this: "Man's capacity for justice makes democracy possible; man's inclination to injustice makes democracy necessary." James Madison at the end of *Federalist* 55, 156 years before Niebuhr, wrote a passage that, without the formulaic parallelism, is very much like that: "As there is a degree of depravity in mankind which requires a certain degree of circumspection and distrust: So there are other qualities in human nature, which justify a certain portion of esteem and confidence. Republican government presupposes the existence of these qualities in a higher degree than any other form."

So republican government, for Madison, rests not only on the need to check and to balance and to restrain human "depravity" but also and more distinctly on those qualities of human nature that justify a certain "esteem," a certain "confidence." It presupposes the latter in a higher degree than any other form of government.

Madison went on to reject cynical notions of humankind: "Were the pictures which have been drawn by the political jealousy of some among us, faithful likenesses of the human character, the inference would be that there is not sufficient virtue among men for self-government; and that nothing less than the chains of despotism can restrain them from destroying and devouring one another."

Madison is taking it for granted that "self-government" requires a certain virtue in the public, and asserting—against cynics, and human egotism notwithstanding—that there is sufficient virtue among human beings to make republican government possible, if you design it right—if you take human egotism as one datum (not the only one) in constructing institutions. The institutions that *recognize,* and *make use of,* instead of assuming away, human selfishness, also *depend upon,* and *assume,* a certain amount of human virtue, a willingness, when day is done, to accept the verdict, to respect the rights of the opponent, to obey the decision of a majority that has gone against you—to collaborate in the service of the public things.

(2) The line taken by some late nineteenth- and twentieth-century apologists for raw capitalism has sometimes been extended in the United States out into law, government, and the press: if each interest group, advocate, or reporter, like each entrepreneur, simply pursues unadorned interest, without worrying about consequences, the result will nevertheless somehow be better than any conscious effort at worthy service to public goods. Justice, truth, and the common good (if it exists) will in this view be served automatically (as by an invisible hand) by the process it-

self. There need be no conscious moral reflection, no attention to worthy goals, no self-restraint; the balance of contending forces will somehow take care of all that. As each bow-maker, butcher, brewer, and baker follows his interest without attending to the public good (but serving it, so it is said, nonetheless) so also (in this view) each lawyer should fight each opposing lawyer without restraint or qualm, and with whatever tricks, because the "advocacy system"—the process—will produce all the justice this world allows; each reporter and news organization should snoop out and write and print and show whatever sensation can be discovered, without listening to any lectures from outsiders about press "responsibility," because the sheer process of the free press will somehow take care of injury in the wash of the public's right to know and elicit whatever truth there may be; when any interest group is asked what it wants, it should should say what Samuel Gompers answered when asked what labor wanted: "more"; the interaction with other "interest groups," it is assumed, will provide whatever restraint is needed, and from the stand-off and balance some rough approximation to the social good may be achieved. This popular attitude, with its homeground in a misunderstanding and overextension of classical economics, borrows something also from oversimplified or mistaken notions of the balance of power, of "pluralism" and of the free press—of free discussion. At the core of such views there is a convenient relocation of life's moral claims; moral responsibility is lifted nicely off our shoulders altogether and placed instead on an impersonal process of balance, conflict, or competition—on the workings of some invisible hand. This demoralization is reinforced by the acids of modernity, which while rightly subjecting our perspectives on social good to criticism, wrongly proceeds to tear them to shreds and blow them away. Who is to say? There is only your opinion and mine.

None of this accords with one's reading of the eighteenth-century student of morals and politics James Madison (or of John Adams, either, or others of the founders). One might say that on this point the implication of the thought of the founders, despite the resemblances on the surface, stood almost at an opposite pole: not removing, but increasing, the moral claim on the shoulders of the citizen. "Republicanism" did that.

They insisted on checking and balancing, on setting ambition to check ambition, not because that would release the participants to pursue their own gain without stint but because even our best efforts to serve the public good beyond our own gain are tainted by our interest. Therefore we need other reasonings (tainted in their turn by other interests) as a counterweight. But these taintings do not—or may not—altogether vitiate the efforts by you and me (and by our opponents) to serve the justice that is and "ever has been" the "end of government" and of "civil society" (*Federalist* 51). Were there no possible moral substance to those efforts—yours and mine and our opponents—then representative government would not work. Those representatives would be nothing but agents of raw interest and power, hard rocks bargaining against each other. Republicanism would not work—would have no meaning, for there would be no "public things" but only the collision of interests.

One way to indicate Madison's implicit accepting of a real moral order (about which we interested human beings argue) would be to quote some of the further references to justice and the public good and the common good and virtue, like the one from *Federalist* 51 quoted above, which are sprinkled throughout his writing. Another would be to draw back and assess his own career—what he chose to do himself, as a free moral agent. One could, if one did that, disagree slightly with Douglass Adair's interesting essay "Fame and the Founding Fathers," which tells the reader that "fame" was their motive. One might say that shrinking their motive to that one surely distorts them, and that that essay applies more to Hamilton than to Madison. One might also hint that that essay tells as much about Adair as about the founders (so it is with all of us—when we write about figures loaded with normative meaning for us and our own time, as the founders always are for Americans).

Or—one might search out the implication of the high place Madison gives to representation—the institution that can filter the purest and worthiest characters from the people.

Or one could look at the kinds of appeals he makes in those moments when he lifts the argument to its highest pitch, as for example at the end of *Federalist* 14.

He discussed representation in *Federalist* 14, the next one he wrote after *Federalist* 10. Hamilton had been pounding away on the advantages of union, the disadvantages of disunion, in the numbers between 10 and 14. Madison in 14 then defended the new fact of *representative* republicanism. In modern Europe, "to which we owe the great principle of representation, no example is seen of a government wholly popular and founded, at the same time, wholly on that principle." But "America can claim the merit of making the discovery [of the principle of representation] the basis of unmixed and extensive republics." Much later, when Madison was writing about the House of Representatives in *Federalist* 55, he was answering the objection that the small number of members of the House of Representatives (sixty-five to start) will be dangerous to the public liberty and the public good. One part of his answer is an appeal to the character of the American people and the ethos of the new nation:

> I must own that I could not give a negative answer to this question, without first obliterating every impression which I have received with regard to the

present genius of the people of America, the spirit which actuates the State legislatures, and the principles which are incorporated with the political character of every class of citizens. I am unable to conceive that the people of America, in their present temper, or under any circumstances which can speedily happen, will chuse, and every second year repeat the choice of, sixty-five or a hundred men, who would be disposed to form and pursue a scheme of tyranny or treachery.

At the end of *Federalist* 14 Madison launched into a long and eloquent rhetorical appeal—unusual for him—which reminds a modern reader—although in its pawky Madisonian way it falls well short of the eloquence of either—sometimes of Lincoln, sometimes of Martin Luther King, Jr., and his "I have a dream" speech.

> Hearken not [wrote Madison] to the unnatural voice which tells you that the people of America, knit together as they are by so many cords of affection, can no longer live together as members of the same family; can no longer continue the mutual guardians of their mutual happiness; can no longer be fellow citizens of one great, respectable, and flourishing empire. Hearken not to the voice which petulantly tells you that the form of government recommended for your adoption is a novelty in the political world; that it has never yet had a place in the theories of the wildest projectors; that it rashly attempts what it is impossible to accomplish.

He certainly appeals to something in his countrymen that goes beyond their self-interest, "vice," and ambition: "No my countrymen, shut your ears against this unhallowed language. Shut your ears against the poison which it conveys; the kindred blood which flows in the veins of American citizens, the mingled blood which they have shed in defense of their sacred rights, consecrate their union, and excite horror at the idea of their becoming aliens, rivals, enemies."

It is in this peroration that he argues, in a passage I have quoted elsewhere: don't be afraid of what is new. And he celebrates the accomplishments so far, appealing to the people's better side. "Happily for America, happily we trust for the whole human race, they pursued a new and more noble course. They accomplished a revolution which has no parallel in the annals of human society: They reared the fabrics of governments which have no model on the face of the globe. They formed the design of a great confederacy, which it is incumbent on their successors to improve and perpetuate."

If the new republic is to be built not on the foundations of a Christian Sparta, where every man is virtuous, (maybe even required to be), but rather upon the awareness of human sinfulness, egotism, and self-aggrandizement—that nevertheless does not pitch all virtue, all sense of common good, all caring for commonweal, out the window. Not as fact, and not as recommendation and requirement of the polity. Human beings

227

are a mixture. Republicanism of the sort that Madison is recommending is built upon that mixture. The task of state-building is to restrain the vice and bring forward the virtue.

(3) One must look at the application—the practical political conclusion—drawn from assertions about mankind's "political depravity."

The most common application throughout the Christian ages was conservative and authoritarian; the sinfulness of humankind requires kings, powers, authorities, order, the majesty of the state, "prescription" to suppress the malevolent tendencies of sinful humankind. The powers that be are ordained of God. Great defenders of monarchy and reaction—deMaistre, for example—applied it in that way. This application tended to find the human vices more blatant in the masses of common people than in the kings and courts and nobles; the radical and leveling movements returned the favor by finding the vices in the kings and nobles courts but not in the people.

But another conservative application of the doctrine of political depravity appeared in the United States even where kings and priests and nobles were overthrown, in the element of populistic traditionalism on the part of the antifederalists.

Unlike the popular republican innovations of the past, which proposed to mitigate, limit, or even overturn monarchical and aristocratic institutions, the innovation which they opposed—the Federal Constitution—came into a situation that was already "republican," where the people already ruled. And they responded warily. Old Amos Singletary, a Massachusetts farmer, self-taught, a sometime member of the state legislature who also was a delegate to the ratifying convention in that state, is often quoted as expressing the epitome of a populist form of that wariness: "These lawyers, and men of learning and moneyed men, that talk so finely, and gloss over matters so smoothly, to make us poor illiterate people swallow down the pill, expect to get into Congress themselves; they expect to be managers of this Constitution, and get all the power and all the money into their own hands, and then they will swallow all us little folks like the great *Leviathan;* yes, just as the whale swallowed up Jonah!"

Thee was the prospect of much swallowing in the fears of the antifederalists: the rich would swallow up the poor; the "consolidated" government would swallow up the states.

It is by no means true that the more numerous and popular side will always be the more progressive; there can be strong "popular" attachment to the way things are. These lawyers and men of learning and moneyed men that talk so finely and gloss over things so smoothly are proposing a change, and they understand it and we don't. One reason for our wariness about it is that we suspect that they will benefit, they will dominate, and we won't. Another is that it sounds like a big change in what we have now. We are attached to the states—or rather, to our state, to our Massachusetts, which is very different from those far-off places like South Carolina. Or to Virginia, which is very different from those "eastern" states. We are attached to the state legislatures, the lower house, the popular house, where we are represented. And these people who talk so smoothly are proposing to make changes that threaten all that we are attached to.

This populistic conservatism included a more rigid attachment than that of the federalists to the received oppositionist radical whig ideology. Where annual elections end, there tyranny begins. Rotation in office. No standing armies. Trial by jury—not only in criminal but also in civil cases. A bill of rights, written down. More generally, a fear of power. A resistance to remote and strong government—like that of London and the royal court. A quick suspicion—even on very small evidence—of a trend toward tyranny. A resistance to anything that smacks of aristocracy. And this Constitution, even though it prohibited titles, or any kind of nobility, still smacks of it; the Senate looked like an aristocracy. Worse, this Constitution even, in Patrick Henry's famous phrase, "squints toward monarchy." The antifederalist opponents of the Constitution, drawing upon the old radical whig ideology with its grumpy suspicion of centers of power, were at least as inclined as the federalists to appeal to humankind's "political depravity"—but as a counsel of suspicion, traditionalism, localism, quietism.

And in its way that antifederalist application of the doctrine of political depravity represents a conservative application that continues down to the present day—the form of it that invokes the unchangeable egotism of humankind as a barrier against all attempts at beneficent change and improvement. Because, it is said, human nature does not change, and because the evil that lurks in the human heart will not be eradicated by any merely external or institutional change, such change is at best of no value—perhaps is perverse. Nathaniel Hawthorne wrote a short story called "Earth's Holocaust"—from a twentieth-century point of view a poignant choice of words—in which after a great bonfire in which humankind destroyed all of the instruments of human evil, whips and chains and handcuffs and prison bars and guns and—by extension— "abused substances" (not Hawthorne's phrase; he included playing cards) and saturation bombers and gas chambers—they were all then after a few years reinvented and restored to place because they had their root "in the human heart." Well into the twentieth century one could encounter crackerbarrel philosophers whose response to proposed changes in society was "you can't change human nature"—therefore do not try to make whatever improvement in the human lot you are proposing, because it won't succeed. That attitude was—or perhaps is—sufficiently widespread to have provoked a response from one of the few in recent times to have carried on the founders' work of public philosophy, the philosopher John Dewey, in one of his best books, *Human Nature and Conduct*. Dewey felt it necessary to attack, at some length, the notion that "you can't change human nature."

And so where did Madison stand on all these applications of the notion of "political depravity"? James Madison did not represent *any* of these conservative applications of that doctrine. Of course, like all his fellow patriots he was an opponent of European Reaction; he did valiant political battle against the antifederalists; he interpreted the limitations of humankind neither to support the order imposed by powers that be nor to dismiss all efforts at beneficent social change.

Madison in fact was actively promoting an immense alteration in the structure of the human lot: one that *did* succeed. In employing a realistic understanding of humankind for a progressive political purpose Madison was standing received doctrine on its head in a much broader way than in that other case in which he was credited with that maneuver, standing on its head the received doctrine that republics had to be small. To be sure, one may say that in this case it was not perhaps Madison alone but many others—John Adams incorporating power balances in his recommendations for new republican state governments, in the decade before, perhaps Puritan thinkers he drew upon from the century before. But now in the arguments of Madison for the Federal Constitution this standing on its head achieves a more particular application. Madison was *not* saying humankind is selfish and vicious, and cannot be changed, *and therefore* you might as well stick with kings and aristocrats. Madison and the pro-Constitution people were not even saying, Yes, the people in the state legislatures under the Articles were "vicious" but that is the way people are, and you cannot change it, and it would be worse under a stronger national government. Although we may guess that he would not have accepted Dewey's view of the malleability of humankind, Madison and his predecessors and successors in the great American constructive collaboration from 1763 to 1791 were undertaking, on different premises, one of the more extraordinary deliberate and considered actions by human beings to *alter* and to *shape* human institutions, and therefore human life, in history. They took "political depravity" as a *datum* that must be taken account of in *designing* such an extraordinary program in human improvement, and a *reason* for designing it, but certainly not as a reason for not undertaking the project.

Madison, at least, also did not apply this doctrine in such a way as simply to reinforce the powerful and the privileged. The doctrine of political depravity may inoculate us against romanticism about today's victims of oppression and injustice; that head of steam of resentment they are developing—justly, to a point—about the injustices under which they labor neither exempts them from common human vices nor insures that they will know when that point has been passed. Many of today's oppressions are carried out by the victims of yesterday's, now risen to power but resentful still. But if the doctrine should thus keep the critical faculties alive with respect to victims, the oppressed, the proletariat, the lowly, how much more should it also keep alive an awareness of the vices of the strong and the powerful. They have the instruments to impose their distorted view, as their victims do not.

Here we may discover Madison to have had nuances of difference not only with many thinkers elsewhere but with others in the founding group—including his collaborator in *The Federalist*. If we look back at *Federalist 6*—the next one Hamilton composed, after the introductory first and after Jay's series, the first one after he got the argument rolling— we find him, in the course of his arguing that the American states, "in a state of disunion," will fall into dissension and tumult, starting right off attacking those who forget human misconduct: "A man must be far gone in Utopian speculations," Hamilton wrote, scornfully, who would doubt that these states would fight with each other, who would forget "that men are ambitious, vindictive, and rapacious." Neither commercial societies nor republics are exempt from the laws of human nature: "Have republics in practice been less addicted to war than monarchies? Are not the former administered by men as well as the latter?" Have we not seen enough of those "idle theories which have amused us with promises of an exemption from the imperfections, the weaknesses, and the evils incident to society in every shape?" Is it not time to adopt as a "practical maxim" for our political conduct that "we, as well as the other inhabitants of the globe, are as yet remote from the happy empire of perfect wisdom and perfect virtue?" But Hamilton seems to apply this shared antiutopian realism in a way that differs in a subtle but important way from Madison. In the flavor of what he writes there is implied by a partial exemption of the rich and well-born, a *particularly* heavy association of human vice with debtors and popular leaders. His one contemporary American example of "personal considerations" affecting public action is this: "If Shays had not been a *desperate debtor*, it is much to be doubted whether Massachusetts would have been plunged into Civil War." Realism about human nature leads him to "high-toned" government, in which the energetic well-born have the governmental power to put down its results.

Madison, on the other hand, although no leveler, and also much concerned about protecting property from those debtors, was nevertheless both more even-handed and more long-term in his application of their shared conviction that human beings in bulk are inclined to selfishness. Douglass Adair, whose articles on these matters were, as the graduate students say, "seminal," made this contrast between the two *Federalist* essayists in an interesting footnote: "It is characteristic of the different outlook of the two men that Hamilton in number 9 advocates the new union because it will make it easier to suppress with military force such outbreaks as Shays's Rebellion, while Madison in number 10 argues that union will prevent the recurrence of any such outbreaks. Hamilton prized the union as an instrument guaranteeing that the rich would win every class struggle; Madison hoped that union would prevent class war from being declared in America."

The United States was not built on the endorsement of selfishness; instead it was built on, among other assumptions, the assumption that selfishness in general will not go away, appearing in the rich and the poor, the rulers and the ruled. Therefore it needs to be endlessly checked and counterbalanced. But counterbalancing the vice of the lowly by the power of kings and nobles, or the rich and well-born, simply leaves the vice of the latter unchecked. Presenting some claimant to the mantle of "The people," on the other hand, as exempt from the vice of collective egotism, leads on to majority tyrannies—at the worse, to the Terror or the Gulag. The solution—insofar as there is one, at the level of power—is pluralism: shifting, cross-checking combinations in an open field of many factions in a big republic.

But that level of power is not the whole story. Republicanism by its name, its nature, and its heritage is more than a balance of power; it is the people's rule, self-government, the shared attention to the public things. By counterbalancing interest in a large republic one may encourage and filter such attachment as there may be to the public good.

The checks and balances are not the sole reason for the longevity and success of American political institutions. We cannot explain the nation's constitutional origins, or its endurance and achievement, by reference to the balance of power, or the restraint of self-love alone; those points taken alone would lead—often do lead—in a quite different direction from that of the American republican government: to the *Leviathan*, realpolitik, a gridlock of power groups, to cynicism.

You cannot explain the persistence and success, or the nature, or American government, by reference solely to the restraining and balancing of power; there was the prior fact of a grant of power, along with its restraint, without which it would be meaningless. And there was an already existent community to do the granting.

Prior to our separating there is the fact of our uniting. Before we can participate in agencies of government that are counterpoised, so that each may shut the door on the other, there must be the single whole and united government of which they are all a part, opening the door to common purpose.

Before ambition is set against ambition there must be the common arena within which these ambitions are juxtaposed, and the implicit common purpose that transcends the explicit contending purposes, the common institutions in which those contending ambitions seek to realize themselves.

Prior to and giving meaning to restraints on power is the grant of power by the community on whose behalf and by whose rules and for whose good it is to be exercised.

Before and after the disunities that the checks and balances recognize and utilize there are the unities that they can be made to serve.

Otherwise the contending powers and interests, contending ambitions and self-loves, would rip the polity to pieces, as it has certainly done elsewhere. It was the purpose of the constitution-makers so to design the apparatus of government as to make these juxtaposed ambitions, interests, and factions, arising both from the difference among human beings and from their self-love, serve not chaos or tyranny but liberty and the public good—make them do so in part by the *design* of their relationship. But also in fulfillment of another potential aspect of human nature, at some times and places, which is not accurately described as self-love—to bring that out and give it place.

The Constitution would not have made it past the first crisis, over the Jay Treaty and the American response to the French Revolution, in the 1790s, if sheer balancing of naked interests were all. In imitation of the American constitutions, constitutions have been written for nations around the world replete with all the restraints on power, all the formal checks and balances, anybody could ask for, and they have failed.

Prior to, and giving meaning to, the restraints on power there must be common purposes of an already existing community. Without that commonality and purposiveness the restraining is empty or destructive. That balancing takes place within a prior and supervening mutual engagement, an engagement to each other to make one people, and to serve the shared good, and to define and to seek it by mutual persuasion.

The endless pursuit of that public good is to be carried on by the method inherited, particularly, from the English, and now given by the

Americans a further elaboration: "free argument and debate," as Jefferson had called it. The capstone of the Constitution was to give that lifeblood of the republic, the great society-wide argument, a written protection in the supreme law of the land.

16

No Just Government
Should Refuse

1787
Thomas Jefferson in Paris to James Madison in New York,
December 20

I HAVE LITTLE TO FILL A LETTER. I will therefore make up the deficiency by adding a few words on the Constitution proposed by our Convention. I like much the general idea of framing a government which should go on of itself peaceably, without needing continual recurrence to the state legislatures. I like the organization of the government into Legislative, Judiciary & Executive. I like the power given the Legislature to levy taxes; and for that reason solely approve of the greater house being chosen by the people directly . . . I am captivated by the compromise of the opposite claims of the great & little states, of the latter to equal, and the former to proportional influence. I am much pleased too with the substitution of the method of voting by persons, instead of that of voting by states: and I like the negative given to the Executive with a third of either house . . . There are other good things of less moment.

. . . . .

. . . I will now add what I do not like. First the omission of a bill of rights providing clearly & without the aid of sophisms for freedom of religion, freedom of the press, protection against standing armies, restriction against monopolies, the eternal & unremitting force of the habeas corpus laws, and trials by jury in all matters of fact triable by the laws of the land & not by the law of Nations. To say, as mr. [James] Wilson does, that a bill of rights was not necessary because all is reserved in the case of the general government which is not given, while in the particular ones all is given which is not reserved, might do for the Audience to whom it was addressed, but is surely . . . opposed by strong inferences from the body of the instrument . . . It was a hard conclusion [for James Wilson] to say because there has been no uniformity among the states as to the cases triable by jury, because some have been so incautious as to abandon this mode of trial, therefore the more prudent states shall be reduced to the same level of calamity. It would have been much more just & wise to have concluded the other way that as most of the states had judiciously preserved this palladium, those who had wandered should be brought back to it, and to have established general right instead of general wrong. Let me add that a bill of rights is what the people are entitled to against every government on earth, general or particular, & what no just government should refuse, or rest on inference. The second feature I dislike, and greatly dislike, is the abandonment in every instance of the necessity of rotation in office, and most particularly in the case of the President. Experience concurs with reason in concluding that the first magistrate will always be re-elected if the constitution permits it. He is then an officer for life.

1788
Thomas Jefferson in Paris to James Madison in New York, February 6

I am glad to hear that the new constitution is received with favor. I sincerely wish that the 9 first conventions may receive, & the 4. last reject it. The former will secure it finally; while the latter will oblige them to offer a declaration of rights in order to complete the union. We shall thus have all it's good, and cure it's principal defect.

James Madison in New York to Thomas Jefferson in Paris, July 24

I returned here about ten days ago from Richmond which I left a day or two after the dissolution of the Convention. The final question on the new plan of Government was put on the 25th. of June. It was twofold 1. whether previous amendments should be made a condition of ratification. 2. directly on the Constitution in the form it bore. On the first the decision was in the negative; 88 being no, 80 only ay. On the second & definitive question, the ratification was affirmed by 89 ay agst. 79. noes. A number of alterations were then recommended to be considered in the mode pointed out in the Constitution itself. . . . The debates . . . were conducted on the whole with a very laudable moderation and decorum, and continued untill both sides declared themselves ready for the question. And it may be safely concluded that no irregular opposition to the System will follow in that State, at least with the countenance of the leaders on that side. . . . But altho' the leaders, particularly H———y—& M—s—n, will give no countenance to popular violences it is not to be inferred that they are reconciled to the event, or will give it a positive support. On the contrary both of them declared they could not go that length. . . .

Among a variety of expedients . . . [much of this paragraph in code] *Col. Mason* . . . endeavored to turn the influence of your *name even against parts of which I knew you approved.* In this *situation I thought it due to truth* as well as that it would be most agreeable to *yourself* and *accordingly took the liberty to state some of your opinions on the favorable side.* . . .

N. Hampshire ratified the Constitution on the 21st. Ult: and made the ninth State. The votes stood 57 for and 46. agst. the measure. S. Carolina had previously ratified by a very great majority. The Convention of N. Carolina is now sitting. . . . The Convention of N. York has been in Session ever since the 17th. Ult: without having yet arrived at any final vote. Two thirds of the members assembled with a determination to reject the Constitution, and are still opposed to it in their hearts. The local situation of N. York, the number of ratifying States and the hope of retaining the federal Government in this City afford however powerful arguments to such men as Jay, Hamilton, the Chancellor [,] Duane and several others; and it is not improbable that some form of ratification will yet be devised by which the dislike of the opposition may be gratified, and the State notwithstanding made a member of the new Union. . . .

July. 26. We just hear that the Convention of this State [New York] have determined by a small majority to exclude from the ratification every thing involving a condition & to content themselves with recommending the alterations wished for.

Thomas Jefferson in Paris to James Madison in New York, July 31

I sincerely rejoice at the acceptance of our new constitution by nine states. It is a good canvas, on which some strokes only want retouching. What these are, I think are sufficiently manifested by the general voice from North to South, which calls for a bill of rights. It seems pretty generally understood that this should go to Juries, Habeas corpus, Standing armies, Printing, Religion & Monopolies. I conceive there may be difficulty in finding general modifications of these suited to the habits of all the states.

But if such cannot be found then it is better to establish trials by Jury, the right of Habeas corpus, freedom of the press & freedom of religion in all cases, and to abolish standing armies in time of peace, and Monopolies, in all cases, than not to do it in any. The few cases wherein these things may do evil, cannot be weighed against the multitude wherein the want of them will do evil. . . . Why suspend the Hab. corp. in insurrections & rebellions? The parties who may be arrested may be charged instantly with a well defined crime. . . . Examine the history of England: see how few of the cases of the suspension of the Habeas corpus law have been worthy of that suspension. . . . A declaration that the federal government will never restrain the presses from printing any thing they please, will not take away the liability of the printers for false facts printed. The declaration that religious faith shall be unpunished, does not give impunity to criminal acts dictated by religious error. . . . If no check can be found to keep the number of standing troops within safe bounds, while they are tolerated as far as necessary, abandon them altogether, discipline well the militia, & guard the magazines with them. . . . I hope. . . . a bill of rights will be formed to guard the people against the federal government, as they are already guarded against their state governments in most instances.

James Madison in New York to Edmund Randolph in Richmond, August 2

I find that [Jefferson] is becoming more & more a friend to the new Constitution, his objections being gradually dispelled by his own further reflections on the subject. He particularly renounces his opinion concerning the expediency of a ratification by 9 and a refusal by 4 States, considering the mode pursued by Massts. as the only rational one, but disapproving some of the alterations recommended by that State. He will see still more room for disapprobation in the recommendations of other States. The defects of the Constitution which he continues to criticise are the omission of a bill of rights, and of the principle of rotation at least in the Ex. Departmt.

John Page in Williamsburg to James Madison in New York, August 6
(Page was a boyhood and lifetime friend of Thomas Jefferson and a Virginia political leader)

Yours of the 27th. Ulto. inclosing the New York Papers, with the joyfull News of the Ratification of the Plan of the foederal Constitution has just come to Hand. I return you many Thanks for communicating to me so early, an Authentic Account of that important & glorious Event. I heartily congratulate you on the brightening Prospect of our Affairs, & the Success of your Wishes & patriotic Labours—they arecrowned with Success, & to your immortal Honor; for it is to you, we are indebted for the Part Virginia took in this great Affair & we see her Influence in the other States. I confess I have always attributed to you the Glory of laying the Foundation of this great Fabric of government; of supporting the Plan of it in Convention & of animating all the States to cooperate in the great Work. I write in such Haste that I can only add that I am my dear Sr. with the highest Respect & Esteem your Friend & most obedt. Servt.

James Madison in New York to Thomas Jefferson in Paris, October 17

My own opinion has always been in favor of a bill of rights; provided it be so framed as not to imply powers not meant to be included in the enumeration. At the same time I have never thought the omission a material defect, nor been anxious to supply it even by *subsequent* amendment, for any other reason than that it is anxiously desired by others. I have favored it because I supposed it might be of use, and if properly executed could not be of disservice. I have not viewed it in an important light 1. because I conceive that in a certain degree, though not in the extent argued by Mr. Wilson, the rights in question are reserved by the manner in which the federal powers are granted. 2. because there is great reason to fear that a positive declaration of some of the most essential rights could not obtained in the requisite latitude. I am sure that the rights of Conscience in particular, if submitted to public definition would be narrowed much more than they are likely ever to be by an assumed power. One of the objections in New England was that the Constitution by prohibiting religious tests opened a door for Jews Turks & infidels. 3. because the limited powers of the federal Government and the jealousy of the subordinate Governments, afford a security which has not existed in the case of the State Governments, and exists in no other. 4 because experience proves the inefficacy of a bill of rights on these occasions when its controul is most needed. Repeated violations of these parchment barriers have been committed by overbearing majorities in every State. In Virginia I have seen the bill of rights violated in every instance where it has been opposed to a popular current. Notwithstanding the explicit provision contained in that instrument for the rights of Conscience it is well known that a religious establishment wd. have taken place in that State, if the legislative majority had found as they expected, a majority of the people in favor of the measure; and I am persuaded that if a majority of the people were now of one sect, the measure would still take place and on narrower ground than was then proposed, notwithstanding the additional obstacle which the law has since created. Wherever the real power in a Government lies, there is the danger of oppression.

Thomas Jefferson in Paris to James Madison in New York, November 18

With respect to the Federalist, the three authors had been named to me. I read it with care, pleasure & improvement, and was satisfied there was nothing in it by one of those hands, & not a great deal by a second. It does the highest honor to the third, as being, in my opinion, the best commentary on the principles of government which ever was written. . . . I confess it has rectified me in several points. (As to the bill of rights however I still think it should be added. . . . I should deprecate with you indeed the meeting of a new convention. I hope they will adopt the mode of amendment by Congress & the Assemblies, in which case I should not fear any dangerous innovation in the plan. But the minorities are too respectable not to be entitled to some sacrifice of opinion in the majority. Especially when a great proportion of them would be contented with a bill of rights.)

1789
The Reverend John Leland to James Madison at Montpelier, ca. February 15

I congratulate you in your Appointment, as a Representative to *Congress;* and if my Undertaking in the Cause conduced Nothing else towards it, it certainly gave Mr. *Madison* one Vote. I expect that Congress will be very busy for some years, in filling a continental Blank with a Code of general Laws. . . . One Thing I shall expect; that if religious Liberty is anywise threatened, that I shall receive the earliest Intelligence.

Thomas Jefferson in Paris to Francis Hopkinson in Philadelphia, March 13

(Hopkinson was an old friend, signer of the Declaration of Independence, musician, author, member of a Philadelphia musical and literary circle that included Benjamin Franklin, correspondent with Jefferson; his widowed mother kept Jefferson's oldest daughter Martha for a time in 1783.)
You say that I have been dished up to you as an antifederalist, and

ask me if it be just. My opinion was never worthy enough of notice to merit citing: but since you ask it I will tell it you. I am not a Federalist, because I never submitted the whole system of my opinions to the creed of any party of men whatever in religion, in philosophy, in politics, or in any thing else where I was capable of thinking for myself. Such an addiction is the last degradation of a free and moral agent. If I could not go to heaven but with a party, I would not go there at all. Therefore I protest to you I am not of the party of federalists. But I am much farther from that of the Antifederalists. . . . I approved from the first moment, of the great mass of what is in the new constitution, the consolidation of the government, the organisation into Executive, legislative and judiciary, the subdivision of the legislative, the happy compromise of interests between the great and little states by the different manner of voting in the different houses, the voting by persons instead of states, the qualified negative on laws given to the Executive which however I should have liked better if associated with the judiciary also as in New York, and the power of taxation. I thought at first that the latter might have been limited. A little reflection soon convinced me it ought not to be. . . .

What I disapproved from the first moment also was the want of a bill of rights to guard liberty against the legislative as well as executive branches of the government, that is to say to secure freedom in religion, freedom of the press, freedom from monopolies, freedom from unlawful imprisonment, freedom from a permanent military, and a trial by jury in all cases determinable by the laws of the land. I disapproved also the perpetual reeligibility of the President. To these points of disapprobation I adhere. My first wish was that the 9. first conventions might accept the constitution, as the means of securing to us the great mass of good it contained, and that the 4. last might reject it, as the means of obtaining amendments. But I was corrected in this wish the moment I saw the much better of plan of Massachusetts and which had never occurred to me. With respect to the declaration of rights I suppose the majority of the United states are of my opinion: for I apprehend all the antifederalists, and a very respectable proportion of the federalists think that such a declaration should now be annexed. The enlightened part of Europe have given us the greatest credit for inventing this instrument of security for the rights of the people, and have been not a little surprised to see us so soon give it up. With respect to the re-eligibility of the president, I find myself differing from the majority of my countrymen, for I think there are but three states of the 11. which have desired an alteration of this. And indeed, since the thing is established, I would wish it not to be altered during the life of our great leader, whose executive talents are superior to those I believe of any man in the world, and who alone by authority of his name and the confidence reposed in his perfect integrity, is fully qualified to put the new government so under way as to secure it against the efforts of opposition. But having derived from our error all the good there was in it I hope we shall correct it the moment we can no longer have the same person at the helm. These, my dear friend, are my sentiments, by which you will see I was right in saying I am neither federalist nor antifederalist; that I am of neither party, nor yet a trimmer between parties.

Thomas Jefferson in Paris to James Madison in New York, March 15

Your thoughts on the subject of the Declaration of rights in the letter of Oct. 17. I have weighed with great satisfaction. Some of them had not occurred to me before, but were acknoleged just in the moment they were presented to my mind. In the arguments in favor of a declaration of rights, you omit one which has great weight with me, the legal check which it puts into the hands of the judiciary. This is a body, which if rendered independent, & kept strictly to their own department merits great confidence for their learning & integrity. In fact what degree of confidence would be too much for a body composed of such men as Wythe, Blair & Pendleton? . . . I am happy to find that on the whole you are a friend to this amendment. The Declaration of rights is like all other human blessings alloyed with some inconveniences, and not accomplishing fully it's object. But the good in this instance vastly overweighs the evil. I cannot refrain from making short answers to the objections which your letter states to have been raised. 1. That the rights in question are reserved by the manner in which the federal powers are granted. Answer. A constitutive act may certainly be so formed as to need no declaration of rights. The act itself has the force of a declaration as far as it goes: and if it goes to all material points nothing more is wanting. In the draught of a constitution which I had once a thought of proposing in Virginia, & printed afterwards, I endeavored to reach all the great objects of public liberty, and did not mean to add a declaration of rights. Probably the object was imperfectly executed: but the deficiencies would have been supplied by others in the course of discussion. But in a constitutive act which leaves some precious articles unnoticed, and raises implications against others, a declaration of rights becomes necessary by way of supplement. This is the case of our new federal constitution. This instrument forms us into one state as to certain objects, and gives us a legislative & executive body for these objects. It should therefore guard us against their abuses of power within the field submitted to them. 2. A positive declaration of some essential rights could not be obtained in the requisite latitude. Answer. Half a loaf is better than no bread. If we cannot secure all our rights, let us secure what we can. 3. The limited powers of the federal government & jealousy of the subordinate governments afford a security which exists in no other instance. Answer. The first member of this seems resolvable into the 1st. objection before stated. The jealousy of the subordinate governments is a precious reliance. But observe that those governments are only agents. They must have principles furnished them whereon to found their opposition. The declaration of rights will be the text whereby they will try all the acts of the federal government. In this view it is necessary to the federal government also: as by the same text they may try the opposition of the subordinate governments. 4. Experience proves the inefficacy of a bill of rights. True. But tho it is not absolutely efficacious under all circumstances, it is of great potency always, and rarely inefficacious. A brace the more will often keep up the building which would have fallen with that brace the less. There is a remarkable difference between the characters of the Inconveniences which attend a Declaration of rights, & those which attend the want of it. The inconveniences of the Declaration are that it may cramp government in it's useful exertions. But the evil of this is shortlived, moderate, & reparable. The inconveniences of the want of a Declaration are permanent, afflicting & irreparable: they are in constant progression from bad to worse. The executive in our governments is not the sole, it is scarcely the principal object of my jealousy. The tyranny of the legislatures is the most formidable dread at present, and will be for long years. That of the executive will come in it's turn, but it will be at a remote period. I know there are some among us who would now establish a monarchy. But they are inconsiderable in number and weight of character. The rising race are all republicans. We were educated in royalism: no wonder if some of us retain that idolatry still. Our young people are educated in republicanism. An apostacy from that to royalism is unprecedented & impossible. I am much pleased with the prospect that a declaration of rights will be added: and hope it will be done in that way which will not endanger the whole frame of the government, or any essential part of it.

17

As Sincerely Devoted
to Liberty

One

A READER TWO HUNDRED YEARS LATER may feel, from knowing the eventual outcome, that Madison's work was essentially finished when the Constitution was written and signed on September 17, 1787, or when he finished his work on *The Federalist* in the following March, or surely when the Virginia ratifying convention ratified the Constitution on June 25, 1788, and the new government was certain to proceed. But there was more. The Constitution at that point was only a skeleton, a sketch of a government in a few broad lines. It has been said that at that point the United States of America consisted of a piece of paper and George Washington. Everything remained to be filled in. There was the matter of the promised amendments. There was also all the specifying in law what was broadly sketched in the Constitution—for example the whole system of the federal courts. And all the precedents that were to be set. There was so much blank paper that the first Congress is sometimes described as almost a second constitutional convention.

Madison wanted to participate in the work of that new Congress launching the new government, but before he could do so he had to win a seat in it. And before he could try to win a seat in the new Congress under the Constitution he had obligations still to the old Congress under the Articles, breathing its last gasp.

Madison left Richmond on July 1, 1788, after the state ratifying convention, to go to New York and the old Congress. He stopped and gave a report at Mount Vernon; he arrived in New York and resumed his seat in the old Congress; he corresponded—as we have seen—with Alexander Hamilton up in Poughkeepsie in the last days of the New York ratifying convention; and he participated in the last piece of business in the four-teen-year history of the expiring Confederation Congress: What would be the location of the government? New York or Philadelphia or where?

The Continental Congress, after all its adventures since John Adams first attended it back in the fall of 1774, expired in October of 1788. It had no quorum, and fizzled out. Madison had hoped just to sit tight in New York, and not have to travel again now that winter was coming, but his friends in Virginia again told him that he had to come home. He learned that Patrick Henry's power was such that he might be denied the chance to take part in launching the new government. Henry, though de-feated in the convention in Richmond, was still enormously powerful in the Virginia General Assembly. George Washington, writing on Novem-ber 18 to Madison, described the situation in the General Assembly as "very unpropitious to federal measures," and said: "that the Edicts of Mr. H—— are enregistered with less opposition by the Majority of that body, than those of the Grand Monarch are in the Parliements of France. He has only to say, let this be law—and it is Law." One Edict that Mr. H—— said should be Law was that the opponent who had defeated him in the convention, James Madison, should not be a senator, and if pos-sible not a member of the House, either.

Against his wishes, Madison was nominated in the General Assembly for a Senate seat. Henry Lee—Light-Horse Harry Lee, companion of the recent battle in Richmond—wrote to him on November 19 some details of his defeat: "The friends to the government exerted themselves to your behalf and altho you was not chosen yet you received strong testimonial of the unbounded attachment of one party and of the excessive jealousy of the other party. Mr. Henry on the floor exclaimed against your politi-cal character and pronounced you unworthy of the confidence of the people in the station of Senator. That your election would terminate in producing rivulets of blood throughout the land." (Perhaps Madison's small stature was the reason his election would produce only rivulets, instead of rivers, of blood) It seems that the Henry forces whispered that "you was an advocate for the surrender of the navigation of the M——" using again those fears about a giveaway, as demagogues might put it today, of the great river. Two solid Antifederalists were chosen as Vir-ginia's first senators—William Grayson, the orator in the Richmond con-vention, source of the anti-Madison rumor about the M—— River, and the old warhorse Richard Henry Lee.

Madison had not wanted to run for the Senate; as between the two houses he preferred the House. One reason was Henry's power in the General Assembly, which would pick the Senators, but Madison gave additional reasons to Edmund Randolph in a letter written on October 17 while he was still in New York: "I mean not to decline an agency in launching the new Government if such should be assigned to me in one of the Houses, and I prefer that latter [the House] chiefly because if I can render any service there it can only be to the public, and not even in imputation to myself." Madison did not want even to appear to benefit himself from the greater possibilities of personal gain that it was thought might accrue to the members of the smaller and more aristocratic Senate. In a later letter to Randolph, from Philadelphia on November 23 on his way home, after he had been defeated for a Senate seat by Henry and his cohorts, Madison wrote that under the circumstances of Antifederal domination, his only surprise was that "my name should have been honored by so great a vote as it received," and then gave another reason for his preference all along for the House: "It will less require a stile of life with which my circumstances do not square."

But Henry's attempted vengeance was not yet complete. The contending groups had agreed that members of the new House of Representatives should be chosen from newly drawn districts. That gave Henry the opportunity for what would later be called, in an honor of sorts for Elbridge Gerry, a gerrymander. Dominating the General Assembly that drew the lines and set the rules, Patrick Henry made sure that Madison's home county of Orange was accompanied by counties that were heavily Antifederalist. He also secured a provision that a representative must have a one year's residence in the district, which meant that Madison could not move his candidacy elsewhere. Further, the Antifederalists put up a strong candidate against him, the young man who had made a good appearance for them at the Richmond convention and who would one day—following Madison—be president of the United States under the Constitution he had opposed, James Monroe.

Madison had hoped that he would not have to leave New York to return to Virginia to go around personally asking for votes. Such electioneering was objectionable to him, and for his health and other reasons he did not want to make the long trip back to Virginia. But his friends wrote to him that he must. He came back to Orange County after Christmas and forced himself to learn how to "campaign," as it would later be put, and became proud to be good at it. He set to work and won this district, a district that had been gerrymandered against him, over formidable opposition, and he won it so convincingly that thereafter he kept on being reelected for as long as he wanted to be.

The big issue used against him was his alleged opposition to any amendments to the Constitution, which meant to any bill of rights, which meant—the most potent claim—to any specific written protection of religious liberty: there were many Baptists and other Dissenters and products of the Great Awakening around Culpeper and elsewhere in this Piedmont district of Virginia. If the campaign had included the negative television campaign spots of a later era there might have been pictures of little children having their Bibles snatched away by the hand of a big government, as a projection of what would happen if Madison, with his adamant opposition to any bill of rights amendments to the Constitution, were elected. In fact (and in private) Madison was adamantly opposed, *not* to amendments, certainly not to religious liberty, but to the second convention that the chief proponents of amendments wanted. Such a convention, in his view, would undo the carefully built structure of constitutional government, and lead to chaos and anarchy.

Certainly James Madison, of all people, the author (as we know now—then it was anonymous) of the Memorial and Remonstrance against Religious Assessments, and the floor manager for Jefferson's Virginia Statute for Religious Freedom, was no opponent of human rights; in fact he is one of a handful of people in recorded history who could truly use that cliché of later political declamation, "I yield to no one . . ." in his support for—his own phrase—"the great rights of mankind." He supported those rights, with an efficacy few in history could match, against the power of government. But he also knew that it was important to *have* a government for those rights to be protected against. Without the ordered liberty of government one loses not only order but also in the end liberty. He wanted to get this government under this Constitution going, and if he had altogether had his own way he would have waited before making amendments and alterations.

Apparently he did accept—or had earlier to some degree accepted—the position which the federalists had worked out and which James Wilson had expressed in his speech back in November in Philadelphia, that since the Constitution created a government of *limited* and *delegated* powers, there was no need to specify rights that were protected against it. Perhaps there would even be some danger in the implication that rights *not* specified were therefore not protected. And he did sometimes deprecate mere "parchment barriers" as protections of rights; religious liberty was effectively protected by the social reality of a "multitude of sects" more than by formal statements on paper.

But this episode is an instance very early in American history of the educational effect that can come from facing the voters. Madison found when he got to Virginia that the sentiment for a bill of rights was strong, and that a picture of him as firmly opposed to *any* amendments had been circulated by his opponents. So Madison set to work to take over the issue, as the Federalists had done in the Massachusetts convention and, with George Wythe's motion, in the Virginia convention.

To take the initiative meant also that he could define the terms: he supported a bill of fundamental civil rights, not a laundry list of objections to the Constitution of other kinds. Some of these common objections—like an amendment changing the taxing power—would go to the heart of the functioning of constitutional government, and Madison wanted to head those off. He also wanted to head off any new, second *convention:* he knew that that soufflé could not be made to rise twice, and that a second gathering assembling all the grievances against the first would be a disaster. He supported—promised—the introduction of amendments in the First Congress, and thus was committed to pursue the more expeditious *congressional* route, instead of the cumbersome (and, he thought, dangerous) method of a new *convention*.

How should he get the word out to his constituents? American politics was very new then, and there were no television studios or press conferences. He did gather himself to make the trip out to the court days in Louisa and Culpeper counties, adjacent to his home country of Orange, and there he did deliver actual political speeches. But for the most part he wrote letters to influential leaders in the county. Two of his letters were published in local newspapers. After his trip to Culpeper County he wrote a letter to a leading Baptist preacher there named George Eve. He did not deny that he had once been reluctant to support amendments. "I freely own that I have never seen in the Constitution as it now stands those serious dangers which have alarmed many respectable Citizens. Accordingly whilst it remained unratified, and it was necessary to unite the States in some one plan, I opposed all previous alterations as calculated to throw the States into dangerous contentions, and to furnish the secret enemies of the Union with an opportunity of promoting its dissolution."

That was his main reason for resisting amendments throughout: he did not want them used as a screen to destroy the Constitution itself. "Circumstances are now changed: The Constitution is established on the ratifications of eleven States and a very great majority of the people of America; and amendments, if pursued with a proper moderation and in a proper mode, will be not only safe, but may serve the double purpose of satisfying the minds of well meaning opponents and of providing additional guards in favour of liberty."

And so now, he tells the Reverend Mr. Eve, he is in favor of the right amendments. "Under the change of circumstances, it is my sincere opinion that the Constitution ought to be revised, and that the first Congress meeting under it, ought to prepare and recommend to the States for ratification, the most satisfactory provisions for all essential rights, particularly the rights of Conscience in the fullest latitude, the freedom of the press, trials by jury, security against general warrants &c."

James Madison had political credit with the Baptists, going back to his leading role in the passage of Jefferson's Statute for Religious Freedom and the defeat of Patrick Henry's bill for a General Assessment for religious teachers in 1784–86. That credit helped him now; pastor George Eve and John Leland and other Baptist leaders came around and actively supported him.

On the snowy election day February 2, 1789, the reduced turnout gave Madison the victory over Monroe by 336 votes out of 2,280 cast. He wrote to Edmund Randolph on March 1 that it had been important for his victory that he came down to Virginia: "I am persuaded that my appearance in the district was more necessary to my election than you then calculated. In truth it has been evinced by the experiment, that my absence would have left a room for the calumnies of antifederal partizans which would have defeated much better pretensions than mine. In Culpeper which was the critical County, a continued attention was necessary to repel the multiplied falsehoods which circulated."

James Madison took seriously the promise he had made to pastor Eve and many others, that he would introduce in the First Congress a set of amendments as a bill of rights. It was a personal promise as part of his election campaign; it was also a party promise, as it were, on the part of the supporters of the Constitution, in the Massachusetts ratifying convention, and in other conventions, including that of Virginia. It must be the most important campaign promise in the history of American politics.

Two

The drafter of George Washington's address to Congress on April 30, 1789, which was also the first presidential inaugural, was James Madison. The House of Representatives, feeling its way, responded after the custom of parliamentary bodies: having been formally addressed by the executive (elsewhere kings and queens), it formally replied. Its reply was drafted by—James Madison. The president, on May 8, responded to the House's response. And who drafted the presidential response? No peeking. Right, James Madison.

Madison was living a ghostwriter's dream, carrying on what the editor of his *Papers* calls a "dialogue with himself." And for good measure Madison drafted the president's response, on May 18, to the Senate's response to the president's address. Madison was like the two-headed lamb that E. B. White found in one of the children's books his wife was reviewing; he could sing in two-part harmony and cross-question himself for hours.

As in the spring and summer of 1789 the inert new machinery of a continent-sized federal republic began slowly to move, clanking and squeaking and testing its joints, Madison was standing at the levers. The "executive branch" was not organized until late in that summer; part of the first business of the First Congress was to provide for its organization. The judiciary, like the executive, existed in March of 1789 only in the few sentences of the Constitution; the Judiciary Act of that First Congress, setting up the federal courts, was one of its major accomplishments. For many weeks there was no government but Congress.

Within Congress the Senate, with Vice President John Adams presiding and pressing the issue, got itself bogged down in a seriocomic debate over whether the president should be called "His Most Benign Highness," "His Elective Highness," "His Highness, the President of the United States, and Protector of the Rights of the Same," or "Mr. President." The House of Representatives took all the important initiatives, except for the Judiciary Act. And within the first House of Representatives the "first man"—the leader—was James Madison. When after the First Congress had been in session for several weeks the newly elected president, George Washington, arrived in New York, in April, he turned to James Madison both as the ghostwriter of his speeches and the chief advisor about his course of action and conduct. Madison had a busy spring.

In Washington's address to Congress on April 30, 1789—the first presidential Inaugural—there were no specific recommendations or legislative proposals; back in February at Mount Vernon, when Madison had stopped there on his way to New York, Washington and Madison had agreed that a very long draft with many specific proposals that had been drafted by Washington's secretary should be set aside. Now in Madison's shorter version there was a dignified invocation of Providential purpose and the seriousness of the occasion, and—the note that Thomas Paine had struck, and that Madison had sounded in Philadelphia and in Richmond and in *The Federalist,* and that many new Americans would strike—an assertion of the distinct historical role of the government whose life was now beginning: "The preservation of the sacred fire of liberty," President Washington said, "and the destiny of the Republican model of Government, are justly considered as *deeply,* and perhaps as *finally* staked, on the experiment entrusted to the hands of the American people."

President Washington's Madison-drafted address suggested that Congress might want to exercise the power delegated by the Fifth Article of the Constitution—the power to propose amendments to the Constitution. The House's Madison-drafted response to the Madison-drafted presidential address said yes, we just might do that. President Washington's very short Madison-drafted response to the House's Madison-drafted response to President Washington's Madison-drafted address did not disagree.

But this intra-Madisonian dialogue did not recommend just *any* amendments; it suggested that Congress consider enacting—perhaps not surprisingly—Madison-style amendments. The president's address recommended amendments that would protect liberty—but not amendments that would endanger "an United and effective government." And Congress cheerfully responded to the president that it would consider amendments "under the influence of all the considerations to which you allude."

Madison in the summer of 1789 was leading the House of Representatives, which was leading the Senate and the government, during the sessions in the day, and advising the new president in the evenings. A note in the *Papers* says that he was acting as a sort of prime minister linking the two branches in the forming of the new government.

Three

In the House itself the amendments question—the bill of rights—was not as we might think today the first item on the agenda or on everybody's minds. Madison had to push to get that matter considered.

The first House of Representatives—wherein, the new Constitution said, money bills should originate—first dealt with, perhaps understandably, the sources of money for the new government, specifically in "imports," or tariffs, and second, perhaps understandably again, with the organization of the executive departments. James Madison took the initiative in both of these matters, doing research on the imports and exports and shipping of the several states—there were to be "tonnage" duties as well as "imposts"—and introducing a motion to establish departments of foreign affairs, the treasury, and war. But while the debates on these large and pressing matters were winding through the first weeks of the new government he remained aware of the importance of taking action, in this first session of the First Congress, on the amendments that would constitute a bill of rights. On May 4, while the House was engaged in its debates about "tonnage," Madison announced that he would bring up amendments to the Constitution on May 25.

There was a certain reluctance to get into the subject on the part of the House. American politicians were already "practical" people; they wanted to get on with the business of setting up the new government and governing, and there was resistance to the whole idea of amendments on the part of some, like Roger Sherman of Connecticut. But Madison persisted; without his persistence the amendments would not have come before the House, and the Congress, and the nation, in these first days.

On May 25 the House was still engaged in debate on imposts and tonnage, and apparently there was an agreement to postpone the subject of amendments for two weeks. On June 8, then, an important date in American history, James Madison rose in the House of Representatives and offered his version of a bill of rights (June 6, 1787, in the Federal Convention in Philadelphia; June 6, 1788, in the Virginia ratifying convention in Richmond; June 8, 1789, in the House of Representatives in New York: three great formative speeches in early June in successive years by James Madison).

Madison had prepared carefully. He used a pamphlet that had been published in Richmond that brought together in a handy way the more than two hundred amendments that had been proposed by seven of the state ratifying conventions, and he sifted out of those his own much shorter list or collection of proposals—nineteen of them at first. This sifting was of enormous importance: here was the chief sponsor of the bill of rights now selecting what shall, and shall not, be included. And in what words. All of the first ten amendments as we have them today were anticipated in Madison's list, and most passed on into the Constitution in his language, or something close to it (his language, that is, usually taken in turn from the language of one or another of the proposals from the states, which in their turn were sometimes taken from colonial or English history: what Madison was doing in this instance was selecting and editing as well as composing).

In Madison's June 8 speech, introducing his proposals, he said: "It appears to me that this house is bound by every motive of prudence, not to let the first session pass over without proposing to the state legislatures some things to be incorporated into the constitution, as will render it as acceptable to the whole people of the United States, as it has been found acceptable to a majority of them."

He was quite candid that a major motive was strategic:

> I wish, among other reasons why something should be done, that those who have been friendly to the adoption of this constitution, may have the opportunity of proving to those who were opposed to it, that they were as sincerely devoted to liberty and a republican government, as those who charged them with wishing the adoption of this constitution in order to lay the foundation of an aristocracy or despotism. It will be a desirable thing to extinguish from the bosom of every member of the community any apprehensions, that there are those among his countrymen who wish to deprive them of the liberty for

which they valiantly fought and honorably bled. And if there are amendments desired, of such a nature as will not injure the constitution, and they can be ingrafted so as to give satisfaction to the doubting part of our fellow citizens; the friends of the federal government will evince that spirit of deference and concession for which they have hitherto been distinguished.

This last point, that the adoption of a bill of rights would reassure "the doubting part of our fellow citizens," the moderate antifederalists, both about the goodwill of the federalists and about life under the Constitution, had been growing in importance for Madison; Thomas Jefferson, among others, had urged that consideration upon him. He was himself notable for a "spirit of deference and concession" (to use his words). He was a conciliator, above all a builder, and now it was time to bring as many as could be into spiritual harmony with the new constitutional order. Among the reasons for a written bill of rights there was this one: that it would go far toward reconciling its erstwhile opponents to the Constitution, and making it work.

Madison omitted all those amendments cast up by the state ratifying conventions that were likely to be seriously controversial, because, as he said in his notes for this speech, in order to enact an amendment it is necessary to "insure passage by ⅔ of congs. and ¾ of Sts." There was a high hurdle, or two high hurdles. He also omitted most of those proposed amendments that did not partake of the nature of great rights of mankind, and all that were in effect disputes about the powers and structure of government (like amendments removing the direct taxing power). He chopped the proposed amendments in two, and included almost exclusively the personal human rights. The exceptions to that rule—amendments adjusting the size and the compensation of Congress, although they made it over the congressional hurdle, failed in ratification by the states. Madison proposed to put a 100-word philosophical statement at the beginning of the whole Constitution—a preamble to the preamble—that would have echoed the Declaration of Independence (in somewhat less graceful language), declaring that all power rests in and derives from the people. This idea was dropped early in the debate in the House, more as a matter of literary than of political judgment: Thomas Jefferson's friend John Page of Virginia said that the phrase "We the People" had a "neatness and simplicity" as the beginning of a constitution that should not be interfered with, and the House, happily, rejected the Madisonian prefix and kept the phrase where it stands today.

Three other Madisonian proposals were also eliminated, either by the House or by the Senate. One would have limited court appeals where the value in controversy is below a certain amount of money. A second would have specifically asserted the doctrine of the separation of powers.

A third—by far the most important loss from Madison's proposals, both in his own eyes and in ours today—would have said that "no *state* shall violate the equal rights of conscience, or the freedom of the press, or the trial by jury in criminal cases"; the emphasis is mine, to point out the important feature of this, as it is sometimes called, "Lost Amendment."

These great rights of humankind were in the end to be protected only against *Congress,* which is to say, against the *federal* government. The states were not covered—not by this federal bill of rights. The states had their own bills of rights, and many would no doubt then have said that those state bills were an adequate protection. But not Madison. He regarded this as "the most valuable amendment in the whole list." This amendment, unlike the others, was Madison's own; it did not come—perhaps it is easy to understand why—from the state ratifying conventions; the states would thereby have placed their own activities under federal restraint. But Madison, who had made his lists of the vices of the state governments and had had extensive experience with those vices as a participant in both state and confederated governments, believed that the states were more likely to violate civil liberties than was the new federal union—a prediction that history has surely proved to be correct. The state governments, in the American federal union, mean also all the smaller jurisdictions, cities and towns and counties and school boards and special authorities, all of which are "creatures of the state"—New York City and what would one day be Cook County, and all of their manifold public actions—have no formal existence under this Constitution that was taking shape back in the late 1780s; they are creatures of New York state and what would one day be Illinois. When one thinks of all the activities that remained with the states under this Constitution—police and education and correctional institutions and highways and indeed, originally, all but a handful of the activities possible to governments—then one can see one reason why there is danger to civil liberty to be found at that level. Moreover, these smaller jurisdictions would have less of the complex cross-checking of multiplicity of groups than would the federal union, and would therefore be more prone to develop tyrannical majorities, oblivious to the rights of small minorities: this was part of Madison's theory in his great *Federalist* papers. But Madison here was relying not so much on any of these theories as on what he had observed in fact in the conduct of the states.

Had Madison's "Lost Amendment" been ratified, the history of American constitutional law—and therefore of human rights in the United States—would certainly have been different. But the amendment was taken out by the Senate—that second branch with its equal representation of states, the product of the Great Compromise! The amendment could not be restored in the conference, to Madison's dismay. This was the change he felt most keenly. The protection of liberties against the states (and all subordinate units) by the federal bill of rights had to wait until after the Civil War. In the aftermath of the victory over the secessionists, the Fourteenth Amendment was added to the Constitution, providing in its most important provision that "no *state* shall deprive any citizen of life, liberty, or property, without due process of the laws." This passage from the Fourteenth Amendment of 1868 was to be the most important addition to the Constitution after these amendments of 1789. It would pick up the term *due process of law* that Madison had already used in what was to become the Fifth Amendment, linked to the three-term series from John Locke: No person shall . . . be deprived of life, liberty, or property; without due process of law." That phrase of Madison's, like the "necessary and proper" clause in the body of the Constitution, was one of those small openings through which passed a vast development of governing, of thought, and of life—in this case, of protections of liberty. And alongside it in its 1868 application to the states, in the Fourteenth Amendment, is the most significant conceptual addition to James Madison's list of 1789: "the equal protection of the laws." That is the point at which the great claim of human equality, which had been a theme in the American political tradition, and in its English sources ("the poorest he hath a life to live as the richest he") was now raised to formal recognition in the constitution of a nation-state.

The application of the federal Bill of Rights to the states, in practical fact, would not follow directly upon the ratification of the Fourteenth Amendment in the late nineteenth century, but would wait until the middle of the twentieth century, when the Supreme Court would interpret the "liberty" one is not to be deprived of without "due process of law" as "incorporating" some, or all—the argument continues—of the liberties protected by the first eight amendments of the federal Bill of Rights. From which interpretation has followed our explosion of constitutional law, and presumably a vast increase in the area of protected liberty, in the last half of the twentieth century.

Most of that would have been obviated, or anticipated—now to return to the late eighteenth century—had Madison's "Lost Amendment" got through the Senate (which killed it on September 7, 1789) and then through the process of ratification. But it was instead—lost.

There is another provision in Madison's list that would have made a difference in American history, had it survived; it, too, was eliminated by the Senate in early September. Madison's version of the provision about bearing arms and a well-kept militia—which became the Second Amendment—read like this: "The right of the people to keep and bear arms shall not be infringed; a well armed and well regulated militia being the best security of a free country: *but no person religiously scrupulous of bearing arms shall be compelled to render military service in person.*"

I have underlined the part that got dropped by the Senate. Had it survived as part of the Bill of Rights, conscientious objection to war, on religious grounds, would have had a constitutional protection. But because this clause was removed, conscientious objection does not rest on any constitutional provision, but upon what lawyers call "legislative grace": Congress may grant, or Congress may take away, the provision for objection to military service on grounds of religious conscience. In fact, Congress has from the earliest days granted such status to those whom Madison presumably had in mind, the Quakers and the members of other historic peace churches. In the twentieth century the list of those eligible for such status has been widened, in the selective service acts, to those who object to war "because of religious training and belief." There has been an intricate interplay between Congress and the courts about the provision, which at one point included the belief in a supreme being, and then later did not. "Religious training and belief" has turned out, in the Vietnam era, in the interpretation of the Supreme Court, to include some folk who are not "religious" at all by conventional definitions, including their own—readers of Spinoza and ethical humanists. Having Madison's provision in the Constitution would not have solved the modern problem of whether there can be exemptions granted to the conventionally religious that are not granted to the equally sincere but less conventional, but it would have lifted the claim of conscientious objection to war to the status of a constitutional right.

That completes the list of the substantive changes that Congress and the states made in Madison's original proposals; given the ramifications of the subject and the complicated multiplicity of the hurdles, and the long list of possibilities, it is surprisingly short list of changes. The Bill of Rights came through to the end essentially as Madison had composed it.

Four

There was an important change in form. Madison on June 8 in the House had proposed to weave the amendments into the body of the Constitution, with his general philosophical statement inserted as a prefix, before the preamble. The main body of the list of civil rights—almost all those that survive in the Constitution today—would have been inserted in Article 1, section 9, between clauses three and four, in the list of the powers (and nonpowers) of Congress. Madison's other proposals would have been sprinkled throughout the Constitution in the places they appeared to fit.

The amendments were still in that form when they were reported by the House Select Committee to whom they were referred. But then Roger Sherman of Connecticut, who was not himself even in favor of the bill of rights, made a proposal that later commentators would endorse: instead of being scattered throughout the document they should all be grouped at the end. "We might as well endeavor to mix brass, iron, and clay," said Sherman, "as to incorporate such heterogeneous articles." Madison objected that there was a neatness and propriety in incorporating the changes into the text, and had his way on that round, but later in the House's deliberations Sherman made his proposal again, and this time carried his point. So the amendments came out of the House in the form we have them today, as attachments to, rather than sprinkled insertions into, the body of the Constitution.

After the June 8 speech by Madison the legislative history of the Bill of Rights is one of those complicated stories that though part of the glory of republican government is nevertheless tedious to recount: You don't want a Committee of the Whole? said Madison; all right then, a Select Committee. No, said the House, we've decided we want a Committee of the Whole after all. But the House did not go into the Committee of the Whole. On July 14, while Parisians were storming the Bastille, the Americans in their new House of Representatives were discussing tonnage, imposts, and the salary of the vice-president ($5,000? Nothing?) On July 21 Madison reminded the House that it was supposed to go into a Committee of the Whole to discuss the bill of rights, and the members decided this time that they wanted a Select Committee after all. Madison was the Virginia representative on that Select Committee (like the Grand Committees of the Federal Convention, a committee with a member from each state). The Select Committee reported on July 28, without having made much change in Madison's draft. On August 3, Madison had to prod them again; events in the summer of 1789 were moving faster in France than they were in the United States. Madison moved that on August 12 the House take up the amendments reported by the Select Committee, and the House resolved that on that day it would. Not on August 12, but on August 13, it did, and met until August 24 as the House itself hearing this report from itself. Through those days in August 1789 these basic constitutional protections of American liberties were debated and put into form, by the fifty-nine members of the First Congress, under the prodding and leadership of the young researcher from Virginia James Madison.

Included among the list of amendments there were versions of what would become the Ninth, which says that enumerating rights is not to "deny or disparage" *un*enumerated ones—a barrier against the misinterpretation about which many, including Madison, had given warnings, and the Tenth, which reserves all unspecified residual powers to the states or to the people. We often speak of the Bill of Rights as the first ten amendments, but strictly speaking these last two are not protections of civil rights but additional points about their location in, and out of, this government. The Bill of Rights, speaking more narrowly, is the first eight amendments.

Twice in the House considerations of the amendments a representative—in the second case Elbridge Gerry—moved that the word *expressly* be added to the provision on reserved powers—the tenth amendment as it would become—so that it would say, "The powers not *expressly* delegated" to the federal government would be reserved to the states. If that motion had carried, American constitutional law, and therefore the history of the United States, would have been altered in immense, incalculable ways. The doctrine of "implied powers," which is another of those hinges upon which the door of the Constitution swings open to the possibilities of an expanding, unseen future, would have been impossible. If that door had slammed shut, the prospects for the American government would abruptly have shrunk. Justice Marshall's portentous decision in *McCulloch v. Maryland,* in 1819, stating there are powers of government *implied* in the Constitution, would have been impossible, if the Constitution itself specified that the federal government had only those powers *expressly* delegated to it. Fortunately, James Madison opposed these motions; he anticipated the later statements of the doctrine of implied powers by saying that "it was impossible to confine a government to the exercise of express powers; there must necessarily be admitted powers by implication, unless the Constitution descended to recount every minutia."

The House on August 24 sent its version of the amendments, still very much at core Madison's original proposals, to the Senate; the Senate, then meeting in private, made the important changes already mentioned—defeating the "Lost Amendment" applying the Bill of Rights to the states—and altering language here and peeling off proposals there and combining provisions in the other place. One cannot quite say that this was only cheese-paring and editorial work, because every word and comma in this fundamental law, this wholesale politics, can make a difference, but Madison's original proposals come through the Senate also, somewhat tightened and perhaps improved, nearly what we have today as the federal Bill of Rights. The combining by the Senate reduced the seventeen amendments of the House report down to the twelve that were to be sent to the states. On September 9 the Senate sent its amended version back to the House, which on September 19 and 21 discussed and voted on that amended version, agreeing and disagreeing, and which then resolved that there be a committee of conference with the Senate. Madison was one of the three House conferees; Roger Sherman was another. William Paterson of New Jersey, the small-state leader who had been Madison's opponent in the first months of the Federal Convention, was one of the three Senate conferees.

The only significant change made by the conference committee had to do with the wording of the religious freedom guarantee, which had been altered this way and that throughout this legislative history. According to the biography by Irving Brant, James Madison wrote the version that the conference committee adopted, which returned the religious liberty provision back more or less to his original intention—if we may use that phrase in this sensitive context—in his June 8 proposal. On September 23 Madison made the conference report to the House, which on the next day by a vote of thirty-seven to fourteen agreed to the conference report. On the next day, September 25, which is one of the dates celebrated as the anniversary of the Bill of Rights, the Senate also agreed.

There were important changes in substance and form and language as these proposed amendments passed from James Madison's hand, on June 8, 1789, through the complicated process in the House, the Senate, the conference committee, and the ratifications by the state legislatures, into the Constitution of the United States on December 15, 1791. But I believe one can say that all of these accumulated decisions, changes, and refinements, from all of these public agencies, were not as important as those that James Madison made in the first place, sitting alone at his desk in New York, with the pamphlet gathering together the amendments by state ratifying conventions before him, picking, omitting, choosing, editing, adding. He formulated his list. Essentially, that list survived, and came to be part of the core of the American government, and has lasted and done its work down to the present day.

18

Bulwarks and Palladiums

One

THE NEW CONSTITUTION, shifting into gear and beginning to move, provided in its Article V two means of proposing amendments to itself—by two-thirds of both houses of Congress, as in the case of the Bill of Rights and in all other actual cases in American history, or by a convention called on the application of the legislatures of two-thirds of the states. The convention method has so far served no purpose except to be another item for students in civics classes to memorize.

The Constitution then proposed two possible methods of ratification, between which Congress could choose: by the legislatures of three-fourths of the states, or by conventions in three-fourths of the states. The second method has been used only in the one instance, unusual in some other ways, of the twenty-first amendment. That amendment, in 1933, repealed the eighteenth amendment that had prohibited alcoholic beverages. It stands alone as an amendment whose only purpose was to cancel another one. It also stands alone in that Congress provided—in February 1933, with the Democrats back on power in Congress, and soon to come into power in the White House in March—that it be ratified in *conventions,* not the legislatures, of the states. These conventions in fact turned out to be little more than recordings of a popular referendum, with delegates already pledged one way or the other; they were not deliberative bodies. In the parched nation in 1933 the thirty-six states then necessary to make the required three-fourths had ratified already before the year was up, "a record," Corwin observes, "for celerity." But that was unusual. All other amendments have taken longer, and gone the other route.

The first to do so were the first ten amendments in 1789–91. Congress, having put together its proposed twelve, requested that the "President of the United States," as it was agreed to call this official, transmit the proposed amendments to the governors of the states, in order that the governors might submit them for ratification by the state legislatures. We do not have good records of the debates in the state legislatures over the Bill of Rights. New Jersey and Maryland were the first states to ratify, early in 1790. Then came North Carolina, which, having not yet ratified the Constitution itself, was able to do two potent ratifications in rapid succession, bang, bang, Constitution, Bill of Rights. In the summer of 1788, the state had held a convention in Hillsboro that echoed many of the themes of the Virginia ratifying convention, but with a different outcome: the antifederalists prevailed. The ratifying convention had refused even to ratify with conditional amendments; it had voted instead to remain in a state of friendly suspension from the union. Now in November of 1789, with the new government already functioning up in New York, North Carolina held another convention, this one at Fayetteville, and ratified the Constitution. The correspondence between William R. Davie, who had been a delegate to the Federal Convention in Philadelphia, and James Madison, indicates that the passage by Congress in its first session of these proposed amendments, this Bill of Rights, went far to change North Carolina's position on the Constitution itself. North Carolina entered the union, and shortly thereafter its state legislature ratified the amendments.

Five of the states that subsequently ratified the other amendments—Delaware, New Hampshire, New Jersey, New York, and Pennsylvania—rejected the first two of the Congress's proposed twelve—the amendments about the size of the House and compensation of Congressmen—so that these were dropped; these housekeeping matters are not a part of the Bill of Rights. Massachusetts had a complicated fight over ratifying, and failed to do so, apparently, on a technicality; two other states, Connecticut and Georgia, did not ratify. These three then existing states that failed to ratify would do so in 1939—the Bill of Rights' 150th birthday—as a symbolic gesture. Meanwhile the amendments—the Bill of Rights—had been the law of the land for a century and a half, since December 15, 1791, when the tenth state ratified. That tenth state, fittingly perhaps, was Virginia, the state with which the whole process of protecting the great rights of humankind with solemn bills and declarations had begun, back in May of 1776, with the Virginia Declaration of Rights.

There had been, as one might guess, a fight in Virginia. The House of Delegates had voted to ratify right away in December of 1789, but not the Senate. The two United States Senators from Virginia, the antifederalists William Grayson and Richard Henry Lee, chosen by the Patrick Henry forces instead of James Madison, had undertaken to write letters to the governor and the state legislature denouncing the amendments as inadequate and "contrary to the wishes of our Country," using the word "country" to mean Virginia. James Madison wrote to President Washington, on December 5, 1789, that this letter "is well calculated to keep alive the disaffection to the Government, and is accordingly applied to that use by the violent partizans." The Virginia Senate, after defeating the ratification of the amendments, explained that they were far short of what the people of Virginia wanted, and by no means sufficient to secure the rights of the people. Patrick Henry and Richard Henry Lee and other Virginians found the list of amendments inadequate, in part, because they did not include amendments providing for the protections of the *states* (as distinct from persons). They wanted those government-restricting amendments that the opponents of the Constitution had included in their long, long list of proposed alternatives from Virginia—in other words, exactly those amendments that Madison had been careful to exclude. Patrick Henry is reported to have said that he would have preferred a single amendment disallowing direct taxes to all the amendments approved by Congress. One might say he and Lee and Grayson were fighting the lost battle of the Virginia ratifying convention all over again. The federalists in Virginia—Governor Edmund Randolph now among them—let the matter lie, and allowed boiling passions to simmer down. Two years later, quietly, both houses in Virginia did ratify the amendments and they became the law of the land.

Two

We Americans in the two centuries since these amendments became part of the Constitution have been inclined to treat them as a list of separated rights each standing on its own. To some extent the several clauses even develop their own constituencies: journalists often seem to think the First Amendment includes nothing except freedom of the press; there is a whole church-state contingent preoccupied with the religion clauses of the First Amendment; the gun lobby makes its special use of the second amendment, detaching the second part ("the right of the people to keep and bear arms shall not be infringed") from the preceding clause, which gives it its eighteenth-century justification, and its qualification ("A well-regulated Militia being necessary to the security of a free people"). Today it is mostly criminal lawyers, their clients, and writers of courtroom dramas who focus on the rights of the accused that are protected in the later articles. One can picture a creative writing class requiring each student to outline a movie script derived form a different provision: unreasonable searches and seizures, double jeopardy, excessive bail, cruel and unusual punishment, trial by jury, a speedy trial, indictment by grand jury, a public trial, the right to have a lawyer, the right to be informed of charges and confront accusers.

But one need not look at the Bill of Rights only in that way, as a list of separate items; one may also see the interconnections, with a few great themes around which these rights and liberties cluster.

One theme is each person's claim to a domain outside the public realm—to be "secure," as the fourth amendment says, in one's person, house, papers, and effects, against those unreasonable searches and seizures, like the British customs agents ripping open your trunks and boxes, and coming in your house and onto your boat to see whether you are smuggling anything. Your premises and effects are not to be invaded without a warrant—and not any "general" warrant, any writ of assistance like those that James Otis spoke against in 1761, but a specific one.

Many of these items have specific causes in American colonial history, or in English history before that. The American colonials, particularly in Boston and New York, had reason to specify the right not to have soldiers quartered in one's house, as is stated in the third amendment. "A man's home is his castle"; presumably a woman's, too. These rights to one's own domain are specific written protections against the peremptory invasions by officialdom, the knock on the door at night, the arbitrary intrusions by power, of which the world, alas, has seen all too much—new forms of it—in the years since these amendments were written. One may not have one's property taken for a public use without just compensation, as is stated at the end of the fifth amendment. The city of New Haven cannot take your house and yard in order to locate a new public school, nor the state of Connecticut level your dry cleaning business in order to run a connector to the interstate highway, without paying you justly for it—so the amendment says—and by implication without public hearings and serious argument demonstrating the necessity for a worthy public use.

On a much larger scale, the most important of all the provisions in the later amendments, the powers that be may not deprive you of "life, liberty, or property" (the trio that goes back to John Locke) "without due process of law"—the immensely important phrase that James Madison picked up, in all probability, from New York's long and rambling list of recommended amendments. That list included a variation on this ancient worthy theme that ended as follows: "or deprived of his Privileges, Franchises, Life, Liberty, or Property, but by *due process of law*" (emphasis mine).

For this Madison could have reached all the way back into English history to a statute of King Edward III in 1335: "No man of what state or condition he be, shall be put out of his lands or tenements nor taken; nor disinherited, nor put to death, without he be brought to answer by due process of law." This ancient statute rested upon the still more ancient foundation of the Magna Carta, which has a famous chapter twenty-nine with a similar protection, but instead of "due process" the phrase "except . . . by the law of the land." This last was also the phrase used in the Virginia Declaration of Rights and in subsequent state declarations and in the proposals from the state ratifying conventions—except those from New York. New York's state legislature had in January of 1787 enacted a statute called "An Act concerning the Rights of the Citizens of this state," which statute had said that no one should be deprived of any right except by "due process of law." The phrase was therefore available a year and a half later, when the delegates to the New York ratifying convention in Poughkeepsie composed their long list of recommended amendments. John Lansing—the same John Lansing who had been a delegate to the Federal Convention, essentially an opponent of the developing stronger Constitution, and who had left early—now in the work of listing recommended amendments, proposed that phrase "due process." It passed the New York ratifying convention that way, and so there it was in the booklet of state recommendations that James Madison a year later (now 1789) took in hand when he sat down to make his list of proposed amendments to the United States Constitution. It was there, alongside all the other state recommendations on the same point, which, like the much more prestigious source, the Virginia Declaration of Rights, not to mention the Magna Carta, all said simply "the law of the land." But Madison quarried the phrase "due process of law" from New York's proposals. This may sound like a merely verbal matter, or a question only of style, but in these constitutional matters the difference in a word, a phrase, even a comma, can turn out to have immense consequences. So much was riding on every nuance of expression that one feels that Madison might find his pencil breaking under the weight of it all. To say "the law of the land" would leave open the possibility that one could be deprived of life, liberty, or property simply by a legislative enactment: if a legislature passed it, then it would be "the law of the land." But the phrase "due process of law" moves the protection up a notch. Now something more than barebones legality is required: a *process* of law, which includes the care and protection afforded by formal and proper—

"fair"—procedures of courts. England, with its strong heritage since 1688 of parliamentary supremacy, could not then have a constitutional provision for due process constraining the legislature, as does the United States. The United States has such a provision—among the most important distinctions of this country as a result of these developments in its first days. The due process clause in the Fifth Amendment was then to be picked up and applied to the states by the Fourteenth Amendment, in 1868, and to be a rich and complicated and very important part of the history of this country.

One great theme was the protection of a realm of the self beyond public claims; another, closely linked to it, was the theme of due process of law. Both of these, looked at negatively, are restraints upon governmental power: ours is a formally self-restraining governmental system, a system that contains limitations upon itself, within itself. Looked at positively, they affirm a dimension of the human person that extends beyond the reach of government and of society, that "transcends" this or any other society, and that this social order tells itself to respect. These themes, like the others we will name in a moment, are the assurance in the nation's supreme and written law, that we are not to be a "totalitarian" government, as the twentieth century would learn to call it, or an absolutism, a despotism, a tyranny of any other kind. Although this is a government in which the people are the foundation of all power, and the majority is to rule, it is also a government in which it is very clear that "the people" can do great wrong, and that "the people's representatives" in the legislature, and in all other branches of government, can do great wrong, and that there are limits to their power, protections of the individual citizen against their power—against "the people's" power. Madison kept saying, in various ways, where power is, there is the threat to liberty, and that certainly included—at the top of his list in fact—"the people," the "majority," the popular legislature.

Three

These are rights and liberties in which the personal or private or individual aspect dominates, and the same is true of another great theme of the Bill of Rights, the protection of those who are accused of crime from arbitrariness or other unfairness in the processes of justice. Edward Corwin, the noted twentieth-century constitutional scholar, wrote that "Amendments IV, V, VI, and VIII constitute a 'bill of rights' for accused persons." These were very important rights for the first-generation republicans who shaped the American government, because they knew what was to *be* the accused. They had suffered, their friends and relatives had suffered, they knew people who had suffered, from the arbitrariness and high-handedness of the royal administration of the colonies. They identified with the accused sufficiently to feel deeply about these protections. They insisted that they be written into the Federal Constitution, as they had already been in most of the states. In those days, the people forced these protections on the elite, because the people knew what it was to be the accused, to be treated unfairly in the courts. Two hundred years later a giant middle-class democracy has grown on these foundations, in which the broad populace, across barriers of class and race, no longer identifies as clearly with the accused. These protections, once the people's own, and at the core of the rights they claimed, no longer have the broad popular support they had in the beginning.

These amendments—IV, V, VI, VIII—give protection against unreasonable searches and seizures, double jeopardy, excessive bail, and cruel and unusual punishment; it is under this last head that many, including judges, have challenged the death penalty. The protection of trial by jury ("that palladium of our liberties," as the founders regularly said), and the right of a *speedy* trial, and indictment by grand jury, and a *public* trial, and the right to have a lawyer, and to be informed of charges and to confront accusers. There could not rightfully be, here, a "victim of nameless accusers." These provisions came to James Madison's desk, by way of the recommendations of the state ratifying conventions, for the most part from the state constitutions and declarations of rights of the decade before—the new constitutions the state wrote after John Adams's resolution in the spring of 1776. Behind those state provisions there were decades and centuries of colonial, and English, history; a few of the provisions—like the antecedent of "due process," as we have seen, and the right to a jury trial and the protection against unreasonable seizures—go all the way back to the Magna Carta, and the right of petition and to bear arms to the English Bill of Rights of 1689. But these historical origins, and in a few cases this great antiquity, should not obscure for us the distinctiveness of the American achievement—that almost all of these protections were first raised to constitutional status by the American states—and of the federal constitutional achievement—that the provisions were sorted, put together, applied, and carried further than they had been anywhere else. The United States, with the ratification of the first eight amendments, went a good deal further than in England, which in turn was ahead of the Continent. Corwin says of protections of accused persons in Articles V, VI, and VIII, that "in more than one respect they represent a distinct advance upon the English law of that time and indeed for many years afterward." Something of the same could be said of the other provisions of a written constitution which as the Supreme

Law of the Land was enforceable by the courts against all the organs of government, including the legislatures, including the people's representatives. In England the great rights from Magna Carta onward were extracted from, and enforced against, the king, as the preexistent sovereign power; there was no comparable protection against Parliament, which was presumed to stand as the expression of the people over against the king. Parliament, so far as the law is concerned, is supreme and can do whatever it wants; there is no written constitution and no judicial review. It is not sufficiently comprehended in the popular democracy, perhaps the mass democracy, that the United States has become, how distinctive a part of our republic it is, that even the people's government itself should be restrained—*constitutionally* restrained—from invasions of those claims of a human being that transcend all societies.

Four

Exactly at the time the Americans were writing their Bill of Rights the French were getting their Revolution underway. While the American congressmen were debating about imposts and tonnage the French were storming the Bastille; one does a cultural double-take to learn that they sent the key they captured, those French revolutionaries, to a great revolutionary across the water: George Washington. When the Americans got around at last to their Bill of Rights, in August, the French were getting ready to write their Declaration of the Rights of Man and Citizen, adopted by the French National Assembly on August 26, 1789.

Where the French declaration was heavy on Ought and Ought Not and Should Be and high aspiration, the American bill was made of homelier stuff: concrete protections and specific commands. They are not speculative or hortatory but mandatory: Congress *shall* make no law, no soldier *shall* be quartered, no person *shall* be held. The American document is not a hope but a law, written by experienced legislators and intended to be enforceable in court, as Americans are still finding out 200 years later.

When the French adopted the constitution of the First Republic, in 1792, it was supposed to be so perfect that it made no provision for amendment. The Americans had made the same mistake in 1781 with the highly imperfect Articles of the Confederation. Upon ratifying the Constitution, therefore, their first step was to amend it. And to amend their ideas about amending it: Madison himself had not originally favored the amendments so soon. He had his mind changed by the merits of the opposing arguments, the realities of power, and the pressure of public opinion. That change of mind was a fitting example of his own ideas, which in turn were the epitome of the American spirit of '89.

Madison had worked out an understanding of pluralism and of checks on power and had planted that understanding in the Constitution that was now creaking into action. At the core of this understanding was an acceptance of the persistence of differences among human groups. There was not going to be a "New Humanity" on the "other side" of the revolution; when you got to the other side, as the Americans had already long since done by '89, you found humanity still loaded with self-interest, and with differing attachments and values. In "republican" politics—in its American, Madisonian variety—those differences were not something to be excoriated, dismissed, or stamped out in the name of "the People" or "the Revolution" or "Justice" or "Virtue." They were not even much to be regretted, these human differences. They were rather to be taken for granted—and turned to the support of liberty and of republican government.

What one reads about the leaders of the French Revolution differs markedly on that decisive point. They did not seem, to put it mildly, to rejoice in the differences among factions. R. R. Palmer wrote this about the influence of Rousseau upon them:

> In the philosophy of [Rousseau's] Social Contract the "people" or "nation" is a moral abstraction. It is by nature good; its will is law. It is a solid indivisible thing. That the people might differ among themselves was a thought that Rousseau passed over rather hurriedly. . . . All struggles were between the people and something not the people, between the nation and something antinational and alien. On the one hand was the public interest, self-evident, beyond questioning by an upright man; on the other hand were private interests, selfish, sinister and illegitimate. The followers of Rousseau were in no doubt which side they were on.

The American leaders did not view "the People" as a simple solid indivisible thing, always right, so that human beings who disagreed were somehow nonpeople. On the contrary Madison was particularly wary about "the people" in their guise as the majority, and about what they would do to those who disagreed. That was a main reason why he became the chief sponsor of the Bill of Rights.

The American leaders did not set about right away "unmasking the enemies of the country" (as Robespierre and St. Just did). What the key Americans did in 1789—Madison in particular—was the opposite: they set about bringing their opponents into the fold.

That the American founders stood, and still do stand, for a different kind of revolutionary politics is suggested by some remarks by the interesting thinker in the Polish Solidarity movement, Adam Michnic. Michnic wrote about their twentieth-century Polish protest movement: "I pray that we do not change from prisoners into prison guards," and worried that "by using force to storm the bastilles of old we shall unwittingly build new ones." And to the same point Michnic wrote that Solidarity never had a vision of an ideal society: "It wants to live and let live. Its ideals are closer to the American Revolution than to the French."

Five

The great themes of the Bill of Rights so far named—the right to one's own domain, the requirement of due process of law, the protections of the accused—are all primarily to be understood, though they play their part in the health of the social whole, under the aspect of the rights of the individual person. The great and fundamental theme postponed until last, however, has much more of a social aspect than these others. The freedoms of belief and thought and speech and press and political agitation are required by, and beneficial to, the society as well as the individual.

The most important of all the items on the lists of rights and liberties were gathered together by the Senate into one amendment, which when the winnowing by the ratifications was complete became our First Amendment. When James Madison first proposed these items on June 8 they came in three separate paragraphs. The one on religious freedom said that "the Civil rights of none shall be abridged on account of religious belief or worship, nor shall any national religion be established." What in the late twentieth century would come to be called the "accommodationists"—that is, those who take some less than absolute position on the separation of church and state—sometimes point to this original Madisonian formulation as evidence that he intended only that a national established religion be disallowed, not impartial governmental aids to all religions. But whatever he may have meant in this political context—an attempt to draft an amendment acceptable to ten diverse state legislatures and appropriate to the Constitution of the new union of thirteen diverse states—it seems clear that Madison himself in other contexts—as a younger man in Virginia composing his Memorial and Remonstrance, and as an older man in the national government taking positions on relevant issues—was inclined to be more like the "separationists" in these twentieth-century controversies. But of course that is anachronistic. In his own time and place these later refinements and marginal issues were not the main point. To say that there should be no national religion, and no civil disability for anyone because of religion, which today's disputants take for granted, was then still of great and central significance.

Madison's original draft had another clause, which got dropped by the Senate: "nor shall the full and equal rights of conscience be in any manner, or on any pretext, infringed." One striking feature of this clause, as the clincher of Madison's provision for religious freedom, is its emphatic elaboration: not just *full* rights, but also *equal* rights, of conscience; not abridged in *any manner* or on *any pretext*. Here was James Madison stomping his foot and naming the root of the entire structure: that conscience be free.

The other two original Madisonian paragraphs that were to become the First Amendment went like this:

> The people shall not be deprived or abridged of their right to speak, to write, or to publish their sentiments; and the freedom of the press, as one of the great bulwarks of liberty, shall be inviolable.
>
> The people shall not be restrained from peaceably assembling and consulting for their common good; nor from applying to the legislature by petitions, or remonstrances for redress or their grievances.

Madison made the subject of the sentence not, as in the version that became our First Amendment, "Congress," which shall make no law abridging these rights, but rather "the people," who shall not be deprived of them. That beginning, and the slightly fuller elaboration of the rights of what we call free speech and free press—"their [the people's] right to speak, to write, or to publish their sentiments"—gives the guarantee a coherence, a clear link to the process of public argument, and a solid location in the people as the agent to whom these rights are assured. Madison gave the freedom of the press—in the context of these *people's* rights—an extra emphasis with his description of it as "one of the great bulwarks of liberty." (*Bulwark* was one of the founders' favorite words for these protections; *palladium* was another.) And peaceful assembly is given a reason and a purpose: "consulting for the common good."

Madison's sentences have the advantage, over the First Amendment into which they were squeezed, of a little more space and a few more words, and Madison's words are able therefore to convey, as the terse phrases of the First Amendment may not, the civic and communal as well as the personal aspect of the fundamental liberties. Madison's version conveys also their interconnection, and their location in "the people," and their role in the great tournament of reason by which a republic was to conduct its life: the people's right to speak, to write, to publish, to assemble and to consult for common good, and—I elaborate on my own—to engage in that endless exercise of mutual persuasion which is the core of the great nation then taking form.

The freedoms of thought and belief and "conscience" and speech and

writing and publishing and arguing and assembling to debate and organize do, to be sure, have their personal or private aspect; no modern
American would fail to see that. That they also have a public dimension
is more likely to be overlooked: that the republic rests on public liberty,
serving the public good.

The great classic of the early stages of the modern development of
these liberties, John Milton's *Areopagitica,* has the oft-quoted sentence,
apparently asserting simply the personal or private need for self-
expression: "Give me the liberty to know, to utter, and to argue freely
according to conscience, above all liberties."

But this uttering according to conscience is not for the benefit of the
utterer only, that his inner self be given expression, though that is part of
the matter; in the uttering and arguing we also serve each other's benefit,
and we do so even when we are in some sense, in somebody's sense, in
some degree, wrong, for the reasons Milton expressed better than Jefferson did: the mingling of the truth with error, the provocation "error"
represents to restate, rediscover "truth" . . . the endless social process of
mutual correction and illumination. Milton and then John Locke, and
then Thomas Jefferson, presented a picture of truth contending with error
in some field of contest—later to be domesticated by Holmes and others
into a marketplace—in which if truth has a chance—a free and open
encounter—and its natural weapons, free argument and debate, it will
doubtless prevail; the surest suppressing of error is its confuting.

But truth's prevailing, and winning out over all the other winds of
doctrine, is not the only purpose of these liberties: governing, deciding
what shall be done in a free society, is another, and a central one. Give
me, and you, too, the liberty to know, to utter, and to argue freely, in
order that it may be by such mutual understanding of our differences, our
different "interest," yes, but our different understandings of the public
good as well, and by our collectively reasoning about it—our "consulting
for the common good," as Madison put it—we may to some important
measure, make reason and not power our governor, and self-government
replace other-government. The model for the governing of free societies
is what happens in a parliament, a legislative body, a jury (that palladium
of our liberties), rather than what happens in a command post, though
many of the latter are necessary in a republic as in any government.

One hundred and forty years after that summer in which James Madison introduced the Bill of Rights, Justice Louis Brandeis looked back at
the American founders and wrote, in an opinion in a case dealing with
freedom of speech: "Those who won our independence believed that in
government the deliberative forces should prevail over the arbitrary and
that the fitting remedy for evil counsels is good ones. Believing in the

power of reason as applied through public discussion, they eschewed silence coerced by law."

Elsewhere in the same paragraph Brandeis wrote "that the greatest menace to freedom is an inert people; that the public discussion is a public duty; and that this should be a fundamental principle of American government." In other words the ground of freedom of speech is not only to protect the "expression" of the private urges of the isolated individual, but also, and primarily, to conduct the business of the common life by deliberation rather than force.

With the addition of these amendments the shaping of constitutional foundations of the American government was almost complete, as nearly complete as such things are in human affairs. Here now was a federal republic in which the people ruled—but through a careful set of divided and balanced powers, checking each other. The people were the foundation of all power—but their interest, will, and mind were filtered through a system of representatives in order that reason and virtue might play a larger role. The people were the sovereign power, not through the vagueness of the "general will" or the impossible means of unanimity, but through the concrete specificity of the larger number of votes in specified election in a particular time and place. The majority rules—but the majority that rules today is formed in an atmosphere of freedom that allows it to be overturned tomorrow. The majority has moral dignity only as it is formed in freedom and maintains itself in freedom: as it is continually overturned and reformed.

With the addition of the Bill of Rights to the Constitution, James Madison completed the work of constructive statesmanship that had begun—let us say, to pick a date—in 1786, when he had made his first research notes, and had introduced the resolution in the Virginia Assembly that led to the Annapolis convention, which in turn had led to the Federal Convention in Philadelphia.

He went on to many other services, to be sure, including the protecting of the essential meaning of the Bill of Rights in the 1798 battle over the Alien and Sedition laws. He went on to serve as key congressman and early advisor to the first president and then collaborator with Jefferson in defending the positions that led to the formation of a great political party, and then as secretary of state, and then as president, and then as elder statesman. But in none of these later roles was he doing anything as distinctive as in this short period when he was in his thirties and by carrying out and making use of some researches he truly did help to make a nation.

The ratification of the Bill of Rights may be taken also as the end— the end of a beginning—of that longer period that began, let us say, as

John Adams said in his old age, on the day in 1761 when James Otis in the old Council Chamber in Boston challenged the general warrants, the writs of assistance, that allowed British officials to enter home and ship, as against the fundamental principles of English law, and against natural equity, and that stirred young Adams to his career ("Here this day, in the old Council Chamber," Adams wrote in later life, "the child Independence was born"). Or the period that began when young Patrick Henry at the tail end of a session of the House of Burgesses in Virginia in 1765 proposed a set of resolutions attacking the Stamp Act, and insisted that only the General Assembly of Virginia could lay taxes on Virginians, and then said something in response to the cry of "treason" that memory and legend would embroider. From the beginnings in the early 1760s through to the end of the 1780s there stretched an extraordinary period of political creativity, in which the American people, in conventions and Congress, and in pamphlets and speeches, and in reflection and study, thought and deliberated and argued themselves into existence as an unusual nation.

Six

Thomas Jefferson sailed from France on October 23, 1789, for a visit home, fully expecting to return for the two years remaining in his term as America's minister, but he never did. He had been there in Paris during the first explosion of the French Revolution, and had greeted it with enthusiasm and showers of proposals for the improvement of the human lot. He came back across the Atlantic supposedly for a six month's leave, but when he landed in Norfolk on November 23, he was greeted immediately with the news that President Washington had appointed him the nation's first secretary of state. He did not want to accept, but he did.

He was in office to receive, as the designated federal official, the notification that North Carolina had ratified the Constitution and joined the union, and then that Maryland, North Carolina, New Hampshire, South Carolina, Delaware, Pennsylvania, and New York, ratified ten of the twelve amendments that Congress had proposed to them as a bill of rights. Thomas Jefferson, the most eminent consistent champion of a written bill of rights, was an appropriate person to be receiving these notifications. Together with the states that had already ratified this group made nine, but by now ten states were required to make the necessary three-fourths of the states. It was not until December 15, 1791, as we have said, more than two years into the life of the new government, that Virginia finally cranked the amendments through the two houses of its General Assembly, and the Bill of Rights became the law of the land.

On the following March 1, in 1792, Secretary of State Jefferson sent to the governors of the states an official notice that the ratification process was complete and that these amendments were now a part of the Constitution. In June 1963 *Harper's* magazine carried the text of this letter of notification under the ironic heading "First Things First." Jefferson's letter went as follows:

> I have the honor to send you herein enclosed, two copies duly authenticated, of an Act concerning certain fisheries of the United States, and for the regulation and government of the fisherman employed therein: also an Act to establish the post office and post roads within the United States; also the ratifications by three fourths of the Legislatures of the Several States, of certain articles in addition and amendment of the Constitution of the United States, proposed by Congress to the said Legislatures, and of being with sentiments of the most perfect respect, your Excellency's &.

By that time the United States government was well under way, and much concerned with fisheries and post roads.

What happened then? The American revolutionaries did not proceed to cut off each other's heads on the glorious guillotine or to kill each other in glorious purges. If they had lived in the age of the photograph it would not have been necessary for them to keep airbrushing out of the group pictures those revolutionaries who later lost political struggles. Two of the greatest collaborators from the earliest days of the American Revolution, John Adams and Thomas Jefferson, both of whom returned from Europe in 1789 to take part in the new government, later bitterly opposed each other. But they did not lead insurgent forces or banish each other to the hills of Kentucky or have each other liquidated. They lived on through each other's depredations and settled down in old age to a renewed correspondence—full of reminiscences but also full of ideas, pounding away still on thoughts about government. They were able to live long enough to astonish their countrymen by dying, both of them, with breathtaking symbolic audacity, on July 4, 1826, the fiftieth anniversary of the Declaration of Independence.

And James Madison? Madison went on to serve his country for almost half a century. In 1836, ten years after Jefferson and Adams both had died, eager patriots tried to persuade James Madison, the last of the fathers, to try round out that miracle by the timing of his demise. He was eighty-six years old and failing, and they wanted him to take stimulants to keep himself alive until the *sixtieth* anniversary of the Fourth. But the modest Madison, never strong on *gloire,* said no thanks and died a week early.

Acknowledgments

Notes

Sources

Index

Acknowledgments

I am grateful to the Lilly Endowment, and in particular to its then Vice President Robert Lynn, for an imaginative grant supporting the larger project of which this book is one product. The grant made it possible to assemble at the Birdwood Pavilion in Charlottesville, on two weekends in the spring of 1987, small groups of scholars and writers and editors who had read parts of my manuscript as it then was. The participants in this enterprise—to name them without further ceremony—were the late Marcus Cunliffe, Roger Shinn, Michael McGiffert, Brooks Holifield, Richard Ruland, Birgit Noll, William Sullivan, John Reed, Rosemary Zagari, Jeff Fischel, Gene Outka, Corona Machemer, Ed Yoder, my colleagues at the University of Virginia Clifton McCleskey and George Klosko, and my colleague both at the University of Virginia and at the Miller Center for Public Affairs James Sterling Young. Michael McGiffert, the editor of the *William and Mary Quarterly,* was particularly helpful after the weekends were over in continuing to give readings and advice. Marcus Cunliffe, who died since his appearance here at Birdwood, also sent helpful books and articles, and comment. John Reed, the sociologist of the South at the University of North Carolina, and Gene Outka, the religious ethicist from Yale, provided particularly detailed and helpful substantive and editorial suggestions, to the benefit I hope not only of this but of additional productions. I am grateful to all those who participated in that undertaking; it was a privilege, and a great help, to have one's manuscript taken seriously in that way. This distinguished group is not in any way to be blamed for what appears in this book, which is in fact some distance from what they read. Andrew Horton Miller gave me exceptional help on that Birdwood project, and on others, and is mentioned in another place.

I have had the privilege of serving, while writing this book and for some years before that, on the faculty of the university that Thomas Jefferson founded, with James Madison as his trusted ally and fellow member of the first Board of Visitors. I had for a time, before the musical chairs of faculty study assignments rotated me out of it, a study in the University of Virginia library, next to the rooms that house the Papers of James Madison. There I sat, scribbling, with the papers of George Washington on one side, and the papers of James Madison on the other side, and an office for the late Dumas Malone, exuding total knowledge of Thomas Jefferson, down the hall, absorbing as by osmosis the spirit of the nation's Virginia beginnings. In addition to these spiritual and intellectual aids from physical location, I have had the benefit of conversation with and support from scholars at this university who deal with America's Virginia beginnings, including the Jefferson scholar and former dean Merrill Peterson, who brought me to the University, and William Abbott, the editor of the Washington papers. Thomas Mason, then an editor of the Madison papers, now with the Indiana Historical Society, was at an early stage very helpful to my efforts to study Madison; more recently John Stagg, the present editor of the Madison papers, was kind enough to read a couple of chapters, and to make exceptionally helpful and detailed suggestions. Robert Morgan, Professor Emeritus of Government at this University, and author of a careful study of Madison on the Constitution and Bill of Rights, and of two influential articles on Madison, was kind enough to read an early version of this book, and to make valuable suggestions.

While working on the larger project mentioned above I was appointed to an endowed chair at the University of Virginia's White Burkette Miller Center for Public Affairs, where then this book was carved out and completed. I have many debts to the Miller Center, which perhaps I can thank collectively, with thanks for particularly gracious help beyond the call of duty to Nancy Lawson and Robin Kuzen. I wish particularly to thank also assistants whom funds available to my new post made possible, who have helped me both with this book and with the larger project, who have ferreted out books and articles that I wanted, and also ones that I did not know I wanted, and in many other ways, with unusual enterprise and inellectual enthusiasm: Brian Menand, then a graduate student in Government, about whom I originally composed those phrases, before perceiving that they applied to them all; Frank Grizzard, then a graduate student in history, who provided not only historical knowledge but editorial skill; Jennifer Bernstein, a student in another institution, who for one summer gave me the benefit of her extraordinary intelligence and energy, and now Holly Redmond, a graduate student in Foreign Affairs, who has assisted me throughout the last stages of the production of this book, and on other projects as well, with unusual grace and generosity.

Linda Moore Miller stood by me, with patient intelligent love, in many ways throughout the production of this book, and some others in the past, and some more I hope in the future.

Notes

Introduction: Big House in Orange County

The editors of the *Papers of James Madison*, and modern biographers, now assign his memorandum on the ancient and modern confederacies to the spring of 1786, when Madison was in Montpelier, instead of the following year.

I discovered the book by Mrs. Scott in the little bookstore on one of my visits to Montpelier. The history of Montpelier comes in part from the excellent descriptions by guides, from phone calls afterward, from Montpelier's own materials, and from the biographies.

The names of Randolph Scott's movies are real; they were quarried by Holly Redmond out of *The World Encyclopedia of the Film*, ed. Tim Cawkwell and John M. Smith, 1972.

"Probably the most fruitful piece of scholarly research ever carried out by an American." Douglass Adair is the source of this remark, in an essay on James Madison reprinted in *Fame and the Founding Fathers*, p. 134.

Chapter 1: A Child of the Revolution Reads Some Books

With respect to Madison's not being as stuffy as the quotation from Witherspoon might imply, modern biographers are at pains to say that in small *private* groups of friends, never in public, Madison told, and laughed at, ribald stories and remarks that made his friend Jefferson blush.

The biographer who observes that Madison was not known to regret his commitment to public life is Harold Schultz, in his *James Madison*, 1970.

The quotation about the leaders of the French Revolution, and their disdain for compromise, comes from Palmer, *Twelve Who Ruled*, p. 19.

I have put together the story of the passage of Jefferson's bill for establishing religious freedom, including Madison's role, in *The First Liberty*, 1986. See the books cited in the text of that book for quotations used here.

The quotations about the supply of books from Jefferson to Madison are taken from Koch, *Jefferson and Madison: The Great Collaboration*, pp. 18–19.

Madison's memo "Notes on Ancient and Modern Confederacies" is to be found in *Papers*, 9: 4–24, together with a valuable headnote.

The quotation from James Wilson about the inutility of references to antique confederations comes from Randolph G. Adams, ed., *Selected Political Essays of James Wilson*, 1930, p. 167. Surely Wilson was implicitly referring to the continual citation of those antique leagues and confederacies by his collaborator Madison.

Chapter 2: "The People" Can Act Unjustly

Madison's memorandum of "Vices of the Political System of the United States" is to be found in *Papers*, 9: 348–58, together again with a valuable headnote.

The jottings of 1791, about slavery, are to be found in *Papers*, 14: 160. Drew McCoy's discussion of these jottings appears in *The Last of the Fathers*, pp. 234–35.

Reinhold Niebuhr would dramatize the theme of the greater moral problem of collectivities, without reference to Madison, in his book and title 145 years after Madison's memo, in the midst of the Great Depression of the twentieth century: *Moral Man and Immoral Society*, 1933.

Chapter 3: Beginning the World Anew, to a Certain Extent

The letters of Madison that are the chief subject of this chapter all appear in the *Papers*, 9: 318, 385, and 369.

Information about Paine came especially from Eric Foner. *Tom Paine and Revolutionary America*, 1976, and Mark Philip, *Paine*, 1989. The "royal brute" quotation from Franklin appears, however, in Moncure Conway, *The Life of Thomas Paine*, 1892, p. 27. For quotations from Paine I used Bruce Kunlick, *Thomas Paine: Political Writings*, 1989.

John Adams's "Thoughts on Government," which is originally a letter written after a conversation with George Wythe, addressed in the first instance to R. H. Lee, and then printed as a pamphlet and circulated, may be found not only in the *Papers* but together with an ordered selection of Adams's political thought in a collection edited, with an introduction, by George A. Peek, Jr., *The Political Writings of John Adams*, 1954.

The quotations about the people as constituent power come from Palmer, *The Age of the Democratic Revolution: The Challenge*, pp. 213–224.

Chapter 4: The Great Seminar in Print; or Founding Scribblers

The quotations with which this chapter begins come from these historians in this order: Forrest McDonald, *Novus Ordo Seclorum: The Intellectual Origins of the Constitution*, 1985, p. 10; Henry F. May, *The Enlightenment in America*, 1976, p. 88; and Adrienne Koch, *Power, Morals, and the Founding Fathers*, 1961, p. 12.

The quotation about the profusion of pamphlets comes from Bailyn, *Ideological Origins*, p. 1.

The observations about print were stimulated by reading Elizabeth Eisenstein, *The Printing Revolution as an Agent of Change*, 2 vols., 1979. She does not apply her reflections to the link between print and liberal democracy, but the points are waiting there between the lines.

Witherspoon's life story has been told in Varnum Lansing Collins, *President Wither-*

spoon, a Biography, 1925, and in Harold Willis Dodds, *John Witherspoon (1723–1794)*, 1944.

Andrew Horton Miller excavated lectures of Witherspoon from the nine sets, more than he expected, of student notes in the Princeton Library.

On James Harrington, see J. G. A. Pocock, *The Political Works of James Harrington*, 1977, and Charles Blitzer, *The Political Writings of James Harrington*, 1980.

The quotation from Henry May about the career of commonsense philosophy come from his *Enlightenment in America*, pp. 63–64.

Hume's essays went through a number of editions, with changes, so that they are difficult to cite swiftly. I have used *David Hume: Philosophical Works*, vol. 1, ed. T. H. Green and T. H. Grose, 1964, and include in the text the titles of the essays.

Douglass Adair's essay is called "That Politics May Be Reduced to a Science: David Hume, James Madison, and the Tenth Federalist." It was published in the *Huntington Library Quarterly* in 1957 and is reprinted in *Fame and the Founding Fathers*.

The quotations from Madison's letter to Trist, about Hume, come from Gaillard Hunt, *The Writings of James Madison*, 1900–1910, 9: 58. Professor Robert Morgan, in his book *James Madison on the Constitution and the Bill of Rights*, has pointed to this comment to suggest discounting Hume's influence on Madison. But the detail of constitutionary machinery the elderly Madison disparaged was not the aspect the young Madison got from Hume decades earlier.

Drew McCoy's *The Last of the Fathers* says in a footnote that "Hume's influence on Madison now appears indisputable, though clearly subject to exaggeration and misconstruction," p. 43. Professor McCoy lists and discusses recent participants in that dispute.

Chapter 5: The Business of May Next

All quotations from the Constitutional Convention, in this chapter and those to follow, are taken from Madison's notes, or in a few cases from the notes of others, as they appear in Max Farrand, *The Records of the Federal Convention of 1787*. I incorporate the date of each citation in the text, for example July 13, when Wilson proposed the cultivation of the human mind as the highest end of government, and omit further citation.

I am aware of the attack on the disinterestedness of Madison's notes by Professor Crosskey of the University of Chicago and others (William Winslow Crosskey, *Politics and the Constitution in the History of the United States*, 2 vols., 1953), but am assured by scholars I trust that that attack has not won assent of the most serious people working in the field. Crosskey's work is discussed, along with other relevant matters, in James Hutson, "Riddles of the Constitutional Convention," *William and Mary Quarterly*, 44 (1987).

I learned about James Wilson from Charles Page Smith, *James Wilson: Founding Father*, 1956, and from Wilson's own speeches in Randolph G. Adams, ed., *Selected Political Essays of James Wilson*, 1930. James Wilson was called the profoundest theorist of the revolution by Professor A. F. Pollard, an English historian, as quoted in Randolph G. Adams's editorial foreword to that book. Max Farrand's placing Wilson second to Madison and almost on a par with him is quoted in that same foreword. John Adams's invidious praise for James Wilson, as against Dickinson, appears in his letter to Abigail on July 8, 1775, *The Adams Papers: Adams Family Correspondence*, ed. L. H. Butterfield, 1963, pp. 252–53.

As to the room in the Pennsylvania State House being hot during that summer, apparently some iconoclastic scholar has discovered, after millions of young Americans have been taught that the framers sweltered in the Philadelphia heat, that the summer of 1787 in Philadelphia was not (compared to other summers) so hot after all. Thus does the disrespectful acid temper of modernity corrode the great traditions, myths, and legends of a people.

Madison's account of his note-taking, written "late in life," including the quotation explaining why he did it, is reproduced in the third volume of Farrand as—in the terrible roman numbering in that appendix—item CCCCI in Appendix A, pp. 539–51.

I have used for the computations about the populations of the states the figures from the federal census of 1790 as they are cited in Appendix II, p. 409, of Winton U. Solberg, ed., *The Federal Convention and the Union of the American States,* 1958.

Chapter 6: The Inadvertent Origins of the American Presidency

This chapter, largely the result of reading the notes on the convention in Farrand's edition, was helped by a presentation given by Norman Graebner at the Miller Center for Public Affairs of the University of Virginia.

The quotation from Hannah Arendt toward the end of the chapter will be found in her *On Revolution,* 1965, p. 16.

Chapter 7: Supreme Law; Unfinished Parts

Max Weber's phrase about government defined as possessing the "monopoly of legitimate violence" appears in his widely reprinted essay called "Politics as a Vocation," which appears in the collection *From Max Weber: Essays in Sociology,* ed. and trans. H. Gerth and C. Wright Mills, 1958.

This chapter, like the two that preceded it, was shaped by reading the notes on the convention in Farrand's edition, and the relevant pages in the *Papers,* Vol. 10, which print with notes Madison's major interventions in the convention. That volume begins with a note on Madison at the Federal Convention.

Chapter 8: Sundays Excepted

For this chapter I have drawn upon a bicenntenial address I delivered at Old Christ Church in Philadelphia, which was reprinted in *Religion and the Public Good, a Bicentennial Forum,* 1988.

James Madison's religious views are well discussed in Ralph L. Ketcham, *James Madison and Religion, New Hypothesis,* which first appeared in the *Journal of the Presbyterian Historical Society,* 1960, and was reprinted in Robert S. Alley, ed., *James Madison on Religious Liberty,* 1985.

I used an ancient pamphlet copy of the Constitution of the Confederate States of America, 1861, available in the University of Virginia Library.

The quotation from Michelet is from Jules Michelet, ed. Gordon Wright, *History of the French Revolution,* 1967, p. 22.

The quotation from John Courtney Murray, S.J., is from *We Hold These Truths: Catholic Reflections on the American Proposition,* 1960, p. 31.

Chapter 9: Other Persons

The three-fifths clause was called a masterpiece of circumlocution by Herbert J. Storing in "Slavery and the Moral Foundations of the Republic," in Robert H. Horwitz, ed., *The Moral Foundations of the American Republic,* 1977, an article from which I have profited.

For the antecedents to the constitutional three-fifths clause, and other matters in this chapter, I drew upon Donald Robinson's *Slavery in the Structure of American Politics, 1765–1820,* 1979, a book, from which I have also profited, which has a different temper from Storing's article.

The quotation about the framer's bifocal view of slavery comes from Don Fehrenbacher, *Slavery, Law, and Politics: The Dred Scott Case in Perspective,* 1981, p. 15.

The quotation from William Freehling comes from his article "The Founding Fathers and Slavery," in the *American Historical Review,* 77 (1972), an article from which I drew much of the material about the end of slavery in the North, and the other points in quasi defense of the founders. It may be that Freehling in his recent book, *The Road to Disunion,* 1990, has somewhat revised, or at least elaborated, what he had written eighteen years before about the ending of slavery in the North.

Bernard Bailyn used the phrase "The Contagion of Liberty" as the title of the last section of his *Ideological Origins.* The effect of the contagion on slavery is the consideration in the first part of that section.

The quotation about what the framers might have done with respect to slavery comes from Donald Robinson, *Slavery,* p. 233.

Chapter 10: Many Hands

On Forrest McDonald, the 3 pages of Madisonian defeats at the convention appear in *Novus Ordo Seclorum,* pp. 206–8; the "forty times" conclusion is on pp. 208–9.

In that book McDonald makes comments about, and criticisms of, Madison that some of the rest of us have a hard time accepting. E.g.: "Madison was an ideologue in search of an ideology: he was a man of doctrinaire temperament, marked by what Jean-Paul Sartre called 'a nostalgia for the absolute'" (p. 203). That does not sound like the Madison one reads in his letters, or in the great *Federalist* papers, or like the Madison one reads about in the biographies and other studies by Ralph Ketcham, Drew McCoy, Harold Schutz, Adrienne Koch, Lance Banning, Robert Morgan, Irving Brant, and others. In fact, as I trust I have made clear throughout this book, my reading of Madison would be rather in the opposite direction: that he was no ideologue, nor a man of doctrinaire temperament, nor marked by any nostalgia for the absolute. That he was free from these diseases was, in my view, exactly one source of the value in his work of political thinking.

If Madison did not speak the most often at the convention, he was a close second to Gouverneur Morris. Counts differ.

Section two of this chapter appeared, in altered form, as part of the essay "The Moral Project of the American Founders," written for the Williamsburg Charter and printed in *Articles of Faith, Articles of Peace,* ed. James Davison Hunter and Os Guiness, 1990.

Chapter 11: The Cloudy Medium of Words

I have taken for granted that the highly entertaining historical argument over who wrote which numbers of the *The Federalist* is now resolved, and basically that Madison's list was right and Hamilton's wrong. Douglass Adair's detective work went a long way toward resolving the matter. His two-part essay "The Disputed Authorship of the Federalist Papers" was published in the *William and Mary Quarterly* in 1944, and reprinted in *Fame and the Founding Fathers.* This essay includes much valuable material about the papers, and the two chief authors, and the history of the various ideological appropriations of *The Federalist,* as well as about the dispute about the authorship. On the last point the general reader needs to know that, as Adair put it in the second part of his essay, "it becomes entirely unnecessary to mark the writer of a single number as uncertain," and "none of the essays in *The Federalist* was composed as a joint product." So if you have one of the older editions that has question marks or double attributions get a new edition. The entire matter, together with further detective work, internal evidence, external evidence, mathematics and logic, is summarized in the extended editorial note in *The Papers of James Madison*, 10: 259–63. The extended note in *The Papers of Alexander Hamilton*, Harold C. Syrett, ed., 1962, 4: 287–301, which has much additional matter of interest about the publication of the essays, understandably gives slightly more credence to the claims made for Hamilton's authorship, and the collection does print as part of Hamilton's papers a few of the once disputed essays (numbers 50–52; 54–58; 62–63). But after doing that, the editors of the Hamilton papers graciously concede that the claims for Madison's authorship are superior to those of Hamilton.

On Hamilton I have consulted, in addition to the *Papers*, Broadus Mitchell, *Alexander Hamilton*, vol. 1, *Youth to Maturity*, *1755–1788*, and vol. 2, *The National Adventure*, *1788–1804*, 1957.

The quotation about the American Creed comes from Gunnar Myrdal, *An American Dilemma: The Negro Problem and Modern Democracy*, 1944, p. 3.

Chapter 12: The Peculiar *Federalist* Paper

The figures on the slave state's extra seats in the House come from the rip-roaring modern abolitionist history by Dwight Lowell Dumond, *Anti-Slavery: The crusade for Freedom in America*, 1961, p. 70. Dumond cites the combined populations of New York and Pennsylvania as 2,352,000, and the total number of representativesin the House for these states as sixty. He cites the combined populations of Maryland, Virginia, North Carolina, South Carolina, Georgia, Kentucky, Tennessee, and Louisiana as 2,554,000, and gives the number of their representatives in the House as eighty-four.

William R. Davie's argument in the North Carolina convention is reprinted from Elliott's Debates in the Ratifying Conventions as item CCXXV in Appendix A, in vol. 3 of Farrand. The quotation will be found on pp. 342–43.

The quotation from Drew McCoy comes from *The Last of the Fathers*, p. 260.

Madison's notes for the articles in the *National Gazette* appear in the *Papers*, 14: 157–68; the notes bearing on slavery appear on pp. 163–64.

Don Fehrenbacher's contrasting description of the two sides of the slavery debate appears in *Slavery, Law, and Politics*, p. 15.

Chapter 13: Traveling toward the Constitution; or Never Turn the Hands Backward

These letters are taken from the *Papers*, on the dates specified, all in vol. 9.

Chapter 14: Rocking Cradles in Virginia

The book from which this chapter is chiefly drawn—Hugh Blair Grigsby, *The History of the Virginia Federal Convention of 1788*, first published in Richmond in 1869, reprinted in 1969—is not only a source, but, as I hope I make evident in the text, a revealing book in its own right.

The quotation from Madison's last major speech comes not from Grigsby but from Madison's *Papers*, 11: 172.

I have been helped in the work on this chapter by hearing a presentation by former

Senator William B. Spong, Jr., at the Miller Center for Public Affairs at the University of Virginia, which presentation was printed by that Center as "The Virginia Ratification Convention of 1788."

Chapter 15: Was the United States Founded on Selfishness

In library copies of *The Wealth of Nations* one will find the passage about the invisible hand marked with the scratchings of many readers—many invisible human hands. In one edition, *An Inquiry Into the Nature and Causes of the Wealth of Nations*, 1904, that quotation appears in vol. 1, p. 421.

The quotations from Bernard Bailyn come from *The Ideological Origins*, p. 59, and, later, the footnote on p. 61.

I have relied most of all, for the antifederalists, on Cecilia Kenyon, *Men of Little Faith*, 1966. I drew also upon Jackson Turner Main, *The Antifederalists*, 1961, and Michael Borden, ed., *The Antifederalist Papers*, 1965.

Douglass Adair's essay "Fame and the Founding Fathers" is the first essay, and the title essay, in the collection already mentioned. The footnote making the contrast between Madison and Hamilton on the point of the class struggle appears, in another essay, on page 61 of that collection.

Chapter 16: No Just Government Should Refuse

These letters are taken from the *Papers*, on the dates specified, all in vol. 9.

Chapter 17: As Sincerely Devoted to Liberty

The letters quoted in the early pages of this chapter appear in vol. 11 of the Madison *Papers*: George Washington's letter describing Henry's power in the Virginia General Assembly on p. 351; the passage in Henry Lee's letter describing Madison's defeat in the General Assembly on p. 356; the sentence from Madison's letter to Randolph indicating his desire to be a part of the new government and his preference for the House on p. 305; his later letter to Randolph after Madison's defeat for the Senate on p. 362; his letter to the Reverend George Eve (from which I give three long quotations) on p. 404; his letter to Randolph after the election was over, saying it had been important for him to come to Virginia, on p. 453. The editorial note on pp. 301–2 gives a summary of the story of Madison's election to the first federal Congress.

Section two of this chapter was extracted to appear, in different form, joined with material from the chapter to follow, in *The New Republic*, June 26, 1989, and is printed here with the permission of that magazine.

Madison's role in the First Congress is described in an extended editorial note in vol. 12 of the Madison *Papers*, pp. 52–64; his role as speechwriter is described in a shorter note in the same volume, pp. 120–21, where it is remarked that he was having a "dialogue with himself." President Washington's Address to Congress, "the sacred fire of liberty," is printed not only in the Washington *Papers* but also in the Madison *Papers* beginning on p. 121 of this volume; the responses of the House and the Senate, and Washington's response in turn, appear in that volume also. The remark about Madison being a kind of prime minister appears in the second of the editorial notes mentioned above.

The events in the First Congress leading to the introduction of the Bill of Rights, and their progress through Congress, are taken chiefly from the *Papers*, vols. 11 and 12; from Ketcham and the other biographies; from Bernard Schwartz, *The Great Rights of Man-*

kind: A History of the American Bill of Rights, 1977; and from Edward Corwin, *The Constitution and What It Means Today,* 1973. Madison's important second speech of June 8, introducing his proposals for a bill of rights, and arguing for their consideration and enactment, as printed in the *Congressional Register,* is reprinted in the *Papers,* 12: 197–210; the quotations, "bound by every motive of prudence," "as sincerely devoted to liberty," appear on p. 198. The *Papers* also reproduce Madison's own notes for this speech on pp. 193–95.

Chapter 18: Bulwarks and Palladiums

The quotation about the celerity of the adoption of the 21st Amendment comes from Corwin, 1973, p. 548. This book was used throughout this chapter; I made some use of a much earlier, 1920, edition of Corwin as well.

I relied even more for this chapter on Schwartz, *The Great Rights of Mankind.* The quotation from the letter by the two antifederalist senators from Virginia, that the proposed amendments are contrary to Virginia's wishes, comes from p. 188. Madison's letter to George Washington deploring that letter, as calculated to keep disaffection alive, appears in vol. 12 of the *Papers,* p. 458.

The statute of King Edward III, including the phrase "due process of law," is quoted from Corwin, p. 326.

Corwin's description of the middle amendments as a bill of rights for accused persons appears on p. 313.

The phrase "victim of nameless accusers" was the title of an article in *The Reporter,* when I was on its staff in the days of McCarthyism.

Corwin's statement that the protections of the accused are an advance on English law comes not from the 1973 edition but from the much smaller 1920 edition, p. 90.

The quotation about the French revolutionaries not rejoicing in differences among factions is from Palmer, *Twelve Who Ruled,* pp. 19–20.

Madison's original version of the ingredients of what would be the First Amendment appears in the June 8 speech mentioned above, in the *Papers,* 12: 201.

The great sentence from the *Areopagitica* should not need a reference, but be engraved on the memory of every lover of liberty.

Justice Brandeis's description of the founders' love of liberty, which almost deserves to be engraved there too, comes form his concurring opinion in *Whitney v. California* (1927).

I learned about Jefferson's letter notifying the governors that the Bill of Rights had passed, and the printing of it, in *Harper's* magazine with the amused heading, from Schwartz, pp. 186–87.

Sources

The most important single source for this book was *The Papers of James Madison,* the thorough and authoritative collection of Madison's Papers that has been issuing forth steadily, volume after volume, since it began in 1956. The early volumes of the *Papers* were edited by William T. Hutchinson, and others, at the University of Chicago. The volumes beginning with the eighth were edited by Robert Rutland, and others, at the University of Virginia. These include the volumes most useful for this book: volume 8 (1784–86); volume 9 (1786–87); and, in particular, volume 10 (1787–88). The Madison *Papers,* now edited by John Stagg and others, as this is written, have reached their 17th volume and the year 1801, where they join with the one volume of the series from Madison's years as secretary of state that had already been published. One volume of the presidential series, skipping ahead in the chronology, has also been published. Because Madison lived so long and corresponded so conscientiously and kept chipping away at public affairs even in his retirement, the series may reach 50 volumes before it is finished; the editors now estimate that the completion of the project may come in something like the year 2012. This kind of thing it is worth doing right.

The Madison Papers project, like that of Jefferson and of Washington, and unlike the much smaller eight-volume collection of Lincoln's Papers, Roy P. Basler, ed., *The Collected Works of Abraham Lincoln,* 1955, include not only the letters the principal wrote, but also those he *received:* a feature obviously of great value when you want to follow something. And the Madison *Papers,* like the Jefferson *Papers,* have in addition to the letters and papers themselves, and to footnotes giving helpful identifications and other information, headnotes on main topics. These notes in the Madison *Papers* have been important to me in writing this book.

For such reference as I needed to the years beyond those that the new editorial project has reached I used the older collection of Gaillard Hunt: *The Writings of James Madison,* 1900–1910.

I sometimes consulted also others of these great editorial projects, in particular the *The Papers of Thomas Jefferson,* Julian P. Boyd, ed., 1950.

For biographical information about Madison I used, most of the time, Ralph Ketcham's *James Madison,* a thorough, one-volume biography originally published in 1971, and for a time very hard to find, but now (1991) happily republished in paperback. Ketcham's book has the advantage, as it seems to me, of an interest in political philosophy that matches that of his subject. The standard larger biography is that by Irving Brant, *James Madison,* 6 vols., 1941–61. Brandt was working away on Madison well before the revived interest of the postwar period, and everyone interested in Madison is in his debt. There is a one-volume biography drawn from Brant's larger undertaking, *The Fourth President: A Life of James Madison,* 1970. There is a good, and somewhat neglected, small one-volume biography of Madison by Harold S. Schultz, *James Madison,* 1970, that makes a virtue of the necessity of compression. During the time that I was working on this book the former editor of the Madison *Papers,* Robert A. Rutland, published his one-volume *James Madison: The Founding Father,* 1987.

Among other books about Madison the most important for my purposes, even though it deals with Madison in years beyond the reach of this book, is Drew McCoy's *The Last of the Fathers,* 1989. This excellent book stands out from the others.

Articles by Lance Banning, who is working on a biography of Madison, that I consulted included "James Madison and the Nationalists, 1780–1783," *William and Mary Quarterly,* (1986) and "The Hamiltonian Madison: A Reconsideration," *Virginia Magazine,* 92, (1984). In addition I read Banning's article "Jeffersonian Ideology Revisited: Liberal and Classical Ideas in the New American Republic," in the *William and Mary Quarterly,* for January 1986, an article that responds to the more recent criticisms, by Joyce Appleby and others, of the theme of "republicanism."

An older book that was also important to me was Adrienne Koch, *Jefferson and Madison: The Great Collaboration,* 1950. Professor Koch was an important voice in the revaluation of Madison, and the founders, after the Second War. She published other books and articles that figured in that fresh appraisal, including *Power, Morals, and the Founding Fa-*

thers, 1961, and *"Advice to My Country,"* 1965, a little book that consists of three lectures, dealing entirely with Madison, that were given at the bicentennial of the Whig-Clio Society at Princeton.

Professor Robert Morgan's careful book *James Madison on the Constitution and the Bill of Rights,* 1988, treats Madison as a political philosopher in a useful way.

Books and articles about *The Federalist,* of course, have much material about Madison's thought. Garry Wills' *Explaining America: The Federalist,* 1981, is, as would be expected, stimulating. One of the most important of the many articles is Daniel W. Howe, "The Political Psychology of *The Federalist," William and Mary Quarterly,* 1987. Two older articles that happened in their day to be important to me are Martin Diamond, "Democracy and *The Federalist:* A Reconsideration of the Framers' Intent," *American Political Science Review,* 1959, and Benjamin F. Wright, "The Federalist on the Nature of Political Man," *Ethics,* 1948–49.

I took for granted, for the purposes of this work of interpretation, not only the revaluation of Madison but also the larger revaluation of the founding period and the founding fathers that historians have been carrying on since the Second World War. It will be evident from the text and the notes that the work of Douglass Adair, a harbinger and stimulant of this revaluation, was important to this book. Adair's essays were collected posthumously in Trevor Colburn, ed., *Fame and the Founding Fathers* (1974). Among the essays in that volume that were of particular importance to me I might mention "The Authorship of the Disputed Federalist Papers"; "The Tenth Federalist Revisited"; " 'That Politics May Be Reduced to a Science': David Hume, James Madison and the Tenth Federalist"; " 'Experience Must Be Our Only Guide': History, Democratic Theory, and the United States Constitution"; and the appreciation of James Madison, called simply "James Madison," written for a Princeton publication.

This book has benefited from the two most important books in the scholarly reinterpretation of the founding period, taking the ideas of the founders seriously again and developing the theme of republicanism: Bernard Bailyn, *The Ideological Origins of the American Revolution,* 1967, and Gordon S. Wood, *The Creation of the American Republic, 1776–1787,* 1969.

Robert E. Shalhope, who wrote a short piece on Adair and the historiography of republicanism in *Fame and the Founding Fathers* has written other articles on the scholarship on republicanism in the *William and Mary Quarterly,* in 1972 and 1976, which I found helpful.

For the Federal Convention I used the four-volume revised edition of

The Records of the Federal Convention of 1787, edited by Max Farrand, that was conveniently and attractively reprinted by Yale University Press in 1966, from the original edition of 1911 and the revision of 1937. This standard source includes not only Madison's notes but the notes of the other note-takers and a valuable appendix, with relevant materials of many kinds, including material from the ratifying conventions. I have referred in the text to the date of the speeches at the convention. I used this source, rather than the *Papers,* for quotations from the convention, including Madison's own speeches. I read books and articles about the ratifying conventions in the big states other than Virginia—Pennsylvania, Massachusetts, and the "Reluctant Pillar," New York—but decided to drop that chapter and therefore that list of sources. Some afterglow of that effort may remain.

I make in passing comparisons to the other great revolution that set the stage for the modern world, the material on which is of course immense. I collected books on this vast subject, too, but in the end the most important source for these comparisons for me was the work of R. R. Palmer, which, because time has passed, has been subject to revision, too, but not so as to alter its value for me: *Twelve Who Ruled: The Year of the Terror in the French Revolution,* 1969, and *The Age of the Democratic Revolution: A Political History of Europe and America 1760–1800: The Challenge,* 1959.

Other sources on specific points are listed in the notes.

Index

___